The Films of Peter Greenaway is one of the first critical overviews of
the work of this controversial contemporary filmmaker. Trained as an
artist, Greenaway began his career in cinema as an editor of government-sponsored films. He began to attract critical attention in 1980
with his epic mock-documentary *The Falls,* the first British film to be
named Best Film by the British Film Institute in 30 years. Since then
he has created the wittily elegant *The Draughtsman's Contract,*
the strikingly unconventional Shakespearean adaptation *Prospero's
Books,* and the disturbingly violent *The Cook, The Thief, His Wife
and Her Lover.* These and several other of Greenaway's most important works are examined and analyzed in depth within the context of
the director's biography and artistic goals. This edition also includes
stills from Greenaway's feature films, as well as the filmmaker's own
drawings.

D1336293

Don Gresswell Ltd., London, N.21   Cat. No. 1208

The Films of Peter Greenaway

CAMBRIDGE FILM CLASSICS

General Editor: Ray Carney, Boston University

The Cambridge Film Classics series provides a forum for revisionist studies of the classic works of the cinematic canon from the perspective of the "new auteurism," which recognizes that films emerge from a complex interaction of bureaucratic, technological, intellectual, cultural, and personal forces. The series consists of concise, cutting-edge reassessments of the canonical works of film study, written by innovative scholars and critics. Each volume provides a general introduction to the life and work of a particular director, followed by critical essays on several of the director's most important films.

Other Books in the Series:

Peter Bondanella, *The Films of Roberto Rossellini*
Ray Carney, *The Films of John Cassavetes*
Sam B. Girgus, *The Films of Woody Allen*
Robert Phillip Kolker and Peter Beicken,
The Films of Wim Wenders
Scott MacDonald, *Avant-Garde Film*
James Naremore, *The Films of Vincente Minnelli*
James Palmer and Michael Riley, *The Films of Joseph Losey*
Scott Simmon, *The Films of D. W. Griffith*
David Sterritt, *The Films of Alfred Hitchcock*
Maurice Yacowar, *The Films of Paul Morrissey*

The Films of
Peter Greenaway

Amy Lawrence

CAMBRIDGE
UNIVERSITY PRESS

PUBLISHED BY THE PRESS SYNDICATE OF THE UNIVERSITY OF CAMBRIDGE
The Pitt Building, Trumpington Street, Cambridge CB2 1RP, United Kingdom

CAMBRIDGE UNIVERSITY PRESS
The Edinburgh Building, Cambridge CB2 2RU, United Kingdom
40 West 20th Street, New York, NY 10011–4211, USA
10 Stamford Road, Oakleigh, Melbourne 3166, Australia

First published 1997

Printed in the United States of America

Typeset in Sabon

Library of Congress Cataloging-in-Publication Data
Lawrence, Amy.
The films of Peter Greenaway / Amy Lawrence.
p. cm. – (Cambridge film classics)
Filmography: p.
Includes bibliographical references and index.
ISBN 0-521-47363-2 (hc). – ISBN 0-521-47919-3 (pbk.)
1. Greenaway, Peter – Criticism and interpretation. I. Title.
II. Series.
PN1998.3. G73L38 1997
791.43'0233'092 – dc21   96-52930
                                                          CIP.

A catalog record for this book is available from the British Library.

ISBN 0 521 473632 hardback
ISBN 0 521 479193 paperback

Illustrations

Contents

Acknowledgments

I would like to thank the following people for their generous help with this book. First, Peter Greenaway for taking the time to speak with me about his career, for providing precise, good-humored, and enlightening comments on the manuscript, and for graciously offering visual material from his own collection to provide some of the illustrations. Special thanks to the invaluable Eliza Poklewski Koziell for her unfailing helpfulness in suggesting sources and sending material I would never have had access to without her. To my editor, Ray Carney, and to Al LaValley, Terry Lawrence, and Mary Desjardins for their helpful suggestions on earlier drafts of the book. To Christa Renza and Bill Pence of Hopkins Film Center and Mary Corliss at the Museum of Modern Art Film Stills Archive for help with obtaining stills.

And thanks to Irene for Mijoux.

Figure 1. Peter Greenaway. (Copyright Medora Hebert, 1991)

Introduction
Encyclopedia Britannica

One of the most controversial and distinctive filmmakers of the 1980s British film renaissance, Peter Greenaway has established himself as a byword in contemporary film studies. With seven feature films in eleven years and a series of award-winning shorts, Greenaway has produced a strikingly beautiful and cohesive body of work during a critical period in British film history.

Greenaway's films are marked by an astonishing proliferation of detail and a remarkable breadth of reference. From theories of history to theories of art, from consumption to construction, his films are best reached through metaphor and paradox – literary concepts that demand we hold in mind more than one thing at a time, that each element illuminate the other, and that those elements be, at the very least, contradictory.

As with the work of any cinematic stylist and innovator, Greenaway's films are easy to recognize and difficult to describe. In writing about Greenaway, some critics feel compelled to adopt the filmmaker's poetic density, his trademark wordplay and puns, struggling to convey a fragment of the unforgettable images crowding each film. In the first twenty seconds of the *titles* of Greenaway's breakthrough film, *The Draughtsman's Contract* (1982), Elizabeth Butz finds clues

> anticipating thematic strains of revolution and cyclicism: light to dark, constancy and alternation, seed to offspring, the long shot pulling away and the close-up closing in, closet to courtyard, awesome catholicity and glorified protestation, artisan to courtesan, orange and pineapple, plum to purge, England and her nether lands.[1]

Another suggests the array of references that come to mind watching a single film: "*Cook, Thief* has the splendor of De Mille and the perversity of de Sade," what "'*Tis Pity She's a Whore* might look like directed by Monty

Python in the spirit of *The Birds*."[2] Even those who do *not* like Greenaway still find it necessary to cite his "diversity (author, painter, art historian), his taxonomical brilliance (games with numbers, alphabets, painterly tableaux, filmic *hommages*, literary allusions), [and] his unconventional narratives."[3]

In an attempt to unify this diversity, many critics look for a central overriding metaphor. Tracy Biga sees eating disorders as an essential structuring element in all of Greenaway's films – from the eating scenes in *The Draughtsman's Contract* through *The Belly of an Architect* (1986) to *The Cook, The Thief, His Wife and Her Lover* (1989). Others argue for abstract organizational systems – numbers in *Drowning by Numbers* (1988), the alphabet in *A Zed and Two Noughts* (1985), both in *The Falls* (1980) – or for the centrality of artist figures: a painter (*Draughtsman's Contract*), an architect (*Belly of an Architect*), a writer (*Prospero's Books*, 1991), or a chef (*Cook, Thief*).[4] We can also find a mordant appreciation of scientific rationalism in the ornithologists and cartographers of *A Walk Through H* (1978), the centralized rural development officials and the documentarians in *Vertical Features Remake* (1978), the zoologists (*A Zed and Two Noughts*), coroners (*Drowning by Numbers*), and scholars (*Belly, Prospero*). But in Greenaway obsessions often overlap. In any Greenaway film, several structuring metaphors are operating simultaneously, no one truer to the essential meaning of the film or more useful than another.

Greenaway's films indulge a taste for the encyclopedic. "I want to make films that rationally represent all the world in one place. That mocks human effort because you cannot do that."[5] Greenaway's films embrace cascades of information. He asserts that

> works of art refer to great masses of culture, they are encyclopedic by nature. . . . [T]he works of art that I admire, even contemporary ones like *One Hundred Years of Solitude* or any three-page story by Borges, have that ability to put all the world together. My movies are sections of this world encyclopedia.[6]

For instance, Greenaway points out that in *Drowning by Numbers* "the coroner's son is named Smut, which begins with the letter S. So there are one hundred things in the film that begin with S. . . ." "You don't have to know that to see the film," he adds, "but it somehow enriches the fabric of it, makes the film again encyclopedic by nature."[7]

The encyclopedia in Greenaway's work is an organizational strategy as well as a philosophical stance as well as an ideological practice. A monumental pastiche, *The Falls* in particular can be seen as a postmodern encyclopedia, an organization of facts and pieces put together in an eminently logical way, laced with the very slightest regret that none of it is actually true. In *The Falls,* Greenaway parodies every technique by which traditional documentary seeks to substantiate its ties to reality. Of course, by the end every aspect of the film has been revealed to be a complete fiction. One critic described *The Falls* as "a paean to pseudo-science; Edward Lear wrapped up in the *Encyclopedia Britannica.*"[8]

A longstanding prejudice regarding experimental films argues that if the pleasures offered are other than narrative (are found, for instance, in visual style, montage, *hommage,* tantalizing juxtapositions, and *ideas*), the films will be cold, distant, pretentious game-playing. "The same accusations (elitism, mannerism, formalism, [and] chilly intellectualism)," one critic points out, were also "levied against the films of Eisenstein, Alain Resnais, Straub-Huillet."[9] Resnais, in fact, is one of the filmmakers Greenaway admires most.[10] "I'd like to think my cinema is somewhere between Resnais and Hollis Frampton, if that's possible. Sort of to the left of field of Resnais but still slightly to the right of Frampton."[11]

Far from chilly in discussing his films, Greenaway takes pleasure in the exuberant range of interpretations to which his work can be subjected. *The Draughtsman's Contract,* he relates,

> has been seen as an essay on fruit symbolism, the political history of Northern Ireland, pro-Thatcherism, anti-Thatcherism, pro-feminism, anti-feminism, and many other things. *Time Out* . . . argued that the film was an exposé of English League Football.[12]

Although he acknowledges that "I am often accused of being an intellectual exhibitionist" (and enjoys repeating Pauline Kael's less than flattering description of him as a "cultural omnivore who eats with his mouth open"),[13] Greenaway emphatically rejects the charge of elitism. "There is much in [my films] to enjoy besides the use of conceit and allegory. It's absurd for people to say, 'Christ, I'm not clever enough to catch all these references.'"[14]

Given such myriad references, some critics feel Greenaway's films fail to develop fully the complex "intellectual, philosophical and aesthetic" ideas they raise.[15] This dissatisfaction frequently centers on what Jonathan Hacker and David Price call the "significant problem of inadequate characterization. The characters are frequently awkward pawns within Greenaway's intellectual game-playing" – leaving the audience with no access to emotional identification.[16]

Greenaway, on the other hand, argues vehemently that cinema should be allowed to serve as a forum for something other than psychological realism. "Most of the films originate essentially as ideas – not as events, not as pieces of narrative, [and] not as a desire to express a character."[17] Like Resnais (who also began as an editor of informational films), Greenaway privileges style, and an epigram associated with Resnais applies equally well to the Greenaway of *Draughtsman's Contract, The Cook, The Thief,* and his other feature films of the 1980s – "Form *is* feeling in its most elegant and economic expression."[18] Greenaway puts it another way:

I do have a genuine interest, I think, in language – cinema language, textual language, imagery. Content very rapidly atrophies and all you're left with is language. It's the manipulation of language which keeps us all excited.[19]

At the same time, Greenaway concedes that his work might be too successful at what could be called a characteristic emotional restraint.

The English are very good at game-playing – they have probably invented most of them – and we are often criticised for hiding behind them. It is said to be a way of ritualizing emotion.[20]

Although his early short films carry a delicate but nonetheless powerful emotional undertow, in his features Greenaway has been especially dependent on actors to introduce and maintain each film's emotional domain. Consequently his strongest films have the best acting: Anthony Higgins, Janet Suzman, and Anne Louise Lambert in *Draughtsman;* Brian Dennehy in *Belly;* Joan Plowright, Juliet Stevenson, and Bernard Hill in *Drowning by Numbers;* Helen Mirren and Michael Gambon in *Cook.* When the acting fails (the main characters in *Zed*) or when Greenaway depends on international stars whose accents detract from the rhythm and wit of the dialogue (Andrea Ferreol in *Zed* or Richard Bohringer in *Cook*), the films risk incoherence (literally, with Ferreol and Bohringer) and lose emotional resonance.

Greenaway's films possess a fundamentally postmodern sensibility. Without underlying myths to endow them with meaning, everything we see is unmoored from history, reduced to the status of signs without referents. History becomes a playground of artifacts, fragments from all periods insouciantly scattered about, incongruous, enchanting, opaque. In *The Belly of an Architect,* an American architect (Brian Dennehy) reels through Rome, his office littered with models, reproductions, props and diagrams, domes and cycloramas, an eerie green-lit Xerox machine spewing forth copy after copy of the marble stomach of Caesar. Outside, gargantuan heads are left sitting in courtyards. A lightweight culture-thief hawks a tray of noses casually chiseled from antique statuary. In *The Draughtsman's Contract,* the dialogue imitates Sheridan and Congreve, the music, Purcell, the images, De La Tour and others. In *The Cook, The Thief,* the characters are dwarfed by the culture they mimic in miniature and to which their every move may be compared. In this grab-bag approach to history, complex relationships can be stated visually in a way that is both dense and widely accessible.

Like Pasolini and Godard, Greenaway is a self-conscious auteur whose work poses the question: How to make art out of *ideas* about art? Despite his loss of faith in explanatory systems, Greenaway holds on to a few basics – the artist, landscape, structure, and the ruins of Western culture – while showing how each has been utterly compromised in the late twentieth century. Artists, for instance, are shown in *Draughtsman* to be inevitably corrupted by the political regimes within which they operate; in *Cook* their skill subjects them to unsolicited patronage. *The Belly of an Architect* and *Prospero's Books* situate the artist amid the rubble of a postmodern consciousness. In *Belly* the modern artist's fealty to the past implicates him in an unending chain of patriarchal authority (corrupt, tyrannical, megalomaniacal) that is ultimately inseparable from his idealistic vision of artistic purity. Prospero's use of books to dominate, subject, and (most stunningly) silence those around him is another indictment of not only the artist but the patriarch.[21]

In criticizing the artist, Greenaway is critical of his own position. After exhaustively listing the mediocrity of each of his major male characters, he concludes, "I suppose they're all self-portraits of a sort."[22] The most autobiographical figure in Greenaway's work, the architect-hero of *Belly,* is a middle-aged man overwhelmed by the endless reproduction of icons of the past as he compares himself to his artistic idols. In *Prospero's Books* and *A TV Dante* (1988), Greenaway does the same, measuring himself against Dante, Shakespeare, and the entire British theatrical tradition as exemplified by John Gielgud.

Like his artist figures, the women in Greenaway's films must make their own way. In films like *Draughtsman's Contract* and *Cook, Thief,* the women and the artists share a social powerlessness, and are valued only for what they can produce to the glory and amusement of the patriarchy. Each must learn to negotiate a hostile world in order to survive. Greenaway's women are frequently more successful at this than the men, and given the corruption of the worlds in which they succeed (*Draughtsman*), this has left Greenaway open to charges of misogyny as well as misanthropy. Although Greenaway occasionally falls into a mythic–romantic view linking women with nature, associating them with childbirth and life (*Drowning by Numbers, Belly, Zed*), the women in Greenaway's films are nevertheless some of

5

the most intriguing in contemporary cinema. Both *The Draughtsman's Contract* and *The Cook, The Thief, His Wife and Her Lover* turn on the intelligence of the women characters. Greenaway's women are also often mature figures, which contributes to the adult eroticism of Greenaway's work: Mrs. Herbert in *Draughtsman* (Janet Suzman), Georgina in *Cook, Thief* (Helen Mirren).

Critical of human failings, Greenaway implicates cinema in the failure of art. In *A Zed and Two Noughts,* cinema's beginnings in Muybridge's studies of animal motion are inverted. Instead of creating the illusion of life, motion pictures create a parodic, grotesque, pseudomovement for the dead. In *The Belly of an Architect,* a camera, employed for surveillance and attempted blackmail, is ultimately revealed to be empty.

Despite this apparent pessimism, Greenaway argues that any tendency toward morbidity is balanced by his love for the English landscape.

> Behind this death, evil, and mediocrity is the natural landscape. These landscapes are magnificent and optimistic. . . . [They] have an ebullient delight in the richness and variety of things and many [of the films] do end with a birth which persistently argues for another try, another chance, another opportunity.[23]

Compared to the urban obsessions of other British filmmakers (from Grierson in the thirties, through the "kitchen sink" realism of the sixties, to Stephen Frears, Mike Leigh, and Alan Clarke in the eighties), Greenaway's films emerge out of the rural British landscape, a setting inseparable from the history of British politics, culture, identity, and art. Evoking the work of landscape artists, Greenaway's short films weave idyllic, nostalgic images of Britain into a witty exposé of man's attempts to "read," interpret, and order nature with a series of grids, maps, and narratives imposed on the land. Films like *Vertical Features Remake, A Walk Through H,* and *H is for House* (1973) uncover a surprising depth of feeling as they reveal the comic futility of man's attempts to explain the richness of the world.

All of Greenaway's films have an unparalleled surface beauty. Consider the southern warmth of *Belly of an Architect,* its underpopulated urban scenes evoking such sixties masters as Resnais (Greenaway was working with Resnais's cinematographer, Sacha Vierny) and the stringent cleanness of Antonioni; the cool, light-filled hospital rooms of *Zed;* an Infanta solemnly jumping rope under a shower of stars in *Drowning by Numbers;* the golden memories of a book depository in *The Cook* and its visual companion in *Prospero's Books* where pages fall like leaves – but upward and in slow motion. The consistent beauty of these films is all the more stunning when one takes into account the speed with which they were made and the limited funding available for experimental film production in England in the eighties. Much of the credit for the "look" of a Greenaway film is due to his production team, which has remained remarkably stable over time: cinematographer Sacha Vierny, composer Michael Nyman, editor John Wilson, and production designers Ben Van Os and Jan Roelfs. This is not to suggest, however, that Greenaway's style is merely the sum of the talents of the people he works with: even when working with others (cinematographer Curtis Clark and designer Bob Ringwood on *Draughtsman's Contract,* for instance, or production designer Luciana Vedovelli and composers Wim Mertens and Glen Branca on *Belly of an Architect*), Greenaway's films are instantly, identifiably, his.

An English Filmmaker

Born in 1942 in Newport, Wales, during "the darkest days of World War II," Greenaway was raised by his mother, aunts, and maternal grandmother in a "working class house in the industrial areas of this South Wales industrial town."[24] When his father returned from the war four years later, the family relocated to London's East End, nearer Greenaway's father's family in Essex. The long-delayed introduction of father and son was the beginning of a difficult relationship.

Greenaway's father's parents were "gardeners, horticultural people, who looked after estates." "Not a million miles away," Greenaway notes, "from the circumstances of *Draughtsman's Contract.*" It was Greenaway's maternal grandmother who introduced him to the cinema.

There was a concession just after the war that bereaved widows (ostensibly war widows which wasn't my grandmother's case) were allowed in cinemas half-price Tuesday afternoon. For some reasons occasionally I was dragged along.

My first cinema experience was of a Western. [I remember] sitting beside my grandmother in her purple hat, eating sweets and watching this movie . . . and not in any way understanding what I was watching. This was all going over my head until suddenly somebody in the film brought in a child – it must have been my age – a girl, long blond hair, I remember this very clearly – and what I thought was black currant juice on her head. Somebody mentioned the idea of scalping which I didn't fully understand but suddenly it dawned on me that that black currant juice was supposed to be blood and the girl was dead – and I panicked because I suddenly understood the conventions. I screamed and was taken out. I remember the backs of my legs being slapped on Corporation Road. I must have been about five years old.

Subsequent ventures proved equally unpromising. Taken to a cartoon theatre in the Haymarket in London, Greenaway at eight was so "enthralled and excited," he did not want to leave. When his parents forced him out of the cinema

> there was a commotion and I ended up on the streets with one shoe. My petit bourgeois parents (who were embarrassed generally in public) were aghast that they had a child walking the London streets with only one shoe on. And ever after there seemed to be an association of cinemas and lost clothing which hung around my head.

As Greenaway grew to adolescence, cinema continued to fail to create a strong impression. "It seemed to be a much more social phenomenon, somewhere you went with your friends."

Like many of his generation, Greenaway's concept of what film could be was formed in the late fifties and early sixties by European auteurs. What he refers to as his "road to Damascus experience" occurred in "a small fleapit cinema called The State. The cinema manager, it would seem, thought that all Swedish films would naturally be sexy so he put on *The Seventh Seal*." Greenaway and a schoolmate "ended up, probably rain-soaked, in the cinema hoping to have a risqué experience and saw this extraordinary movie."

> That was an amazing revelation. All the movies I'd seen before were not like this. This was something completely different. This really engaged in some questions I was interested in – superstition, religion . . . But it had the hallmarks of something which was highly watchable, [with] a story you wanted to know what happened next. It was about medieval history which was my passion. It had a strange musical language, beautiful Swedish, you had to read the subtitles which gave it a certain distancing (both characteristics of my cinema again). So I think that it was the big turning point.

Greenaway saw it "nearly two performances a day for five days."[25]

This led to "a crash course in European cinema," focusing on "Antonioni, Pasolini, Godard, and Resnais. I saw their films eagerly as they arrived in England – with Godard that was regularly."[26]

That was what I wanted – to make films regularly. I bought my own camera, a clockwork 16mm Bolex, and I applied to the Royal College of Art film-school.[27]

When Greenaway failed to be accepted at film school, his education followed a different path, one that "irritated and antagonized" his parents: "I was supposed to go to university. I got myself placed at Cambridge and I decided that wasn't what I wanted to do. I wanted to be a painter instead."

After he graduated from Walthamstow Art School, Greenaway's employment in film began inauspiciously. Unable to find a position as a film critic ("writing totally unreadable articles like 'The Relationship between Chirico and Alain Resnais'"),[28] Greenaway "got a temporary job as a doorkeeper at the BFI." Working in the British Film Institute's distribution department for eight months, he quickly moved on to a position as "'third-assistant-editor-on-trial' in the broom-cupboard cutting-rooms of Soho" until he "got a proper job at the COI [Central Office of Information] – nine to five, paid at the end of the week, union-supervised film-editing."[29] For the next ten years, Greenaway worked first as an editor and then as a director of informational films.

> [Having been] trained, I suppose, in an elitist way in terms of literature and art theory and painting, I entered as a minion sweeping up trims off the floor, determined to learn a craft. . . . So this rather, as they saw it, highly overeducated young man with grand ambitions and no practicality was trying to get into this system. I spent a lot of time climbing up the hierarchy.

The Central Office of Information was a branch of the Foreign Office producing informational films about life in Britain for distribution abroad. "We all had to sign the Official Secrets Act." Greenaway was one of "twelve editors employed in house."

> There must have been thirty people . . . pushing out these programs all over the world. You never knew what happened to them. There was no feedback. It was calculated that a third of the world's population was seeing these films – I mean the biggest audience I could ever hope for.
>
> I'm sure a lot of the stuff was terrible. I remember making programs supporting DDT for spreading on fields in South Africa. I remember making documentaries about dried milk for babies in India. All these horrendous – Another program which I at the time thought was very dubious: farmers were encouraged to grub out their hedges and make

bigger fields, put more and more fertilizers, take down the forests and fill in marshes. . . . I had a little hand in all that propaganda.

Despite reservations about content ("It's not exactly Goebbels but it's retrospectively not to be proud of"), Greenaway found employment at the COI conducive to his own work.

I should have left earlier but I was well paid, extremely well paid, and with that money I could buy cameras, I could buy stock, and in the evenings I could use all the facilities I was using professionally. . . . So it was a useful little sort of nest for me – decent salary, facilities at my beck and call, and, within the COI, a certain amount of freedom.

Throughout his stint at the COI, Greenaway was making his own "very modest 16mm films, [and] developing theories" about non-narrative cinema – "largely determined by my absurdly meagre means of production."[30] For Greenaway, these films were also the last time he was able to create films dictated exclusively by the image.

Those films were very much created from the camera. I went out and found the shots according to compositions that amused, excited, or delighted me, then came back with all this amorphous material and structured it in the cutting room.

None of the shots last longer than fifteen seconds – the capacity of Greenaway's wind-up 16mm Bolex.

Most of Greenaway's short films were influenced by his taste for avant-garde film and the work of structuralists like Hollis Frampton.[31]

I was also studying for a BA in film theory at the BFI [and] spending a lot of time in the archives. . . . I had the key to the projection room and the archive, and could go and see films when I wanted to.

At the time, "there was great concern for anti-narration in cinema in general," and Greenaway was particularly struck by the work of North American "underground filmmakers – Hollis Frampton, Brakhage, Snow and all those other people. . . . The sense of freedom, the liberation that all their work indicated was powerful stuff." For Greenaway, their work provided

great encouragement. Not because I wanted to make films like they did, but because here was an alternative. You didn't have to have a Hollywood budget to make a movie. You could make a private movie that had philosophical legitimacy, concerning ideas which were happening in terms of post-Pop American or Western art [and yet] related intimately to experiments going on in literature.

What struck Greenaway most was that these films

had no truck with all those other difficulties like a star system; the pretense of acting (which I had great problems with); had no desire for objective truth that would exist in terms of a Grierson tradition. So here was a way through.

The study of classic documentary traditions at the BFI (perhaps coupled with his own work at the COI) led Greenaway to a growing disillusionment with the concept of "documentary truth."

It seemed to me more ethically acceptable to say "This is a lie, this is a fiction, but let's try to tell the truth within fiction" (always acknowledged as fiction). None of this pretense of the English system.

However, despite his antipathy toward classical documentary, Greenaway's early work in particular is clearly shaped by the industrial filmmaking practice and style of government-sponsored informational films. Early films such as *H is for House*, *Windows* (1974), and *Dear Phone* (1976) (his thesis film at the BFI) can be seen as virtual parodies of the kind of work done at the COI. For Greenaway, *Windows* in particular marks the beginning of his career as a filmmaker.

Truffaut suggested that a filmmaker's subsequent career is always made manifest with his first acknowledged film – and all the characteristics are there: the statistics, the wordplay, the black humor, the idyllic countryside, the music, structure, [the] formulation of a very deadpan, flat, static image, carefully framed. All the characteristics are there.

Windows epitomizes what someone once called "the pathos of statistics." The narration is made up of a list of progressively more specialized "facts."

In 1973 in the parish of W., 37 people were killed as a result of falling out of windows. Of the 37 people who fell, 7 were children under 11, 11 were adolescents under 18, and the remaining adults were all under 71, save a man believed by some to be 103.

As we listen to the increasingly convoluted statistics, we see a series of windows, each shot from inside a house. Some compositions gaze through windows onto the landscape, others emphasize the frames. At times there are unexpected correspondences between the seemingly arbitrary images and the narration. When the narrator notes that "among the 19 adults who fell" was "a seamstress," we see a woman sewing. Told that of the eleven adolescents who fell, "Five were students of aeronautics, one of whom played the harpsichord," we hear harpsichord music. A single statistic may be a fact, but two together form the beginnings of a story, a character, or a conspiracy.

At sunset on the fourteenth of April, 1973, the seamstress and the student of aeronautics who played the harpsichord jumped into a plum tree from a window in this house.

With a phrase, the image takes on a sudden significance. The audience's position shifts and instead of coolly considering mathematical probabilities, we find ourselves at the heart of the space in question.

Despite the ironic distancing, these early short films are also Greenaway's most overtly personal films in terms of both content and mode of production. On *Windows,* Greenaway notes, "I did everything, I was the cameraman, I did the narration, I certainly edited it. I expect it must have cost me five hundred pounds."

Each of Greenaway's short films is built on the radical disjunctions of sound and image, stasis and movement, narrative and nature. *H is for House, Windows,* and *Water Wrackets* (1975), for instance, are made up exclusively of a series of idyllic pastoral images whose connection to the fanciful stories, lists, and fictional histories on the soundtrack is delightfully tenuous.

In *Dear Phone, A Walk Through H,* and *Vertical Features Remake,* the narrative space is segregated from sections of "pure cinema." As the elaborate verbal commentary unfolds, still, man-made images fill the screen: photographs, charts, letters, maps. But at other moments the talking stops and we see moving images of nature: the unoccupied landscapes of *Dear Phone* and *Vertical Features,* the images of birds in *A Walk Through H.* "Nature" exists outside any attempt to impose order through storytelling; presented without commentary these segments are accompanied by music (*Vertical Features Remake*) or unobtrusive ambient sound.

Greenaway then begins to break down the various *kinds* of storytelling. In *H is for House* there are three different kinds of narration. In the first, a narrator (Greenaway) tells stories about naturalists and developers. The second kind of voice-over is a pedagogical dialogue between a father (Greenaway) and his young daughter. As he asks "A is for . . . ?" "B is for . . . ?" she blurts out her favorite answers – "Butterfly!"

The third kind of narration comes in the authoritative voice of Colin

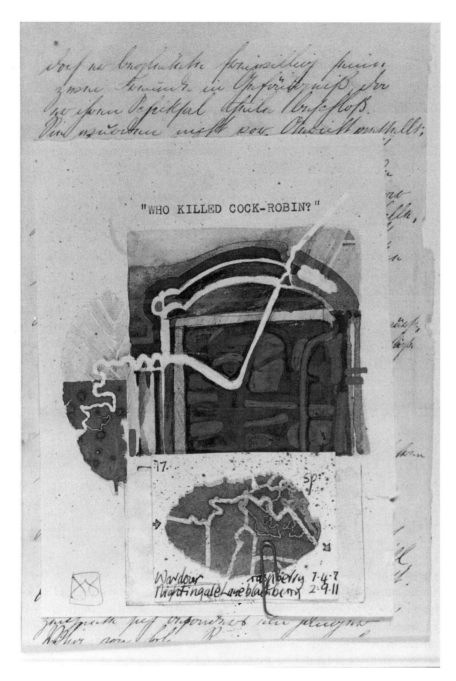

Figure 2. "Who Killed Cock-Robin?" *A Walk Through H* (1978). (Peter Greenaway).

Cantlie (who would narrate most of Greenaway's early films, as well as parts of *The Falls* and *Four American Composers* [1983]). Cantlie recites words that begin with the letter H. Some are related series: birds ("H is for hawk, hoopoe, hawfinch, heron, harrier") or plants ("hawthorne, heather, hemlock, holly, hellebore, and hazel"). As the lists continue, the organizational principle of "things that start with H" leads not to order but to chaos. "H is for health and happiness, hearse, hepatitis, heretic, heaven, hell, horror, holocaust and His Holiness." The arbitrariness of such lists is underscored by the willful inclusion of nearly anything: "H is for bean – haricot bean. And has-been."

The charm of Greenaway's short films comes from the coexistence of a high-spirited playfulness and a lingering emotional effect. In Greenaway's work, both wit and feeling are produced the same way: the inclusion of blissfully irrelevant detail, the development of character through throwaway lines and non sequiturs, a sense of resignation when confronted with the universe's lack of meaning balanced by a taste for the absurd. The delicacy of these films results from Greenaway's use of indirection; what makes them so moving is harder to pinpoint. Intangible and evanescent, their special quality exists in the space between images and words. The rapt stillness that marks the contemplation of sun-filled landscapes in *Dear Phone* and *Vertical Features* is combined in *Windows* and *H is for House* with the pure pleasures of domesticity: a toddler plods across a lawn, bees hum around a table, a woman dozes in the sun.

Both *H is for House* and *Windows* were shot in the same house in the village of Wardour, a setting discovered by Greenaway "almost by accident." A "friend of some people Michael Nyman used to know" had gone skiing.

> It was suggested that I should spend a fortnight down at these people's house, looking after their animals. I had just met my wife. It was a quite idyllic time.

Greenaway married in 1969 and his oldest daughter was born in 1970. Commenting on the "home movie" quality of *H is for House* ("H is for home movie"), Greenaway points out that "that was early family life. My children were very young. I spent, certainly, some extremely beautiful times down there." The area around Wardour, on the Wiltshire–Dorset border, became a personal landscape for Greenaway.

> Every landscape I have since encountered has to measure up to this landscape's history, mystery, variety, drama, and charm, though I am

not in any doubt that its ten square miles have been largely re-fashioned in my imagination.[32]

Greenaway's emotional attachment to the English landscape began in childhood. "I had a minor English public school education and hated it but we had incredibly long holidays, about three and four months." Returning to his grandmother's house in Wales for his summer holidays, Greenaway explored the "extraordinarily beautiful countryside." "A lot of my memories are very strong there." In contrast to the mountains of the west, Greenaway locates his "delight in the flat landscape" in East Anglia, which is for him "the nearest you can get to the flat skies, two-thirds sky, one-third land, characteristic of Dutch painting."

Around 1978, Greenaway moved closer toward writing and directing his own work full time, motivated in part by changes in his personal life. On the making of A Walk Through H, Greenaway writes simply:

My father died. His ornithological knowledge, never collected or collated in anything like a comprehensible book – it was five suitcases and two trunks of scattered notes – died with him. A loss of knowledge. I made a film in small part reparation.[33]

Greenaway identifies the tension that existed between him and his father as being

part and parcel of why I'm a filmmaker still – the desire of a young child to prove the love of his father . . . to placate him or attract him. All those early films I can say without the slightest blush are attempts, I suppose, to create a bond that was never there.

Substantially longer (forty-one minutes) and more expensive than anything Greenaway had done before, A Walk Through H, or The Reincarnation of an Ornithologist was financed by the BFI at a cost of £7,500.

A Walk Through H combines all the characteristics of the earlier films. Narrator Colin Cantlie describes a journey illustrated by various "maps" made up of Greenaway's paintings. (Greenaway studied painting in art school and has continued to exhibit his work from the 1960s through to the present.) Because of the journey's increasingly metaphysical character ("perhaps the country existed only in maps"), the landscape had to be "fantasized – not photographed."[34] Abstract evocations of a spiritual journey, the maps can be emphatic, red lines tracing a clear path through neatly divided fields, or they can be as mysterious as a fading impression on the back of a stolen envelope. Enigmatic signposts, blurs of ink seeping into paper, emphasize the material fragility of the marks people make, the indecipherable traces of their attempts to say where they have been. Only the birds, seen in clips kept separate from the ornithologist's tale, need no maps. Unlike the film's unnamed hero, birds are not given to making mistakes, being misled, caught in pointless repetition, or slowed by the warnings of signposts. Unlike human beings, their way is unmarked but utterly clear.

Greenaway's application (and subversion) of structuralist principles is apparent in the film's structure. "There were ninety-two maps in all – an act of homage to . . . John Cage, and most especially to Cage's 1940s *Indeterminacy Narrative*, whose ninety parts I had counted incorrectly."[35]

The making of *A Walk Through H* also coincided with Greenaway's leaving his position as a director at the COI. "It was maybe in practical terms the worst time to become freelance. . . . My second daughter had just been born." The break with the COI was not abrupt.

> For about three years [roughly 1975–78] I was doing my own films, making things like *A Walk Through H, Vertical Features Remake,* editing other directors' films, and also making my own COI films as well.

He was able to pull away permanently with the making of *The Falls* in 1980.

Produced "on an impoverished budget" of £80,000, *The Falls* was "the first British film to win the BFI award for Best Film for thirty years."[36] A monumental three-and-a-half-hour parody of the British documentary, *The Falls* presents government-produced documentaries as highly developed forms of fiction whose value lies somewhere between the paranoid comforts of conspiracy theory and the zany absurdity of Monty Python. *The Falls* also shows why Greenaway locates his most important British influences outside cinema. "My literary interests," Greenaway points out,

> were strong on lists, classifying, encyclopedias, and the nouvelle roman. . . . My films perhaps relate [best] to an English literary tradition that also includes Edward Lear and Lewis Carroll, and to English landscape painting.[37]

The Falls is also the culmination of the Tulse Luper saga begun in *A Walk Through H* and continued in *Vertical Features Remake*. Greenaway recalls, "I'd previously created this character called Tulse Luper." Greenaway and his wife "came across this cache of old photographs in a trunk" at a "carboot sale" (or flea market).

Figure 3. A signpost on a map in *A Walk Through H.* (Peter Greenaway)

> You could virtually create an entire history of the family (I'm sure it's highly fictional the way that we did it). Most of the photographs were of this gentleman with a face that looks out of Beckett.

The weathered countenance that actually resembles Samuel Beckett himself came to personify Greenaway's favorite fiction, Tulse Luper. "He's an ornithologist basically. Back again to the same phenomenon – my relation to my father. But he was also an excuse, a classic alter ego figure."

Hints of fiction proliferate whenever Luper appears. In *Vertical Features Remake,* members of the fictitious IRR (Institute for Restoration and Reclamation) endlessly debate the veracity of three separate reconstructions of a Tulse Luper film about verticals in the rural landscape, concluding at one point that Luper, his film, and all its documentation are fiction. Through a deliberate confusion of Luper's work with his own – by situating Luper as filmmaker, author, and bird fan – Greenaway deconstructs the figure of the author at the very moment he is establishing himself as an auteur.

Greenaway's deconstruction of structuralism, playfully redefined, is central to *The Falls* and to all his films made before and after. "I was much too cynical about structuralism to be a good, down-the-line structuralist as *Ver-*

tical Features Remake, I hope, indicates." For the former editor and director of informational films, the explanatory power of organized data (mathematical, visual, linguistic, scientific, and artistic) becomes progressively less tenable the more it is insisted upon. All of Greenaway's feature films are obsessed with the way principles of organization (alphabetical, numerical, statistical) have a tendency to become ends in themselves. *A Zed and Two Noughts* (the title itself breaking a word into its component parts) takes us from apples to zebras, each item rotting picturesquely so scientists can study its decay. *Drowning by Numbers* counts the ways (literally counting the scenes) men and their science are overwhelmed by women and their mystical ties to nature: number 1 is plastered on a tree, 100 on a sinking ship. Despite his deep response to Vermeer and the work of other artists (especially painters), Greenaway finds that art does not serve humanity any better than science does.[38] Both *The Draughtsman's Contract* and *The Cook, The Thief, His Wife and Her Lover* organize the world as a series of artworks only to find that the rules of consumption still reign.

Despite the attention garnered by *The Falls,* it was the immediate international success of *The Draughtsman's Contract* in 1982 that established Greenaway as a commercial filmmaker.

> I realized that I could go on making obtuse, recherché films for ever and ever that would never be seen beyond the converted. I also had the feeling that I was coming to the end of my subsidized life. So there was a certain pragmatism involved. I certainly wanted to come out of the experimental-movie closet and seek a wider audience.[39]

Financed by the BFI and Channel Four, *The Draughtsman's Contract* played every major film festival (Edinburgh, Venice, New York, Rotterdam, London, and Berlin) and established Greenaway's reputation as a world-renowned filmmaker. When the film played the London Film Festival in 1982, the opening-night screening at the National Film Theatre had particular significance. "The National Film Theatre represented art cinema, not commercial cinema," and Greenaway found himself following in the steps "of a hero like Bergman – who was always on at the National Film Theatre." It was because of *The Draughtsman's Contract's* popularity at festivals that Greenaway met his producer, Kees Kasander, who was working as an assistant to Hubert Bals, the director of the Rotterdam Film Festival. *Draughtsman's* proven international appeal also made it possible for Greenaway and Kasander to find financing for future films.

Greenaway's films since *The Draughtsman's Contract* have been financed by combinations of international money (*Prospero's Books,* for instance, was made with British, French, and Dutch financing and technical assistance from Japan). Where *The Draughtsman's Contract* cost £300,000, the films in the mid-1990s have an average budget of "about 2 million pounds." "All the money, I think, is up there on the screen," Greenaway insists. "I know it sounds incredibly wet, but these films are essentially made for love. They have to be."

Such tight budgets require a high degree of professionalism. One gets the impression that Greenaway and his production team are not ruffled by much. Greenaway notes that during the filming of *Drowning by Numbers,* for instance, when "England was hit, as it is about once every hundred years, by a hurricane [that] absolutely wiped our set away and ripped all the leaves off the trees," the production lost a mere three days. This sense of equanimity extends to the cast as well as the crew.

> Gielgud always used to say how extraordinary our sets were because nobody ever shouted, nobody lost their temper, everything was on an even keel. Even though in some sense it wasn't brilliantly organized, the thing got done with a sense of affability and ease.

Such a disciplined approach to filmmaking also makes it possible for Greenaway to be famously prolific. In addition to writing and directing feature films, he continues to produce short films as well as works for television, publish screenplays and novels, mount exhibitions throughout Europe, and stage his first opera – making Peter Greenaway the model of a contemporary auteur.

I

The Falls (1980)

The National Landscape and All That Was in It

In *The Falls,* the benign surface of the national landscape has been rent by a catastrophe of such magnitude that it can only be held together by a phalanx of quasi-official government reports, to wit, the most recent English-language version of *The Falls.*

Like *Vertical Features Remake, The Falls* is ostensibly a film made by a committee. In its every aspect, *The Falls* is a tribute to bureaucratic zeal, a monument to systems for the organization of data and those who use them. Like any good government document, *The Falls* carefully sets forth its own methodology, a scaffolding riddled with flaws upon which the story blithely rests.

Unlike direct cinema, which seeks to convey "life as it happens," *The Falls* presents itself as the kind of documentary that foregrounds its own construction, its authenticity as document guaranteed by its format, a format strictly adhered to throughout the film's 186-minute running time. From the first Fall to the last (Orchard Falla and Anthior Fallwaste), each segment begins with a black title card bearing a large white number and the name of the subject.[1] The same music brightly announces the beginning of each segment.

By contrast, the material contained within each segment and the style in which it is presented are largely unpredictable. Living lives beset by incongruity, explainable solely by non sequiturs, redundancies, odd emphases, and the errant detail, the subjects of *The Falls* exist in a conceptual landscape out of Borges via Lewis Carroll.

There is an ever-present tension in *The Falls* between containment and chaos. In his preface to *The Order of Things* (originally entitled *Les Mots et les choses,* or "words and things"), Michel Foucault describes a "'certain Chinese encyclopedia'" in which "it is written that" 'animals are divided into: (a) belonging to the Emperor, (b) embalmed, (c) tame, (d) sucking pigs, (e) sirens, (f) fabulous, (g) stray dogs, (h) included in the present classification, (i) frenzied, (j) innumerable, (k) drawn with a very fine camelhair brush, (l) *et cetera*, (m) having just broken the water pitcher, (n) that from a long way off look like flies.'[2]

For Foucault, this "passage in Borges" shatters

all the familiar landmarks of my thought . . . breaking up all the ordered surfaces and all the planes with which we are accustomed to tame the wild profusion of existing things.[3]

As in Greenaway's world, "the wonderment of this taxonomy,"

what transgresses the boundaries of all imagination, of all possible thought, is simply that alphabetical series (a,b,c,d) which links each of those categories to all the others.[4]

In *The Falls,* as in Borges, the implied logic of the system is systematically undermined by its eccentric contents. Simply put, the victims of what comes to be known as the Violent Unknown Event are turning into birds.

In Greenaway's film, the logic of the format (orderly, sequential) is precariously balanced against the progressively more incredible tale contained within it. The more information we receive, the harder it is to believe what we hear. We soon begin to see that the very system that so confidently imposes order on the impossible is itself insane. But in a film whose title evokes both water at its most chaotic (plunging off the edge of the world into the abyss) and an originary biblical catastrophe, we must also remember that the preeminent fall is apostasy – the falling away from faith and the loss of the ability to believe in a universal explanatory system.

In any serious parody, method is all. The more incredible the story, the more essential it is to relate it with a completely straight face and in a method beyond reproach. Drawing on his years of experience as an editor and director for the COI, Greenaway constructs his film out of a nearly encyclopedic array of documentary styles. For staged interview scenes and shots of "talking heads," Greenaway relied on mostly nonprofessional on-screen help. *The Falls*

used the services of practically everybody I knew – my friends, my acquaintances, their children, my many Yorkshire in-laws, Michael Nyman's Estonian in-laws, *Time Out* critics, my neighbour's doctor's receptionist, local shop-keepers, travel-agents, fellow editors and their wives and grandparents and dogs, film cameramen and their ex-wives, an accountant coerced by a film-appearance, a passing car-mechanic and his son, child-minders.[5]

In a parody of cinema verité, Greenaway himself puts in an appearance as a filmmaker interviewing Armeror Fallstag (#81), a Bob Dylan–like rock star, in the backseat of a car, in a parody of D. A. Pennebaker's *Don't Look Back* (1967).

> I was interested in the whole cinema verité thing but again I found that just as phony because the documentarist became too egotistical. Somehow his subjectivity became not just out of the frame but inside the frame. That, again, I found unacceptable.[6]

But, without question, the style Greenaway favors most is the one that carries the implicit and unquestioned authority of the BBC: the use of a voice-over narrator – traditionally known as "voice of God" narration (if God is in fact a higher authority than the BBC). Greenaway's favorite narrator, Colin Cantlie, is himself a kind of fiction, not being a professional announcer at all but another of Greenaway's colleagues at the COI. A researcher, scriptwriter, and producer, Cantlie "occasionally wrote the commentaries" for the COI films Greenaway edited. For Greenaway, Cantlie "had an excellent voice, deep, authoritative, and he read well," but above all, "he sounded more BBC than was possible."[7]

Through narrators such as Cantlie, Greenaway wanted to invoke the "authoritative documentary BBC voice." This and all the other ways documentaries guarantee their authority through something as insubstantial as style become one of *The Falls*' preeminent themes.

As a list of ninety-two names scrolls over the opening shot we are told that the

> names are taken from the latest edition of the Directory, published every three years by the committee investigating the Violent Unknown Event – the VUE for short.

The directory lists all known victims of the VUE, of which the ninety-two figures represented in *The Falls* constitute a small if certifiably random sample. "The ninety-two people represented in this film all have names that begin with the letters F – A – double L": Fallaby, Fallfree, Fallanway, Fallstoward, Fallusson, Fallwaste (numbers 5 and 6, 63, 13, 82, 89 and 92, respectively). "The names are presented in the alphabetical order in which they stand in the directory" and thus "represent a reasonable cross-section of the nineteen million other names that are contained there."[8]

The VUE Directory Commission itself gains its authority and its aura of objectivity by maintaining a certain bland innocuousness characteristic of bureaucracies, a willed anonymity that means safety. Acronyms bestow authority (even if they are parodic, meaningless, unattached) by presupposing widespread familiarity. For instance when Mashanter Fallack, #9, lists a group of well-known institutions, initials suffice ("The IRR, BFI, COI, the European section of the WSPB – not to miss the VUE Directory Commission"). Many of those listed, such as the World Society for the Protection of Birds, evidently need no introduction, although others have undergone small but telling changes. The BFI, for instance, is not the British Film Institute, producers of *The Falls,* but the Bird Facilities Investments [sic]. The fictitious IRR and the actual COI both already possess ideal monikers, names at once all-encompassing and blissfully uninformative: the Institute for Restoration and Reclamation and the Central Office of Information.[9]

The anonymity of the Directory Commission fails to protect it from attack and does not guarantee omniscience. As soon as the biographies start, problems arise around the issue of representation. Consider the subject of the first biography:

Orchard Falla is a Kapistan speaking young male man. He suffers from perpetually aching teeth, gross anemia and a marrow deficiency.

"There is no known photograph" of Orchard Falla. In the absence of images we haunt the locations he is said to have haunted, though it is pointed out that the view we see (which replicates his habitual gaze eastward) is in fact in error. Orchard would "stare fixedly to the south east"; however, what he wanted to look at (the Lleyn peninsula of Wales) was in fact 45 degrees to the north, or due east. Instead he faced Pembrokeshire, which is "much too far to the south." Whereas fiction calls upon the reader to suspend disbelief, a documentary depends on belief; its scrupulous methods evoke it. And so when a shot of the horizon is replaced with a shot of a presumably different horizon, we have to trust that the images represent what the narrator says they represent – Wales and Pembrokeshire – though, as both are images of the sea, it is hard to tell.

The fictitious makers of *The Falls* are canny enough to authenticate their work by calling attention to their fallibility. As the camera tracks past row after row of mobile homes, we are told that

Standard Fallaby has a DC-3 single berth caravanette with a glass roof. In winter he hides it among hundreds of other caravans on sites in the west of England, ostensibly that it might escape the scrutiny and examination of his sister Tasida Fallaby, whose attentions, according to Standard, are *not* ornithological and exceed those of an orthodox brother and sister relationship. The VUE Directory Commission have as yet not been able to locate Standard Fallaby or his caravan.

Number 69 cannot be discussed because the biographical material is owned exclusively by Crow Films. Numbers 72 and 73 (Castan Fallochery and Cottes Fallope) "have been temporarily blue-pencilled" by the BFI (the Bird Facilities Industries). Allia Fallanx (#14) cannot be described because "the publication of personal biographical details of VUE commission employees is forbidden." Allia's wife, Starling Fallanx (#15), is profiled instead.

And some lives are simply complicated. Twin sons of different mothers (twin sisters), "Ipson and Pulat Fallari were brothers in fiction or half-brothers in fact or, thanks to Tulse Luper, maybe the other way around." The fourteenth edition of the VUE directory said they were dead,

> shot in Medina Sidonia by the only legitimate son of their father. The directory is silent for 2 years, only to resurrect them in the 17th edition, this time spelling Ipson as Ipsan.[10]

The authenticity of the directory is ironically verified by its mistakes, the commission's power reinforced by its ability to acknowledge and recuperate error. Joyan Fallicary #66 is a place not a person, David Fallcash #47 was "entered due to false representation," Merriem Falltrick #84 is "insubstantial," while Wrallis Fallinway #69 is "a typing error – see #13." Any attempt to foil the compilers of *The Falls* brings down the full wrath of the law. When we reach #80, Ascrib Fallstaff, the narration is blunt: "Pernicious inclusion of a fictional character. Criminal charges pending."

Names

As the incongruities pile up, basic identification of each subject becomes less and less certain. Names get changed and the explanations for how and why point to conspiracy, fraud, and the heavy hand of the commission itself. After the Violent Unknown Event, Cathine Fallbutus (#41) reverted to her maiden name and legally changed her children's names. Propine Fallax #27, on the other hand, is included in the directory precisely because of the "accident of a marriage license." "To underline her aversion to the darkness of cinemas and in order to make a clean break with her past reputation" as a patron of the Goole experimental film society, Propine (otherwise known as the third Cissie Colpitts) changed "her Christian name by deed poll and her surname by marriage." Some are just restless: #53, Orian Fallcaster, changed his name several times – on his birth certificate, his driver's license, and his swimming license. Having since been adopted, he is now out of the directory – much to his regret. Number 48's "Bewick Fallcaster," we're told, "is a name of convenience for which the directory commissioners are responsible, only knowing at the time of the first edition the maiden name of his wife. Since there have been no objections from himself or his family, the name has been ratified and is legal."

Some identities are too popular. Five people claim to be #59, Ostler Falleaver. Fraudulence hangs heavy in the air as all five read a prepared statement denying the Boulder Orchard as one of the epicenters of the VUE. After demonstrating its ability to bestow and withhold legitimacy (noting succinctly that the statement was in an "unauthenticated" VUE language), the commission diagnoses the five as having "compound schizophrenia" – a scientific-sounding term as bureaucratic as it is psychiatric, which pretends to account for things without actually specifying what. There is photographic documentation of Ostler Falleaver as well; we are told he or she is one of five people in a photograph with five people in it, giving this identity an abundance of pretenders while calling the reliability of visual evidence into question.

The unreliability of names is not helped by those who wish to hide their identities: Affinado Falleur #62 also changed his name, although "according to his wife [he] was paid £5,000" to do it at the request of FOX (the Society for Ornithological Extermination). He might also be in league with the IRR: "The Institute for Restoration and Reclamation wanted a character without a history to represent them at the repeal of the European Landscape Bill." The commission itself participates in concealing people's names by giving them a selection of pseudonyms to be used for the film. Falleur chooses "Nathan Isole Dermontier," the aviation pioneer. (Taking the name of a famous aviator, his wife suggests, might have made it easier for him to get a pilot's license.) As if Affinado's fluidity wasn't enough, the VUE commission "offered Falleur/Dermontier's wife anonymity" and we see a woman leafing through a collection of potential identities. "After perusing the possibilities, she declined."

With these pseudonymous photos, people can choose not only the name they will be known by but the image that will be shown while we hear their story. The narrator calls attention to the "delicate matter" of doing a biography of a living person and stresses the directory's consideration in providing subjects with a choice of pseudonymous identities. For the story of Squaline Fallaize #10, a hand sifts through a packet of ten black-and-white photos arranged like a stack of cards. Some are photographs of famous peo-

Figure 4. Possible identities (Tulse Luper is fourth from left, top row). *The Falls* (1980). (copyright British Film Institute)

ple, some are photographs of allegedly real but less familiar people (the short-story writer Tulse Luper), and some are famous representations of historical figures (Jean-Louis David's portrait of the assassinated Jean-Paul Marat). In some, "real" images (actual photographs) have been appropriated to support fictitious identities (Gang Lion, Van Hoyten, and Cissie Colpitts). And some are of real people *playing* fictional characters (Tippi Hedren in *The Birds*). Squaline Fallaize chooses the latter, identified on the soundtrack as simply "another bird victim." When Aptesia Fallarme (#18) chooses the same photo, it is identified as a picture of "a bird victim who is also an actress." Anteo Fallaspy (#20) and Hasp Fallbazz (#33) choose to be represented by more abstract representations, the latter by the picture of Marat and the former by the blank head of the chart used for graphing VUE symptoms. What's one fiction more or less? Convention thus allows patent fictions to stand as legitimate corroboration.[11]

Languages

The most noticeable effect the VUE has on its victims is the instant production of new languages (or "compound articulacy"). This new linguistic knowledge can cause difficulty, as with #5 and #6, Standard and Tasida Fallaby, who are brother and sister yet find themselves speaking radically different tongues. He (Standard) speaks Curdine, a language that is evasive and ever changing, whereas Tasida's Katan is blunt, coarse, and to the point.

The wholesale invention of languages gives Greenaway a chance to indulge his interest in names (Catalan B, Betelgeuse, Metropolitan Kath-a-ganian).[12] The descriptions are even more charming. Curdine, we're told, is a cursive language that "deliberately fosters ambiguity and encourages punning." Tulse Luper has said that it is "a superlative language" and in the larynx of the right speaker would be "an antidote to all the world's feathers."[13] Tasida Fallaby (a native speaker of Katan) "learned a mechanical Curdine" to be able to speak to her brother, being particularly sure to pronounce bird names with accuracy; however, her efforts were considered a failure as Curdine is "antipathetic to being spoken mechanically."

Ninety-two languages and ninety-two subjects suggests a connection between identity and language to the extent that each human being's use of language is so distinctive, it becomes an idiolect. Fallaver, for instance, is the ninety-second VUE language; its only and last speaker was #26, Agropio Fallaver.

Being restricted to only one language, though, can be a kind of trap. Despite being a victim of the VUE, Coppice Fallbatteo (#30) spoke only his native Italian, although he "tried very hard to learn one of the VUE languages."

> Ambitiously he had chosen Betelgeuse, the language of unlimited vocabulary and rapidly changing grammar and syntax. As fast as he had mastered one small area of its possibilities, he found that the same small area had developed, realigned itself with a new set of meanings, or had indeed become obsolete. Dispirited, Coppice had made a hesitant start at Katan.

Several people are multilingual, finding themselves at home with various combinations of languages. Mashanter Fallack (#8) speaks English and Karnash with Allow-ease. Appis Fallabus (#4) is a "Regest-speaking young man" who is also fluent in "Metropolitan Dutch" (which on the soundtrack sounds suspiciously like pig Latin). Many VUE victims have a particular affinity for Welsh, including Musicus Fallantly #12, Bird Gaspara Fallicutt #67, Cathine Fallbutus #41, and others. French also has a special status. Astraham and Loosely Fallbute (#38 and #39), French catalogue researchers, do not suffer much despite being near one of the epicenters of the VUE. In fact, few in France were affected, a stroke of luck attributed to either

(1) France's sacrifices in the early days of experiments in flight, or (2) the French language itself.

One of the by-products of the proliferation of VUE languages is an explosion of experts, linguists, and translators, many of whom are consulted throughout the course of the film. Musicus Fallantly (#12) has written an Allow/Welsh dictionary. Bird Gaspara Fallicutt (#67) translates the "Star Fighter 143 flight manual from the VUE language of Hapaxlegomena into French."[14] Bwythan Fallbutus "could interpret nine [VUE languages] at a diplomatic level" and wrote the definitive book on the subject, "*A View from Babel.*" (Bwythan himself becomes a subject of *The Falls* as #42.)

But as all expertise is suspect, authorities being particularly well positioned to perpetrate frauds, the post-VUE interest in languages includes "fictitious languages." The major language credential of "trained philologian" and "energetic traveller" Anteo Fallaspy #20 "is as the inventor of the language of Hartileas B," which he designed in order to further "communication with other vertebrates, mainly birds and their precursors, the reptiles." Not content with his VUE symptoms, Anteo promotes elective surgery in order to make the human mouth more like that of the starling. He "chose the starling because of the wide variety of noises it can make, its ability to mimic, its dual plumage and its sociability."

The Body

The chaotic effects of the VUE are different for each individual. In addition to recording names and languages, it becomes the VUE commission's responsibility to chart the mélange of positive and negative effects the VUE has had on the body. Under ordinary circumstances, the body insists on changing. Puberty and aging presage sexuality and death respectively, and a host of "cosmetic" changes such as balding, graying hair, wrinkles, and sagging denote the effects of time. The changes wrought by the VUE are even more dramatic and unsettling.

The most extreme result of the VUE is immortality. Betheda Fallbutus (#40) has said it was the "excitement about immortality that kept her from cutting her wrists." Number 25, Ardenaur Fallater, has "nine lives, four of which he used diving off cliffs in Gabon, saving VUE suicides," the last being lost when he dove into a barley field during a VUE flying exhibition. Several VUE figures seem to have been murdered (despite their immortality) by FOX. Often the victims are those who have threatened to expose the VUE as a hoax.

Other basic tenets of humanity are thrown into question as well. Take, for example, Canopy Fallbenning (#34), who has been "immortally 83" since the VUE. After being told that her favorite Tulse Luper story is "The Cassowary" and that she can time an egg by the tinnitus that strikes her hearing at regular thirty-second intervals, we learn that she has written extensively on the "sexual quadromorphism" that is a hallmark of the VUE.

A core element of identity, gender is riddled with contradictions, a fact heralded in the film by simple redundancy. Subjects are identified as a "male man," a "female woman," a female man, or a male woman.[15] Inspired by Tulse Luper's "Quadruple Fruit," Canopy rails at an incompetent God (or an inadequate catastrophe) that transformed "two orthodox sexual units into a heterodox form," and thus failed to work out fully the upheaval in gender. However, Canopy has decided over the years to "reserve her splenetic attacks for agents of the VUE commission, especially those who believed in the responsibility of birds."

In addition to immortality and gender quadromorphism, there are numerous other physical changes to be charted. Recited, along with name and language, at the beginning of each segment, the VUE symptoms become part of each subject's basic description. People are defined by their symptoms, as surely as by their names, age, or gender, as identity becomes a form of illness.

#60: Edio Fallenby was classified as an elderly female woman. She spoke Untowards with a Yorkshire accent and suffered from fluttering eyelashes, excess numeracy, and a high blood temperature.

The most disturbing of these symptoms are those that transform the body in graphic, painful ways. "The VUE has contracted [#5 Standard Fallaby's] intestine and paralyzed his legs." Standard's sister, Tasida, suffered "one partially collapsed lung, a singing-tinnitus . . . a doubling of the menstrual cycle, and . . . a twisting of the intestine into tighter coils" resulting in "intense cramps" and "malodorous breath."

The VUE commissioners, authorizers of *The Falls,* adopt various organizational strategies for containing or explaining this physical mutability. Most notable is the invocation of science, through terminology (language) and diagrams (providing visual representation of changes through the use of line and color, i.e. mapping the body). When we are told that Anteo Fallaspy #20 "received retractable thumbs, soft serrated fleshy earlobes and a six-part heart," scientific diagrams illustrate what has happened. Charts of hands, feet, and a torso appear, marked with arrows, splashes of color, lettering, and numbering, to indicate where VUE symptoms have appeared on the subject's body. For Anteo Fallaspy, a huge red blotch is splattered over his heart, numbers 1 through 6 pointing to its illegible divisions.

As the symptoms become progressively more fantastical, they begin to form a pattern. We find our dependence on logic leading us to a conclusion almost impossible to believe. Some of the most elaborate symptoms are suffered by #4:

> Appis (Arris) Fallabus is a Regest-speaking young male man. He is partially blind, sensitive to temperature change, and has poor circulation.

Arris Fallabus's most persistent symptom is parasites: "Ticks, lice, termites, tapeworm, you name it." Although he is "obliged to lubricate himself with Spanish oil" every evening, the parasites are "impossible to get rid of at sea level." Although Appis holds birds responsible for his condition, he feels an affinity with the swallow. "A single bird of that species could be preyed upon by no less than a dozen different types of parasites at any one time and that was punishment enough." For #3, Melorder Fallabur, the physical changes are more pointed.

> The muscles along his arms and his chest and back had become enlarged, engorged and strengthened. His doctor referred to the phenomenon as "patagium fellitis" or "skin-wing aggrievement."

As with Borges's encyclopedia, the key to the insubstantiability of *The Falls* is not to be found in its use of categories, its documentary form, in the unreliability of authority, or even the inconsistencies, but in its content. As the VUE's unexplainable effects begin to coalesce into a comprehensible pattern, we find that VUE victims not only have four-part genders and are linguistically profligate, they are being radically re-formed by their symptoms. They are becoming birds.

Obsession, Category 1: Birds

> Boids. Dirty, disgusting, filthy, lice-ridden boids.
> *The Producers* (1967)

Increasingly, *The Falls* can be seen as the flight of fancy of an avian monomaniac. If we do an ornithological survey of *The Falls*, we find nature and culture riddled with overt and covert avian influence. Birds occupy the landscape but cannot be said to be quite in it. As migratory birds, they are for the most part passing through. But their trace is everywhere, particularly in things man-made. Mashanter Fallack pickets The Golden Egg restaurant on Birdcage Road. Anteo Fallaspy's second wife was killed by an electioneering van in the Rue des Oiseaux. The Goldhawk Road is a possible epicenter for the VUE; twenty-six people were found dead at The Raven. Names like Starling, Bewick, Catch-Hanger, Grastled, and Crasstranger evoke bird names common and un–.[16]

Birds are clearly in some danger from man, their corpses scattered across the landscape as we hear grisly tales of their deaths (#55). In #1, Orchard Falla collects "the skulls of seabirds." He cuts their heads off with a penknife and hides them in the toe of a pair of wading boots. ("Concealment is necessary in case he's challenged.") #57 Agrimany Fallchester, accused of selling samples from the Boulder Orchard, spills out his bag for inspection; it contains skeletons of birds, including "a crow's wishbone in Swansea." Not even that much is left of entire species rendered extinct, from archaeopteryx to the earthbound dodo. Time-honored folk tales in the form of nursery rhymes (#49, #77) are used to teach children to fear and disdain our fine feathered friends – a phrase that curiously occurs nowhere in *The Falls*.

Most of *The Falls* dwells on the danger to man from birds: #76 was killed by Hurricane Birdie #1. The VUE commission itself endlessly circles the issue of avian influence. When asked what he thinks of the theory of the responsibility of birds, Appis Arris Fallabus says that "the coincidences seem inexhaustible, obviously – but I leave it entirely to the experts." Orchard Falla "is very noncommittal about any opinion concerning the responsibility of birds, though in an unguarded moment he has described his enemy as the fox."

An interest in ornithology can begin quite young. Despite his large family (#48 through #53), Throper Fallcaster (#54) seems a lonely little boy. An "infant polymath" and collector of bad jokes in several languages, Throper sits in a spare modern room, wearing thick glasses and telling chicken-and-egg jokes as an egg swings back and forth on a string. The loneliness of an exceptional child is accentuated by his having been born in an egg.

The VUE offers worse dangers for children than loneliness. Arris Fallacie (#8), who like Throper Fallcaster appears to be about nine, "gave evidence of being a persistent dreamer of water, Category 1: Flight." A chubby, friendly boy represented by a black-and-white still photograph, Arris "spoke Itino Ray" and "developed a stammer around the letter H." One night while traveling home to London from Perth by rail, he opened the wrong door while looking for the toilet and "fell into the path of an oncoming train."

The oppressive conjunction of children and death marks the darkest aspect of "the VUE's malevolence." The children's premature awareness of death hits with sudden force in the story of Cathine Fallbutus's daughters, Menenome and Olivine (#43, #44). Blond and perpetually ages eight and four, they play with their backs to us, throwing rocks at the sea while standing near a red chair from their favorite storybook. Both girls speak Maudine and have the following symptoms:

> [Menenome was] prone to toothache and nosebleed and was happiest hanging upside down like a bat. She sang a lot, swam well, and like a velvet scoter, could stay under water for five minutes. Olivine spent much of her time asleep. When awake she would join her sister in an extended dance, song, and talk marathon with [a] red folding chair.

English lingers as an archaic trace.

> Menenome remembered one word of English which she taught her sister, though Olivine may have remembered it for herself. They used the word to describe the VUE's malevolence. They pronounced it with a fierce, short, monosyllabic stab. The word was "clout."

When the children learned this word from their mother (referring to a rag hanging on a line outside their farmhouse), they "were amused at such a dead-sounding, monosyllabic word. That night the VUE struck."

Flight

These four children illustrate three different possible relationships to flight: those who are fascinated but remain firmly on the ground (Throper Fallcaster, the little boy with the egg), those who "take wing," if only in a dream (the "dream of flight") (Arris Fallacie), and the ambivalence toward water (Menenome and Olivine throwing rocks at the ocean). The children's relationship to water is important because one of the prime myths about flight in the film centers on the relationship between a child and parent – Icarus and his father, Daedalus.

Of the four classical elements – earth, air, fire, and water – Greenaway in *The Falls* focuses especially on air and water. Water is associated with Pluto/ Neptune and death. Those drawn to the water are linked with death: Orchard Falla drives "at least once every twenty-four hours to the coast, ostensibly to collect the skulls of seabirds." Those from ships or in the navy are associated with violent death so frequently it can hardly be a coincidence. Several women drowned in ship's swimming pools and #55, former ship's navigator Raskado Fallcastle, has one of the most disturbing stories in *The Falls*.[17]

Earth, on the other hand, is defined mostly in relation to water. The most frequent references to land (besides the Boulder Orchard) are to islands or the coast, for example, the Lleyn peninsula (#1), or the beach (#43, #44). Being on an island (such as Great Britain) is not threatening in itself, but in order to leave you must undertake a journey over water.

Flight is also defined by its relation to water, a golden, soaring possibility linked to science (Da Vinci, Icarus's father, the French aviators) and man's urge to outsmart nature through reason. Reason is associated with the Enlightenment coming from France. Following the metaphor of enlightenment, the light of the sun draws people to the sun god, Apollo, the god of reason. The flight of Icarus is poised between light (sun, fire, burning) and water (dark, engulfing). Those who would fly (Melorder Fallabur, Ipsan and Pulat Fallari, etc.) are fated to fall, flights over water being particularly hazardous (see Arris Fallacie).

Not Falls themselves, Icarus and his father sneak into the story through the back door, being referred to usually at the end of segments, by way of illustration.[18] First mentioned in story #3 (Melorder Fallabur), Icarus pops up again, seemingly in passing, at the end of segment #12 (Musicus Fallantly). "Guller," we are told, "is an Allow word" meaning flight over water. "Icarus was a guller."

Greenaway's taste for the non sequitur lends much of the information the quality of a throwaway – until the casual asides begin to add up. For instance, segments #2 and #3 are the first time we hear the story of the Frenchman who jumped off the Eiffel Tower in an early attempt at unaided flight. Unlike the story of Icarus, the running gag about the Eiffel Tower transposes myth to the realm of history, where aspects of the story can presumably be verified by research. Each time we are told about the Eiffel Tower, the information is accompanied by newsreel photography showing a man in heavy gear on a ledge, giving a last salute toward the camera, presumably immediately before jumping. Yet as we watch this (to all appearances) authentic historical artifact/document, the accounts of what we see vary.

In story #2, we are told that Constance Fallabur named her house "Le Nid, after the initials of Nathan Isole Dermontier, who threw himself from the Eiffel Tower in 1870." (We see archival footage of Dermontier drinking tea, presumably before his flight.)

Melorder, Constance's husband, said the story was a fabrication, not least because the Eiffel Tower did not exist until 1889. Constance replied that Dermontier must have jumped from the roof of Les Invalides.

Musicus Fallantly (#12), a singer and the author of an Allow/Welsh dictionary, dedicates his choral work on ninety-two early flight pioneers to Van Riquardt, "the French patriot and pioneer airman who threw himself from the Eiffel Tower in 1889." We see another piece of archival footage of a man in a huge padded suit, standing on a railing, ready to jump. "Cadence, Musicus's wife, said that the film was a reconstruction, not least because the moving picture camera wasn't invented until 1895."

Vaceta Fallbutus (#45), the second son of Betheda Fallbutus (#40), who suffered from motion sickness when the light was brighter than F11, had as "his personal hero" "Reichfeldt, the patriot airman who threw himself off the Eiffel Tower in 1909." (As illustration we see the man on the railing.) "Vaceta's family scorned the hero worship because they knew Vaceta was afraid of heights." To prove them wrong he jumped off a bridge in broad daylight. Stumbling around in the dark under the bridge, he was run over by a van marked CROW (apparently the same one that killed his brother Bwythan, #42).[19]

Crasstranger Fallqueue supplies the presumably definitive version of the Eiffel Tower story in #78. Crasstranger is an "aeronautical journalist and flight historian," and his "knowledge of the facts, figures and feats of air pioneering were rarely contested."

> [He] knew for example, that the man who threw himself off the Eiffel Tower in April 1911, was not the patriot airman Nathan Isole Dermontier, nor the Welsh baritone called Van Riquardt, but was in fact an Austrian clothing manufacturer called Richelt, testing a parachute coat of his own design. Any amount of historical inaccuracy, misguided heroic identification, and misrepresentation could not disguise what was for Crasstranger a supreme example of the folly of aspiring to emulate the birds.

We see the footage of the man on the ledge one last time. Dermontier/ Riquardt/Richelt jumps, and with a cut we see him, unfortunately, land.

Ironically, the heavy concrete ledge we see the patriot airman–clothing manufacturer standing on *does* look like Les Invalides. But when he hits the ground, he clearly lands at the bottom of one of the iron supports of the Eiffel Tower.[20]

Why does it matter? Because this is our entry into the era of scientific myth, of hero-inventors rather than gods, of actual men who take on challenges with means of technology and science, practical applied science made to produce quantifiable results. Icarus and the Eiffel Tower are the two competing myths that recur throughout *The Falls*. Yet it is the myth of science that gets harder and harder to pin down, whereas what we accept as myth (Icarus) remains an ideal.[21]

The concept of human flight, whether mythical or scientific, functions as a metaphor for many relationships in *The Falls*. Distilled into their essence, the complex series of interwoven biographies are often stories about marriage.[22] As a historian, a fantasist, and a debunker of myths and conspiracies, Melorder Fallabur (#3) recounts his plan to jump from a tall building to prove man can fly. Because of his VUE symptoms, he believes it will now be possible; it was the physical changes resulting from the VUE that "persuaded Melorder that his historical and theoretical knowledge of human flight should be put to practical use."[23] In an interview recorded at the Crane Hotel,[24] he raises the issue of conspiracy by suggesting that historians have only reported the failed attempts at human flight, not the successes, Icarus's fall but not his father's skill.

Told of her husband's plans, Constance Ortuist Fallabur is reported to have commented, "Too much entertainment, not enough research." Unlike her husband, Constance refuses to fly. Her symptoms have rendered her "earthbound," and "having an exaggerated respect for gravity, she shuns flight for herself."[25] Although we never see Mr. or Mrs. Fallabur, their houses stand in for them, unassuming, eccentric and stalwart, side by side near an airport. Constance's house (Le Nid, or "the nest") is crowded with furniture thrown out of airport lounges from around the world.[26] Because Melorder has sterilized himself as a result of the VUE, it is implied that he and Constance have grown into a companionable if unpassionate routine, characterized by a certain formal distance.

As with Constance and Melorder, issues of flight are threaded through the story of the twins Ipson and Pulat Fallari and Ipson's wife, Stachia (#17). The VUE put a stop to the brothers' connection with flight (first as air couriers, then as parachutists) because of their tendency to suffer synchronized blackouts. Now Pulat taxis his plane in circles around a runway until the fuel runs out. Bwythan Fallbutus (#42) tells us that like the unfortunate brother and sister Standard and Tasida Fallaby, Ipson and Pulat spoke different languages: Ipson spoke Allow-ease while Pulat was fluent in Capistan. "Allow is terse and impersonal, full of abbreviations and imperatives, as though invented for use on the parade ground or at best for the writers of instruction manuals," while Capistan is "a lazy, gentle language requiring unusual amounts of saliva and above average exposure of the tongue."

"Either way they were inseparable" – until they met Stachia. Like Icarus, Ipson fell out of the sky. Walking a tightrope, he slipped and landed on Stachia. When they ran (or flew) off to be married, a bereaved Pulat began

35

making flights to towns without airfields. A near-fatal crash brings Ipson hurrying to his side, vowing to break with his wife, but his resolution does not last. The three try living together, but Stachia walks out.

Stachia's fate is unenviable: she suffers a rare symptom of the VUE, the "reopening of old wounds." Every scar begins to bleed afresh so that she requires constant transfusions and extensive hospitalization. What is perhaps worse, she meets Van Hoyten, head of the ornithology department at the Amsterdam zoo, and is living with him at the time of the VUE (see *A Walk Through H*). Like Ipson, Stachia speaks Allow "but she scarcely uses it," finding it "antipathetic to her sympathies." The last we hear, she is learning Capistan.[27]

The marital ideal is encapsulated in those who work together and who share a similar attitude toward flight, such as Astraham and Loosely Fallbute. (Mrs. Fallbute's identification as #39 slips without a ripple into Astraham's story as if the two are one.) Catalogue researchers working for "a film company specializing in ornithological films," the Fallbutes are among the very few VUE victims whose symptoms are visible; red splotches placed symmetrically on either side of their faces provide a clue to the Platonic ideal of their match. They drive through the countryside telling their story, cars (especially those driven in circles) frequently appearing in the film as safely grounded airplane substitutes (see #75).

But even those drawn to the same field can be pulled apart. Number 67 Bird Gaspara met her husband Obsian Fallicutt (#68) at an air force cinema at Birdlip.[28] Bird Gaspara weaned Obsian away from a taste for technical films and steered him toward narrative features by depending on his taste for ornithological subject matter. Obsian did not respond until he saw "A. J. Hitchcock's *The Birds*."

With his wife, Obsian viewed all the ornithological material available so he could make a thorough examination of Hitchcock's film. He joined a film lab to learn how to produce cinematic illusion, built an illicit film library, and did a frame count of a new 35mm print of *The Birds*.[29]

Conspiracy envelopes Obsian. Having disappeared, he is traced to Bel Air, where he writes articles for an obscure ornithological journal funded by the Hitchcock estate. His VUE injuries are said to keep him from answering the directory commission's inquiries.

As in the cases of Bewick Fallcaster #48 or Wrallis Fallanway (#13), wives are left to answer for missing husbands. Bird Gaspara believes hers is being blackmailed by FOX. Since Obsian's disappearance, Bird Gaspara has been working with a fellow researcher (male) cataloguing film titles that deal with birds: *Three Days of the Condor, The Owl and the Pussycat, Only*

Angels Have Wings, Four Feathers, and so on. Many of the films are British–Hollywood coproductions (*Where Eagles Dare, The Seagull, The Flight of the Phoenix*). Hitchcock himself was perhaps the ultimate British–Hollywood coproduction.

A Note on A. J. Hitchcock

There are many subtle (and overt) references to "A. J. Hitchcock" in *The Falls,* the most prominent encompassing *Psycho* (1960), *The Birds* (1963), and *Marnie* (1964). The Crane Hotel, where Melorder Fallabur was interviewed, collapses *Psycho's* main character Marion Crane with its legendary setting in the Bates Motel. The Crane pops up again in segment #62, the story of Affinado Falleur (another aviation historian and experimenter), who was said to have a grid (*Vertical Features Remake*) tattooed on his palm from a window (*Windows*) at the Crane Hotel. (The crane is a water bird and thus, like the gull, particularly ominous.)

The Falls also values taxidermy, a skill reserved in *Psycho* primarily for birds (sometimes not). Afracious Fallows #75 is sacked from his position as headmaster for, among other things, "incompetent taxidermy." The shadow of the large bird hovering over Cathine Fallbutus (in #41 and #32) recalls Marion's interview with Norman in his study, where he talks about his hobby of stuffing birds (a British joke, and an Oedipal one if the bird in question is his mother).

Marnie is the only Hitchcock film besides *The Birds* that stars Tippi Hedren ("an actress who is also a bird victim"). Like Marnie, Stephany Falltrix (#85) has an obsession with the color red; she refuses to cooperate with the survey because she does not think it will help her condition. Instead, she supplies a book of blank pages dyed a deep shade of red that progressively lessens as the pages move slowly toward white. One of the most powerful scenes in *Marnie* occurs when Marnie is discovered in the pool of an ocean liner, having tried to drown herself after her honeymoon, a scene echoed in *The Falls* by all the stories of wives and mothers who drowned in ships' swimming pools (#31, #53, #67).

As in Hitchcock's work, criminality covers up or stands in for the frequently violent and often sexually disastrous relationships between men and women. *Marnie* alone filters male–female relations through such crimes as embezzlement, blackmail, the use of aliases and disguises, prostitution, child molesting, rape, and more.[30] In *The Falls,* the innumerable crimes, disappointments, and misunderstandings between men and women mirror the hostility of the universe. Death colors everything.

The story of Raskado Fallcastle #55 palpably describes, without irony, someone's mounting hysteria in the face of mortality. A ship's navigator (and thus associated with the sea, site of chaos and catastrophe), Raskado made maps from the black and white patterns on the hides of his dairy herd. (Reproduced in watercolors on graph paper, the maps are leftovers from *A Walk Through H*, the numbered livestock foreshadowing those in *Drowning by Numbers*.) Accused of the scalding death of a close friend (a cartographer mapping owl habitats), Raskado became unhinged, slaughtering his herd and using tar to cover the white on the cows' corpses. A fanatical believer in the responsibility of birds, he began slaughtering birds in reconstructed washhouses (water boding ill for flying creatures), and finally set himself on fire at a bird sanctuary.

Although there are attempts to explain the physical and psychic violence in *Psycho* and *Marnie* (attempts widely found wanting and unpersuasive, dismissed as "dollar-book Freud"), in *The Birds* we are beyond psychology. At times *The Falls* seems like an extensive elaboration on the one scene in *The Birds* where it becomes clear that some things have no explanation. At the diner, the townspeople of Bodega Bay discuss the question of the responsibility of birds. Those superstitious and fearful are eager to believe the birds are actively hostile, the ornithological expert (a tough old bird herself) pooh-poohs that theory, while Melanie Daniels (Tippi Hedren) argues the evidence of her own eyes. She was attacked in a boat by a bird (see the death of Anteo Fallaspy's first wife, Sashio Fallaspy #22). The diner scene also raises the issue of guilt: has human irresponsibility (from Melanie's carelessness in the bird shop to the very existence of birdcages) brought this about? In *The Birds*' diner scene even the solution put forward by FOX is expressed: ornithological extermination. "Wipe 'em out," a drunken sailor shouts, "wipe 'em off the face of the earth!"

Artist-Conspirators

As a couple, Bird Gaspara and Obsian Fallicutt are torn apart by his obsession. Even more important (or possibly less) is Obsian's allegation that the VUE is a cinematic fraud, a hoax played out through cinematic means. While others debate the responsibility of birds, Obsian argues for the responsibility of *The Birds* – that the VUE (accepted, absorbed into the bodies and minds of millions) is, in fact, an elaborate and expensive "hoax perpetrated by A. J. Hitchcock to give some credibility to the unsettling and unsatisfying ending of his film *The Birds*."

And so, roughly two-thirds of the way through *The Falls* (about the same placement as the diner scene in *The Birds*), an explanation for everything is floated and summarily abandoned (though not refuted). The film continues as if nothing happened. We move on, the air of conspiracy thick on the ground as more extensive frauds wait to be revealed.

As Obsian suggests, *The Falls*' greatest conspiracies, hoaxes, and frauds are self-reflexive, turning in on the film and its maker. Obsian's allegations both fortify and undermine the narrative strategy (or any narrative principle) that makes us think that, through careful study of the details, it is possible ultimately to reach the truth. On the contrary, the more we learn – especially about characters who are artists or experts of any kind – the more doubt is cast on everything around them. Not content with unraveling hoaxes, Greenaway's protagonists have a tendency to perpetrate hoaxes as often as they expose them. Take Ashile Fallko. "Novelist, historian, and ornithological journalist," Fallko is the first of whom it is said, "If the VUE hadn't happened, he would have invented it."

Art so often becomes life – or, at the very least, indistinguishable from it – that representation begins to have the same weight as reality. Represented by David's portrait of the murdered Marat, Fallko's pseudonymous photo literally becomes him. "Ashile Fallko, like Marat, died in his bath." The VUE struck him with considerable force, but he survived. Taken first to hospital, he was found to be "suffering from exposure, congested lungs, shock, and a rapidly developing eczema." Like Marat, Ashile took to his bath to alleviate his skin irritation. He had "all the rooms in his house connected to a tape recorder" so that, like Marat, he could "dictat[e] letters from his bath."

As with the revolutionary theorist and martyr, Fallko's death attains the weight of assassination. A toy duck swirls on the water as a soundman records the sound of the tub filling with water and we hear of Ashile's contributions to social upheaval.

> A furious scourge and a shrill critic of institutions, Ashile hounded the VUE commission, and in total succeeded in getting five directors removed or dismissed. And it is reported that he had developed a strong case against Van Hoyten and FOX and was waiting for an opportunity to use it.

Unfortunately for Fallko, "It was said that Fox had trapped him in a technical hypocrisy."

> Persuaded into the role of a contemporary Marat, Fallko only needed a zealous executioner or a celebrated painter to complete the neces-

sary cycle. The execution he had to commit himself. . . . The suicide weapon appears to have been a 2-bar electrical fire.

Instead of the sun's flames causing this would-be Icarus to fall into the sea, the fire falls on him. As we gaze at the painting of Marat, we hear Fallko's last words – "Arghhhh" – said to be "as poignant as anything ever written by a pen that was also a feather."

Intellectuals in *The Falls* are routinely subject to "accidents." Bwythan Fallbutus (#42), the VUE languages expert and author of *A View from Babel,* is run over by a van marked CROW, evidently the action branch of FOX. (The van has a license plate that reads "NID 92.") His brother Vaceta Fallbutus is run over by the same van (#45). Vaceta was particularly interested in exploring sites along the Goldhawk Road, a possible VUE epicenter. Agostino Fallmutt #71 (also known as La Solitaire), was a hermaphrodite who wrote the biography of the man who found archaeopteryx.[31] Accused of "avian blasphemy" for promulgating the theory that birds orchestrated the VUE as calculated revenge against mankind, she becomes the object of intense persecution. Living in caves and driving in circles, La Solitaire is also the model of the artist as misunderstood loner. Her body was found in a boathouse, the cause of death impossible to determine.

The political nature of the work (and perhaps the deaths) of Fallko, the Fallbutus brothers, and La Solitaire forms a thread that continues throughout *The Falls.* Crasstranger Fallqueue, whose knowledge as a flight historian is seldom questioned (#78), comes from a family that is unusually familiar with political murders, having experienced "a fair share of under-planned flying from tenth storey windows" of police departments. Such "defenestration" was attributed by the relevant bureaucracies to a (fictitious) "desire for flight." Crasstranger escaped by hijacking a plane, a quintessential political act. He survived as a refugee by juggling eggs and by posing as a blind ornithologist – in other words, his connection to flight was forced, artificial, unorthodox, and possibly illegal. Greenaway's antipathy to the antiornithological stance of FOX and CROW is underscored by associating them with the methods of the secret police and right-wing death squads.

Other members of the "Falls" are silenced by means short of assassination. Some are bought off like Obsian Fallicutt (#68). When we hear that Affinado Falleur (#62) "was paid five thousand pounds for changing his name" at the request of FOX, the first reason his wife gives for his adoption of an alias is that FOX needed the identity for a saboteur. Bewick Fallcaster #48, whose name is already an alias supplied by the commission itself, has disappeared and the first explanation *his* wife offers is that the "information is false, supplied by FOX."

Some are blackmailed: Ashile Fallko #70, Affinado Falleur #62, and Sitiarch Fallding #58 ("information unavailable due to blackmail by FOX over a tar and feathering incident"). Sometimes the information has been co-opted: "CROW Films owns the biographical material [on Erek Fallfree #63] exclusively." And sometimes FOX actively spreads disinformation, muddying the waters, as with the five people who claim to be Ostler Falleaver (#59). There are strong indications that Ostler Falleaver has been manufactured by FOX in order to deny that the Boulder Orchard is a possible epicenter for the VUE.

The Boulder Orchard is owned by relatives of Rappaport Gull.[32] Anti-intellectual and anti-art, Gull is a kind of counterexpert, brought in to contradict the experts in the name of journalistic objectivity and bureaucratic fair play. Gull, for instance, dismisses Melorder's and others' plans for unaided human flight (#3). Identified as a "photographer, embryologist, saxophonist, firewatcher, and writer of egg tales," Gull, like FOX, is most of all an obstructionist, stopping the story in its tracks (and possibly some of the characters) nearly every time he appears. (Gulls eat the eggs of other birds, including their own.)

"Experts" like Gull and his shady associate, Cisgatten Fallbazz #32, are frequently presented as hostile figures. An avid exploiter of interest in birds, having made bird novelties until the theory of the responsibility of birds made them unpopular, Cisgatten has an unsettling tendency to turn into an owl as he is being interviewed, courtesy of slow dissolves. (Nocturnal predators, owls hold a special, dark place in Greenaway's personal mythology; Van Hoyten was keeper of the owls at the Amsterdam zoo (#17, *A Walk Through H, A Zed and Two Noughts*).) There is also evidence that Cisgatten's scientific and ornithological talents have been put to darker uses. His enemies

> accused him of conducting experiments on birds to make the species interchangeable and suggested he kept owls illegally at the back of the house, and that his brother had committed suicide for fear of prosecution.

Not surprisingly, the power wielded by these historians-turned-critics can be quite menacing. Coppice Fallbatteo (#30) is an art historian who "had wholeheartedly taken to the idea of the responsibility of birds." He "dutifully" goes through the history of Western art tracing the representation of avian issues until he zeroes in on a Piero della Francesca painting of the vir-

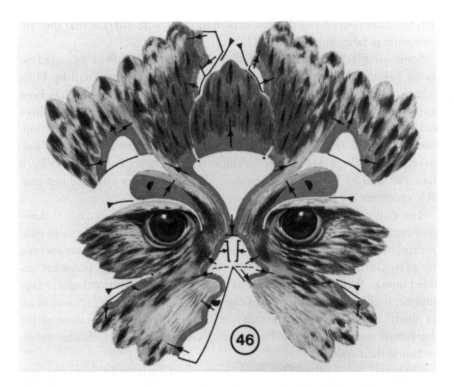

Figure 5. #32: Cisgatten Fallbazz, *The Falls*. (copyright British Film Institute)

gin with an egg suspended above her. Coppice (pronounced like the Italian word for understanding)

> knew everything there was to know about this painting: its conception, its mathematics, the mineral constituents of its colors, the hagiography of its saints, its value in lira, dollars, gold and osprey feathers.

He had his students make copies,

> some bad, some indifferent, some eccentric, some three or four inspired, two almost impossible to tell from the original, and one considerably better.

This last was painted by a woman who spoke Betelgeuse and whose name was Adioner. Their developing relationship is traced through the shifting definitions of a word. "Adioner" could be translated into Italian as "yellow" at the time Coppice started to learn Betelgeuse; when he became interested in the Piero della Francesca the word had shifted to mean "yolk";

when Adioner told him her name it meant "embryo." This collection of co-incidences inspires Coppice to want to marry, possess, and own this girl whom he seduces. When she has a son he takes the child, "fosters" him out to his sister, and names him "pera Adioner" which by that time means "egg." (Throper Fallcaster #54 believes he was born from an egg. Perhaps he was adopted.)

The Conspiracy of Authorship

Conspiracy theory underpins much of the way in which Greenaway constructs narrative. In Greenaway, conspiracy theory becomes a theory of reading.

Conspiracies (planning and carrying out frauds and hoaxes) become models for how artists work and, in return, for how spectators make sense of fact *and* fiction. In watching a film, we reconstruct characters, events, and their authors by imaginatively fusing the evidence presented into a coherent unified whole. The perception of character, event, and author is dependent on faith; characters, whether "real," based on fact, or entirely fictitious, are the product of *our* imaginations. As Greenaway reveals, the process is thus open to illusionism or sleight-of-hand. Documentary in particular becomes a magic act that Greenaway is at pains to undo. Like the canniest of magicians, first Greenaway performs his trick, shows you how it was done, then he does it again. To explain how he reveals the fallacy of "non-fiction," we should return to Greenaway's use of documentary technique.

In a documentary like *The Falls,* characters exist in neither the image nor the soundtrack, but in the interstices. Nearly every character in *The Falls* is a missing subject, re-created or conjured up through effects, artifacts, or unreliable testimony. The image most frequently stands in for an absent subject. We see locations where people have been or may be: the seacoast for #1, Orchard Falla, Constance Fallabur's house (#2), the airports where Pulat Fallari circled his plane until it ran out of fuel (#16). Or we see locations *like* the locations associated with characters: various trailer parks emblematic of the trailer parks where Standard Fallaby (#5) lives.

People can be represented by their work: Anteo Fallaspy's black-and-white footage showing "his enthusiasm for the written word" (#20), Geoffrey Fallthuis's tree film (#83) (both excerpts from Greenaway's early films). They can be represented by the things they liked: Lacer Fallacet #7 by photos of her dogs named after famous female aviators, Carlos Fallantly #11 by slides of his beloved turkey.[33] Characters can even be represented by something we know to be nonrepresentative (pseudonymous photos) or by a declared absence of evidence – because of a mistake (#66), typing errors (#69), false representation (#47), or late-developing symptoms (#37).

Events are as insubstantial as characters. The most notable absence in the film is the VUE itself. Like the characters, the VUE is re-created from its effects. We infer that it must have happened because we can list, catalogue, chart, and analyze the effects it produced. As the film draws toward an end, Greenaway reveals that the central event around which the film is constructed may be a construct.

Given the vast numbers of people involved, the VUE begins to loom as a huge conspiracy. Conspiracy theory assumes there is a guiding intelligence behind any unexplainable event. Is there, then, an author of the VUE?

Suspects

Certainly the most prolific and diversified artist in *The Falls,* Tulse Luper is the author of short stories ("The Cassowary" in #2 and #34, "The Photographer's Dog" #7, "Sparrow Week" #9) and of the essential work on VUE-induced sexual quadromorphism, *Quadruple Fruit* (#34). He also wrote the definitive book on migratory birds of the northern hemisphere, featured in *A Walk Through H* and translated here by Catch-hanger Fallcaster (#49). Luper is a filmmaker (*Vertical Features*), even if, according to critics (#56), his films are "cinematic guano." A teacher of film, his shortest and youngest pupil was the arborist Geoffrey Fallthuis (#83). A near-mythical figure and "hobbyist of the absurd," Luper is a hero to some: #81, Armeror Fallstag the rock star, has come all the way from the United States to meet him, and #61, Shey Fallenby, modeled his life on Tulse Luper's. Others, such as Gang Lion and Van Hoyten, call him a fraud.

In *A Walk Through H* and *Vertical Features Remake,* where the rivalry between Luper and Van Hoyten begins, Luper is also a thief, cartography expert, ornithologist, conspirator, hoaxer, as well as spiritual advisor and guide. To this list his enemies would add charges of forgery, deception, manipulation, and the giving of ambiguous and possibly unreliable advice. They find him fraudulent and his methods for obtaining information questionable.

He may even be fictitious.

According to "some members of the public" (including Gang Lion, a friend of Van Hoyten's and thus an admitted enemy), "Tulse Luper" is a pseudonym. Luper is actually Audubon.

The name Audubon appears several times in the film before it is attached to Tulse Luper. In segment #40, Betheda Fallbutus owns a house in the

Goldhawk Road where Audubon once lived. This passes, early in the film, as an untroubled reference to Jean-Jacques Audubon, the historical figure and bird painter. In #87 (the story of the calligrapher Vassian Falluger), we are told that Audubon and Tulse Luper must be two separate people because Audubon replaced Tulse Luper as master strategist and cataloguer for the VUE. Yet the description of Audubon fits Tulse Luper to a tee. This Audubon made a film about trees based on the number eleven. (The inset films in *Vertical Features Remake* are edited to multiples of eleven.)

If Audubon is Luper, Luper chose well. The name Audubon is, of course, synonymous with the study of birds. The Audubon Society is a group devoted to the protection of birds and the preservation of their habitats. Audubon himself is a near-mythical figure, artist and scientist in equal measure, and the supreme (and most likely the only) example of a man who achieved lasting fame by drawing birds. Jean-Jacques Audubon left a legacy of work, highly prized and much sought after, of rare and expensive drawings of birds. A superb draughtsman, Audubon conjoins artistic excellence with scientific precision.

On the other hand, Audubon also left a legacy of questions about his business practices, his background, and his very identity: That he got money under false pretenses from a syndicate of European investors for his *Birds of North America* folios. That the name Audubon is an alias either (a) to escape creditors and a string of bad debts that seemed to track him wherever he went, or (b) to hide the fact that he was the Dauphin, the son of Louis XVI and Marie Antoinette, hiding out in the French New World to avoid the fate of his parents in the Revolution.[34] (A product of the Age of Enlightenment, the French Revolution unleashed the Terror, its own version of the VUE.) A signifier slipping between the fiction of the film and a reality that is itself fraught with ambiguity, "Audubon" evokes a history at once true, highly unlikely, and impossible to confirm or contradict.

Once the possibility is raised that Tulse Luper could be operating under a pseudonym, the possibility of him starts popping up everywhere. Given his many different skills and professional identities, he is almost certainly the Audubon mentioned in #87 who replaced Tulse Luper as the VUE's master strategist and cataloguer. He could also be #88, Erhaus Bewler Falluper, the "master cataloguer, enumerator and compiler of statistics," whose work on the natural landscape resulted in seventeen incomplete surveys (the project partly illustrated by Tulse Luper's "lost" film, *Vertical Features*). Then again Luper could be #89, Grastled Fallusson, of whom it is tersely stated that he has "invented so much fiction about himself that the directory is unable to vouch for any version of his biography."

Of course Tulse Luper, author of *Birds of the Northern Hemisphere*, might be #90, Castral Fallvernon, the keeper of photos for the VUE and possessor of a wealth of bird anecdote, with an interest in flying machines (illustrated by the work of Leonardo da Vinci – another artist-scientist-inventor-naturalist), and an interest in zoos, especially birds in zoos (*A Walk Through H*). And like Audubon (the real one), Fallvernon is adept with a brush when it comes to retouching or re-creating illustrations of birds. Or Tulse Luper might be #91, Leasting Fallvo, an alibi hunter who catalogues the library of VUE productions, with its poor fiction section containing all the Tulse Luper stories we have seen, including "A Walk Through H," "The Tulse Luper Suitcase," "The Red Chair," and "A Turkey for a Wife."[35] It is said of Leasting Fallvo, "If the VUE hadn't happened, he could have invented it."

Of course, like Dr. Mabuse, a man of many disguises, Luper could be any or all of them. As Luper's possible identities multiply, we get the gratifying sense (as we do with a conspiracy) that all the stories are starting to come together. Bit by bit we create Tulse Luper, and when the picture is nearly complete, we seem to have found the chief conspirator, the one who holds all the strings and knows how all the pieces fit (because he put them there himself). And yet as soon as he comes into focus, he comes into question as part of the fiction. The closer we get to Tulse Luper, the more elusive he becomes, the master inventor who himself turns out to be invented, created from a series of dropped hints and pieces of evidence that were always highly questionable.[36]

Unlike many of the other profiled subjects (of which he is not one), there is an actual photograph of Tulse Luper. With penetrating gaze, a Gallic cigarette raffishly dangling from his mouth, Luper stands clad in a World War II leather trenchcoat that signals membership in the RAF or possibly a branch of British intelligence. Perhaps he worked in reconnaissance. (If he was in the RAF, he would have been a flyer. Crossing the Channel, he would have been a guller.)

The same photo appears in *Vertical Features Remake*. As we gaze in the earlier film at this alluring figure, redolent of mystery, we are told that there *is* no Tulse Luper. "Tulse Luper" is the product of a conspiracy. The photo used to ground the references to such a person, we are told, is actually a picture of the editor's wife's father. The photo no longer represents Tulse Luper but, unhinged from representation, becomes an artifact, "the photo in question." Once this revelation is made, the film goes on as if it never happened.[37]

"Tulse Luper" (in and out of quotation marks) may be, in fact, a meta-

46

phor for authorship itself. As with cinematic characters and events, a film's "author" is someone deduced from effects.

> The auteur is a construction that can only be located provisionally at the "head" of a series of shifting marks: it is a series of texts that retrospectively creates an auteur, rather than an auteur who creates texts.[38]

We chart "his" effects and deduce from them a person who made them. We have already been told that if the VUE is a hoax, the perpetrator could well have been a filmmaker (A. J. Hitchcock). Let us return, then, to #88, Erhaus Bewler Falluper.

Number 88, by virtue of his numerical symmetry and his many biographical resemblances to both Peter Greenaway *and* Tulse Luper, brings together most of the key themes in *The Falls*. Falluper, it goes without saying, is notorious for manufacturing fictions and deliberately confusing identities. Like Tulse Luper, he cannot tell a good joke from a bad one (though this comes from the possibly unreliable calumnies spread by Gang Lion). A filmmaker, he is responsible for the surveys scattered throughout *The Falls* testing people on their knowledge of birds ("In 30 seconds name all the birds you can think of that start with the letter W"). Like his creator, Erhaus demonstrates an effervescent desire to "draw maps, index disaster, and break chaos into small pieces that he might arrange them in a different way, perhaps alphabetically." His desire to chart "the natural landscape and all that was in it" led to only partial works, but "all seventeen incomplete surveys spawned others." (A catalogue of Greenaway's early films lists fifteen short works before *The Falls,* several of which led to later works.)[39] But in place of the rigorously structured surveys demanded of an anthropologist or social scientist or even a structuralist filmmaker, Erhaus Bewler Falluper "preferred random choices." And, like Greenaway, Erhaus ultimately "changed his identity and became a catalogue clerk, working nights in an office in Whitworth St., London, W1."

We can discover much of Greenaway's presence in the traces left by Tulse Luper, a.k.a. Audubon, a.k.a. Falluper. However, the critic's job, like that of the cartographer, is to design a clear route through a maze of detail. When the terrain is fictitious (as in *A Walk Through H* where "perhaps the country existed only in maps"), can cartography/criticism be anything less?

As a librarian, Leasting Fallvo, cataloguer of all VUE productions (charts, maps, illustrations, photographs, stories, and films), links *The Falls* to a Borgesian "Library of Babel," which holds "the translation of every

book in all languages [and] the interpolations of every book in all books."
The library contains "all that it is given to express," including

> thousands and thousands of false catalogues, the demonstration of the
> fallacy of those catalogues, the demonstration of the fallacy of the true
> catalogue.[40]

As in *The Falls,* in Borges's library, criticism is as fictitious as fiction.[41]

The encyclopedic scope of Borges's library finds its match in Greenaway's
ambitions for future editions of "The Falls Directory."

> There was to be a later version with 124 entries that persuaded the
> publishers to make a more sensational volume to increase book-sales;
> there was to be an edition assembled by medical specialists frightened
> of epidemics; a version under brown-paper covers assembled by por-
> nographers; a highly politicised version trying to prove international
> conspiracy; and then three last editions – the first doubted the exis-
> tence of the VUE; the second criminalised the dwindling 60 represen-
> tative victims; the third proved the whole affair was a hoax.[42]

The Falls is the exhaustive, thorough documenting of an event that did
not happen, which affected people who do not exist, verified by experts who
also do not exist, and ultimately invented by an array of possible authors,
none of whom exist either. As the film ends we see that the figure of the author is simultaneously everywhere and nowhere, a fiction that can seem particularly sturdy or can dissolve before you. Whether Tulse Luper or Peter
Greenaway, the author at the very least has something in common with #92,
Anthior Fallwaste, a character who, we are told, has finally succeeded in ter-
minating his relationship with birds.

He might even be found posing as a simple catalogue clerk working
nights in an office in Whitworth Street, London.

2

The Draughtsman's Contract (1982)

"Ah, that was clever."

For Greenaway's first mainstream feature film, producer Peter Sainsbury (head of production at the BFI) made a strikingly modest stipulation: that the characters speak to one another.[1] Consequently, the film opens with a monologue, a close-up of a character addressing the camera. A stylistic red herring (close-ups will be rare, dialogue overflowing), the first shot condenses an astonishing range of the film's major themes. It is a shot of a man telling a story.

Mr. Thomas Noyes, 1694 (Neil Cunningham), sports a powdered eighteenth century wig framing a powdered face, the red of his lips more a product of artifice than of nature. Smacking his lips over a juicy piece of gossip as he eats a juicy piece of fruit, he tells us about "a man who spent more time with his gardener than with his wife." Gardens and wives will prove the poles of attention (or neglect) characteristic of (and fatal to) the ostensible subject of the draughtsman's contract. "They discussed plum trees – *ad nauseam.*" The fruit of the garden will be central, as will the fruit of matrimony. The Latinate aside shows off the speaker's erudition and language's function as a field for exhibitionism and gamesmanship. The people of the gardening gentleman's estate, we are told, were "regaled" every year with the fecundity of his plum trees, "until their guts rumbled and their backsides ached from overuse." Not all fruit nourishes, often passing directly into excrement with much discomfort for the unpleasantly surprised epicure. Greenaway's insistence on the body's inescapable vulgarity at once liberates it (and him) from the strictures of middle-class respectability and lowers it by calling attention to the less exalted attributes of the human animal. The gentleman farmer eventually built a chapel where the pews were made of plum wood (express-

Figure 6. Greenaway on the set of *The Draughtsman's Contract* (1982). (copyright Steve Pyke)

ing his desire to control the landscape as a patron of architecture). The teller concludes with relish that those who visit the gentleman's chapel "still have cause to remember him through their backsides, on account of the splinters." Thus proving that there will be a joke in the end.

The opening scenes of *The Draughtsman's Contract* are framed by titles, the characters' names written in large red baroque signatures as the actors' plainer names appear below, small and white. The fragments of narrative we see begin to accumulate meaning, plots are laid, so that by the time the film's title finally appears, the story proper is well under way. In the murky candlelit interiors of a late seventeenth century salon, Mr. Neville (Anthony Higgins) brags of his ability as a draughtsman to grant a husband "delight or despondency" in both his house and his wife as a result of the way Mr. Neville depicts them, showing one in sun or shade, the other dressed or undressed. Mrs. Herbert (Janet Suzman) is eager to have Mr. Neville stay at Compton-Anstey, her husband's estate, and make a series of drawings of the house that she can present as a gift to her disdainful husband, who is leaving that evening for two weeks. Twelve drawings in twelve days. Reluctant, Mr. Neville eventually agrees. "Your terms are exorbitant, so must mine be." As they sit opposite each other at a small table, Mrs. Herbert dictates the contract for a watchful Mr. Neville, Mr. Noyes acting as notary: eight pounds a drawing, food for Mr. Neville and his servant, and Mrs. Herbert's agreement to meet with Mr. Neville in private and "comply with his requests concerning his pleasure." The game is afoot.

As the title appears, flushed with the zest of Michael Nyman's mock-Baroque score, the film bursts into the open air. The black fancy dresscoat and satin breeches that set Mr. Neville apart from the cascades of amber-hued white ruffles worn by everyone else, provide a dynamic contrast, an exclamation point in the center of a landscape defined by greens. Discussing the use of color in *The Cook, The Thief, His Wife and Her Lover*, Greenaway points out that although the restaurant set may seem red, it is in fact "many different types of red and they all interact, balancing each other."[2] The exteriors in *Draughtsman* celebrate greens, emeralds, olives, yellow-greens and apple greens, Irish and Kelly greens, the grass of an English lawn, the scum on the surface of a pond.

From our first view of it, this quintessentially English landscape is subjected to a program of systematic organization.[3] As a draughtsman, Mr. Neville does work characterized by precision, a near-scientific fidelity to the physical world underscored by the apparatus he uses. A wire grid within a black frame serves to frame the view. Transferring the grid to paper, Neville ensures the correct proportional relationship between objects in space. Balanced on a black lacquered tripod, the frame metonymically figures the film screen, whose perfectly composed images are fixed by Greenaway's static camera. The sharpness of the light makes manifest the nearly fetishistic dependence on sharp focus. As the incisive lines are carefully inscribed by Neville's hand, the paper fills the frame as the drawing literally takes the image's place. A frame within a frame, Neville's grid is the most ubiquitous emblem of the film's concern with restricted vision.

The constraints on seeing what is there to be seen go beyond the visual. The first exterior shot bears a voice-over as Neville announces the regimentation of sight. "Curriculum for the execution of the drawings at Compton-Anstey. For Drawing Number 1: from seven o'clock in the morning until nine o'clock . . ." Listed by number, restricted by time, subject to a rigorous schedule, the draughtsman's work is not the product of inspiration or personal expression as it would be with the Romantic artist a century hence. Mrs. Herbert's son-in-law, Mr. Talmann (Hugh Fraser), notes that Neville has organized his work as if it were a military campaign, ordering members of the family about as if he were "an officer in a hostile billet." Stepping in front of his grid at one point (lined up exactly with the camera's line of sight), Neville blocks the view of the formal garden, refusing to let us see until the busy scene is cleared of intrusive human subjects. Neville's nemesis Talmann wryly notes that Mr. Neville seems to "have the god-like power of emptying the landscape." In voice-over, Neville continues to court charges of arrogance: "Such animals as are presently grazing in the fields will be permitted to do so."

Arguing that all his characters are in some way "mediocre people,"[4] Greenaway does not stint his criticism when the hero is an artist. Arrogant, opportunistic, contemptuous of his employers, sadistic toward women, Neville nevertheless serves as a figure of identification for the audience. Greenaway pulls this off, despite the unpleasantness of much of Neville's behavior, by positioning Neville as our eyes. Except for slivers of information salted throughout the film and left ambiguous, nearly every scene centers on Neville. We know what he knows as he serves as our guide to this world.

Despite his pretensions, Neville is an underdog. In an interview, Greenaway noted that "in a way, all my films are about outsiders."[5] Affecting the weariness of a gentleman while boasting of his prior commitments ("I have work to do up and beyond this year's apple season," with no end in sight until next year's apples have all been "drunk as cider"), Mrs. Herbert reminds him bluntly, "But you can be bought, Mr. Neville." Taking great pleasure in sending his servant to tell the exalted family members to clear out of "his" landscape, Neville is careful to insist on decorum: "Go and ask those people to move. Ask them nicely. Smile. Don't trot." In an intentionally static visual world, Neville moves: chasing sheep, striding up a hill sans wig and coat, or tossing a fallen apple at the garden statuary. Having shooed away Mrs. Herbert's company, thus proving his temporary authority, Neville dashingly tosses his drink aside and bows with a flourish (being sure to glance up and check his effect).

An outsider, Neville takes the opposing side in political disputes, usually sparring with the German-born Mr. Talmann. Neville's distaste for Germans is inextricable from his constant friction with the snobbish Talmann. Where Talmann refers to Neville as "the son of a tenant farmer," Neville shows a drawing to Mrs. Herbert, saying, "Look, madam, this man has no head – a typical German characteristic." He scoffs at Talmann's accent: "You talk, Mr. Talmann, like one who has learnt abroad an archaic way of speaking that became unfashionable in England when my grandfather was a young man." And insults Talmann's clothes. Complimenting the fruit the gardener has brought him, Neville tells Talmann, "I congratulate you on today's raspberries, but not on yesterday's damsons. They were tasteless, *geschmacklos*. Like your coat, Mr. Talmann."

Figure 7. Mr. Neville in the garden. (Museum of Modern Art/Film Stills Archive)

Talmann's presence represents a moment in British history when civil and religious conflicts, abetted by the lack of legitimate male heirs, resulted in a group of British nobles requesting that William of Orange "invade" England and depose Charles II's Catholic son, James II, in 1688. The Dutch William was childless, and his reign set the stage for the Hanoverian succession, when English kings would be German-born. At the first of several open-air dinners, Talmann notes that the English "can raise colonies but not heirs to the throne." When Neville points out that "some of England's oldest colonies have heirs aplenty," Mrs. Herbert's daughter, Sarah (who is also Mrs. Talmann), inquires, "Do we have an indication of Scottish sympathies?" Seeing a little boy surrounded by servants, Neville learns that he is Talmann's nephew Augustus, brought to live with them when his father died and his mother became a Catholic. "He was an orphan, Mr. Neville, and needed to be looked after," Mrs. Talmann insists. "An orphan, madam?" Neville says with disgust. "Because his mother became a Catholic!" During a heated discussion with Talmann about Ireland, Neville's sympathies are more pointed. Sparring with Mrs. Talmann (Anne Louise Lambert), Neville opines, "The Garden of Eden was planned for Ireland, for it was there that St. Patrick eradicated the snake."[6] Talmann sneers, "The only useful eradication that ever happened in Ireland, Mr. Neville, was performed by William of Orange four years ago on my birthday." Enraged, Neville snaps,

– Then happy birthday to you, Mr. Talmann. If you are not too old to receive presents, perhaps the gardener and I can find a snake for your orangerie.

After a long pause, Talmann responds: "What?"

Talmann scores points in their ongoing battle by insulting English painting and painters.

If the best Englishmen are foreigners, Mr. Neville, then the best English painters are foreigners too. There's no English painter worthy of the name. Would you agree that to be an English painter is a contradictory term?[7]

In the wake of the German Hans Holbein (the older and the younger serving as court painters for the Tudors) in the sixteenth century, and the Flemish Van Dyck in the first half of the seventeenth, and born too soon for the century of Hogarth, Gainsborough, and Sir Joshua Reynolds,[8] Neville does not have a strong cultural tradition to support him and Talmann has a point. Instructing little Augustus, Talmann stresses that Mr. Neville is not to be imitated: "Drawing is an attribution worth very little – and in England, worth nothing at all." Neville, however, admits his failings only when to do so puts him above Talmann. Drawing an obtrusive, whistling Talmann in place of Mr. Herbert (the proposed recipient of the drawings and the owner of the estate), Neville remarks, "It is beyond my powers to describe a whistle pictorially, whether it comes from an Englishman or a German dressed like an Englishman."

Sanguine about his abilities (he does depict the whistle and with amusing ease), Neville's statements on art are almost always about himself. Insisting that his instructions about the grounds be followed to the letter, Neville explains: "I'm painstaking enough to notice quite small changes in the landscape." Asked to disguise something in one of the views of the house (a shirt left hanging in a tree), Neville replies, "I try very hard never to distort or to dissemble" in drawing. As the earlier exchange about William of Orange illustrates, however, language grown too elaborate can trip you up and become a trap. Neville's every boast is hoarded and used against him.

For Greenaway, linguistic intricacy is often cheek by jowl with intrigue.

The edifice of language, with its structured complexities, is as central to Greenaway's (de)construction of representation in *The Draughtsman's Contract* as the image is. The image may even, at times, seem to take second place.

One of the essential conceits of the film is that the camera does not move. . . . [W]ith a still camera you throw the emphasis on the dialogue and soundtrack.[9]

Defending the film against the accusation that it is too talky, Greenaway asserts, "I am in no way apologetic for having made a 'talkie.' I would like to stand up and say this very loudly, clearly!"

It is extremely important that all the words are heard – not just heard, but listened to, because of the puns, conundrums, word plays, red herrings and so on.[10]

In *The Draughtsman's Contract,* the film "play[s] with the whole business of conversation."[11] The elaborate repartee, characterized by labyrinthine syntax, studded with allusions and conceits, conceals as much as it reveals.

In Greenaway's pastiche of Restoration England, language must be carefully attended to because of "what words don't mean, or appear not to mean."[12] Language disguises what it reveals, as the legalisms of the original contract make clear. At another late evening banquet, Neville states to Talmann and those assembled:

I am permitted to take my pleasure without hindrance on [Mrs. Herbert's] property and to enjoy the maturing delights of her country garden. And gentlemen, there is much there to be surprised at and applauded.

Double entendres, of course, point simultaneously toward and away from illicit sex. When Mrs. Herbert tries to break their contract, Neville, uncharacteristically, expresses himself directly. "The peak of my delight, madam, is obtained in those short minutes when we are together. I would regret losing them." But he quickly reverts to brusque (if specious) fact and insists the contract continue: "It would take the consent of both signatories to make it void."

Many of the film's double entendres stress how easily language confuses one thing with another, the metaphorical richness of language being held accountable for its slipperiness. When Neville first exercises his right to abuse Mrs. Herbert's body, he gives her an impromptu lecture on pears. As she tries to close the shutters so no one will see, he roughly pulls her back, rudely yanking off her clothes. Inquiring about the grafting of the estate's pear trees, he holds her arm out straight to the side and observes her naked torso.

The angle between the branches and the main trunk is too steep. But the original work is good and what of the pears themselves? Are they presentable?

Rejecting the flavorfulness implied by his speech, Mrs. Herbert is next seen alone, clutching her stomach and vomiting.

Assaulting Mrs. Herbert on another occasion (asking her to kneel, he pushes her with a sharp jab in the back so that she falls bent over a pile of pillows), Neville pursues an interest in citrus. She should ask her gardener, he advises, "what can be done with limes – by doing as little as possible. Limes, madam, can smell so sweet. Especially when they are allowed to bloom without hindrance." As Mr. Neville's actions are hidden by a large umbrella that nearly covers the screen, we are left to imagine a corollary to his sensual imagery.

The association of women with fruit soon expands to include the entire garden. Either way, the comparison is never to a woman's advantage. Mentioned in the same breath with fruitful gardens, women find themselves objects of barter. Flirting with a Mrs. Pierpont, who considers herself not strictly "of the company but a part of its property," Mr. Noyes parries that "since that is what the company is here to discuss and revel in, you should be well-favored. I should favor you myself," he continues, offering her, say, "two parterres and a drive of orange trees." Brushing aside the lace decorating her décolletage, he recommends the orange: "They smell so sweet. They are so . . . invigorating."

Symbolically replaced by things horticultural, women may disappear altogether. Relating another cautionary gardening tale, Mr. Noyes enlivens an afternoon repast with the case of a man who planted fruit trees whenever his wife conceived. While the wife miscarried or the children died, the trees thrived. "Today there are eleven trees in his fruit garden – and he knows them all by their Christian names."

It is the family name, however, that counts. Absorbed by their husbands' legal standing, Mrs. Herbert and Mrs. Talmann are confronted with issues of inheritance. Rudely "persuaded" by Neville in a hayloft (he enters her so roughly, she screams in pain), Mrs. Herbert reveals the limits of her position. Unable to inherit as a woman, she was married off by her father to Mr. Herbert, who coveted the estate. (Upbraiding Mr. Herbert earlier for his "indifference" to her mother, Sarah Talmann recites his true priorities: "a house, a garden, a horse, a wife" – in that order.) Sarah, in turn, was married to Mr. Talmann, a man referred to by Mrs. Herbert as being "without airs [heirs] or graces." Talmann has left the second generation of Compton-Anstey women without the firm connection to property guaranteed by having a son. Sarah, who has little patience with any of the men in the film, openly accuses him of being impotent.

Enjoying once more the maturing delights of Mrs. Herbert's garden, Neville introduces a painting into the scene of seduction, directing Mrs. Herbert's attention to it as he snips open the laces at the back of her dress. The composition of this shot showing an image within an image is one of Greenaway's most subtle evocations of seventeenth-century painting. Invoking Dutch scenes of debauchery (later expanded by Hogarth) as Neville undresses Mrs. Herbert on the left, Greenaway shifts the dominance of that trope to one side, balancing it with the painting on the right. Staged this way, the composition calls to mind the seventeenth- and eighteenth-century genre of the "conversation piece." "Derived from the Latin *conversatio*," the generic name refers "to 'familiar discourse . . . [as] opposed to a formal conference,' and even to connotations of sexual intercourse."[13]

A reaction against portraits of single figures, the conversation piece shows groups posed in seemingly casual arrangements that nevertheless scrupulously inscribe each member's status in the social and familial hierarchy. For instance,

> there is a tendency in seventeenth-century conversations for the husband to be both emphatic and separated by some distance from his wife and children.[14]

Objects typical of the genre's iconography would include "a deed or legal document" under the father's hand "and (toward the women) a bowl of fruit."[15] According to Ronald Paulson, "the sitter's status is emphasized by the presence of artifacts he has gathered, including his manor house."[16] Although Mr. Herbert is absent throughout the film, he is present everywhere through his legal standing, signified at all points by his property, especially the house enfolded by its gardens. Because it positions the socially constructed family "within a natural setting" (where nature is "ordered by art or tilled by husbandry"), the conversation piece naturalizes patriarchal authority.[17]

An innovation within the genre of the conversation piece involves the introduction of frames within frames. In Hogarth's *The Fountaine Family* (1730), an idyllic country scene surrounds a trio of men discussing a painting of an idyllic country scene, oblivious to the natural splendor all around them. Two women sit off to the left, privately discussing something, possibly the blindness of the men.[18]

Greenaway's scene likewise pulls our eye back and forth between the scissors working their way up Mrs. Herbert's bodice, exposing her bare flesh, and the vaguely Renaissance scene propped up nearby, its mysteries obscured by an aged varnish. The scene also works as a pun on the current meaning of "conversation piece," that is, an object serving as a pretext for conversation. "Are you not intrigued by it," Mr. Neville presses. "What do you think?"

"Your husband surprises me with his eccentric and eclectic tastes," Neville insists. "Perhaps he has an eye for optical theory – or the plight of lovers – or the passing of time." With each phrase the narrative's image is replaced by a detail of the painting (a woman cowering in a temple, a brightly dressed young man pointing the way), just as Mr. Neville's drawings routinely supplant the view, rapid cutting stating a comparison between landscape and representation. "Perhaps, madam," he continues, "he had – and I would stand by him in this – an interest in the pictorial conceit." Practical, perhaps fighting her characteristic nausea, Mrs. Herbert dismisses this tribute to her husband's nonexistent taste. "It is of a garden, that is probably reason enough." But Neville persists, "Let us peruse it together."

Seeing only the painting now, Neville, in voice-over, leads us deeper into interpretive mists.

> Do you see, madam, a narrative in these apparently unrelated episodes? What intrigue is here? Do you think the characters have something to tell us?. . . . Madam, could you put a season to it? Madam? Do you have an opinion? What infidelities are portrayed here? Do you think that murder is being prepared?

As the mist encloses Compton-Anstey, a man leads a white horse toward the house.

Murder is in the air, introduced as a matter of art interpretation. Mrs. Talmann approaches Mr. Neville one day when he is halfway through realizing his commission. "Let me make a little speech." One by one, she points out from memory the incongruous details scattered throughout Neville's otherwise pristine (and uninhabited) depictions of the grounds. Her father's boots, his shirt, a ladder leading to his room, "a jacket of my father's, slit across the chest." (There are so many, at one point Neville quips, "Someone's getting careless. The garden is becoming a robe room.") "Do you think that before long," she asks, "you might find the body that inhabited all those clothes?" "Four garments and a ladder do not lead us to a corpse," Neville counters. "Mr. Neville, I said nothing about a corpse." ("Lying crimson on a piece of green grass," Neville ventures fancifully. "What a pity your drawings are in black and white," Sarah retorts.)

Leading him step by step, Mrs. Talmann explains how, through misinterpretation, Neville might be suspected of being "a witness to misadventure" – "more than a witness, an accessory." For the first time in the film, Neville is speechless. Blocked, he repeats her words, unable to grasp the meaning. "Misadventure, madam? What misadventure? There is no misadventure." "Perhaps, Mr. Neville," she suggests later, "you have taken a great deal on trust."

Sarah is superior to Neville verbally and visually throughout the scene. As he bows his head in concentration, her face looking down on him from the upper half of the frame, she taunts him on the subject about which he is most sensitive.

A really intelligent man makes an indifferent painter. For painting requires a certain blindness, a partial refusal to be aware of all the options. An intelligent man will know more about what he is drawing than he will see, and in the space between knowing and seeing, he will become *constrained,* unable to pursue an idea strongly.

Accused of artistic impotence, Neville surrenders. "You're ingenious. I am allowed to be neither of the two things that I wish to be at the same time."

Knowing of her mother's contract with Neville and assuring him that her mother is a woman of "few words and not incapable of a few stratagems," Sarah offers a contract of her own – one that "might protect you and humor me." Following her, as instructed, to the library, where Noyes awaits, Neville repeats after Sarah the terms of the new contract. Echoing her phrases like a wedding vow, Neville promises to "comply with her requests concerning her pleasure." As he draws his next image of a geometrically designed walk lined with yew trees, Sarah glides with impunity into his line of vision. Disappearing and reappearing behind the trees, she sheds her clothing one piece at a time, brazenly stuffing a slip into one of the yews, until she stands directly before the camera, centered in the draughtsman's frame, blocking his view. "It is time, Mr. Neville."

This is not the first occasion when Mr. Neville has been unable to see. When Mrs. Herbert comes to break their contract, she takes his place behind his optical frame. Dismissing her request that he consider the contract void, he dismisses her, adding, "I feel that from this position I cannot adequately see what I am supposed to be seeing." Aware that there is more to the grounds of Compton-Anstey than meets his eye, Neville begins to play art critic and interpreter. Showing the painting to Mrs. Herbert, he inquires

Figure 8. Mr. Neville (Anthony Higgins) and Mrs. Herbert (Janet Suzman): frames within frames in Super16. (Peter Greenaway)

about the one thing the painting cannot tell him, the motivations of those around him. "Would you know, madam, if your daughter had any interest in this painting?"

Preparing to leave on the day of Mr. Herbert's scheduled return, Neville is called to answer for the "unexpected" details in his completed drawings. Neville insists that whatever is in the drawings was actually there, and appeals to Mrs. Talmann to confirm it. Attesting to the presence of the ladder, she is complimented by one of the gentleman, "You have an exact knowledge." "– As exact a knowledge as though you placed it there yourself," Neville muses. As Sarah denies it, her father's body is dragged out of the moat.

Last Year at Marienbad

Resnais's *Last Year at Marienbad* (1961) comes up frequently in discussions of *The Draughtsman's Contract*. Fighting off comparisons with *Barry Lyndon* (1975), Greenaway himself told an interviewer, "For me, the temperament is derived much more from French cinema – for example, *Last Year at Marienbad* by Alain Resnais."[19] To measure the differences between the films, one need only consider their gardens.

Figure 9. A French formal garden: *Last Year at Marienbad* (1961). (Museum of Modern Art/Film Stills Archive)

The formal gardens of *Marienbad* mock the feverish, romantic angst of the film's main character. Obsessed with memory and fantasy (distinctions that will not hold), he struggles to connect (or reconnect) emotionally with the woman for whom he says he has waited. Sometimes he meets her on the grounds outside their luxury hotel. Laid out in harsh straight lines, the French formal garden is paved with gravel and anchored with classical statuary. Subduing the landscape with a cold, stony rationalism, indifferent to puny human affairs, the garden reduces those who pass through it to shadows in black and gray.

The "poetic garden . . . developed by Englishmen in the first half of the eighteenth century," on the other hand, "was a reaction against the formal geometry of the French and Dutch."[20] *Draughtsman* revels in its landscapes. According to one source, "it is in landscape design that . . . the true Englishness of English art is revealed."[21] Greenaway's enthusiasm is boundless:

> These landscapes are magnificent and optimistic. If the films do not celebrate the lives of individuals, they do celebrate life . . . [with] an ebullient delight in the richness and variety of things.[22]

Given Neville's demand for complete control of the landscape, Talmann comments, "It's a wonder the birds still sing." But sheep continue to flock across the image and birdsong peppers the soundtrack, talismans of Greenaway's hope for a natural world indifferent to social control. As much a romantic in his way as Resnais, Greenaway persists in this hope for a natural world – "Behind this death, evil, and mediocrity is the natural landscape,"[23] the desire to believe reinforced by the knowledge that such a thing does not exist.

Although the language is excessive in both films, in Resnais's film the words tumble out in poetic modernism's lush stream of consciousness, the main character's voice-over weaving an incantatory spell, reverberating with totemic phrases as if speaking a private language connected directly to desire. The language of *Draughtsman* is at the other extreme: exhibitionistic, designed for formal public display, removed from feeling and employed for the fun of scoring points and besting your betters.

Marienbad is a deeply serious film where troubled characters struggle to infuse romantic love into a world patterned on cold reason; *Draughtsman* takes an ironic, analytical stance, where characters, quite satisfied with a neat surface, conspire to persuade themselves their world is "natural." In *Marienbad*, it is a question of finding depth in flatness, profound feeling behind the riot of reflecting Baroque surfaces. In *Draughtsman*, Neville colludes with his patrons to make a world of eddying depths look flat, denying depth by transforming it into surface. Looking at the moat, covered with a scummy yellow-green algae, Neville asks Mrs. Herbert why Mr. Herbert doesn't have it cleaned. "He doesn't like to see the fish. Carp live too long. They remind him of Catholics." Besides, she adds, when covered with scum, the water's troubling depths (swirling with intimations of mortality and ineradicable political conflicts) can be confused for the reassuringly solid surface of an English lawn.

The man in *Marienbad* wants to escape the repetition of surfaces, to break through predictability into change. Neville jettisons the landscape's ever-changing colors and fixes its naturally shifting contours in black and white. While both plots feature triangles and murderous impulses centering on a husband (too present in one film, absent in the other), in Greenaway's film relationships are ruthlessly de-romanticized, de-sentimentalized, reduced to blunt action epitomized by sex stripped of emotion.[24] Feelings persist, but like fish glimpsed under the surface, they are seen for a moment then gone, still present but rarely visible.

Each film's style explores these dichotomies between surface and depth. Sacha Vierny's camerawork in the Resnais film dwells in movement. With or without characters to motivate it, the camera wanders restlessly through

Baroque halls, making sudden turns to discover a new detail in the garden, someone standing by a hedge, the opening of another path. Panning, re-framing, dollying ever deeper into the shot, the camera may just as suddenly reverse direction and pull away at dramatic speed.

"One of the essential conceits" of *The Draughtsman's Contract,* Green-away stresses, "is that the camera does not move."[25] When the woman played by Delphine Seyrig in *Marienbad* searches, lost in the garden, carry-ing her broken shoe, the camera lures her onward, choreographing its move-ments to each sudden stop, each sign of curiosity or hesitation. When Mrs. Talmann crisscrosses the path in the yew garden, the camera waits. Hiding and revealing herself at a deliberate pace, taking a circuitous route toward a fixed point, Mrs. Talmann knows how to exploit static features – go around.

At a central point in each film, the narrative stops as the characters con-template a work of art: a statue of a heroic couple and their dog, the paint-ing of the young couple's stormy expulsion from the garden. Debating its meaning, they find no clear answer or, rather, too many answers, none with greater purchase than another. Surrounded with ambiguity, each work of art entices but remains opaque, offering the endless pleasures of unanswerable questions. Is it all then a matter of interpretation? As a producer of art, Ne-ville resists interpretation, but his attempt to take refuge behind material re-ality ("whatever it is, it was there") fails. Caught up in endless speculation as to what he knows or wants, and what his drawings "mean" ("it is akin to pursuing some complicated allegory," one gentleman insists), Neville finds that interpretation is not a game, but can be a matter of life and death.

For both films games are richly evocative. *Marienbad* is famous for its game. Two players pick up rows of matchsticks until one is "stuck" with the last piece. A seemingly simple set of random choices nevertheless lead inevitably to the main character's loss. Audiences of the day would try to play at home, to prove (as the character tries to prove) that it is possible to beat the game. The characters in *Draughtsman* play few overt games (remarkably few, considering it is a Greenaway film), but game playing per-vades the film on other levels. On one level, *Draughtsman* is a simple enter-tainment, a whodunnit in the grand British tradition of murder-in-the-manor-house. (Its French title was *Death in an English Garden.*) Because it evokes board games like *Clue,* people speculate endlessly about whodunnit. (Greenaway's own choice for a model mystery is Agatha Christie's *Murder on the Orient Express.*)[26] Such games are built on murder. As with the game in *Marienbad,* in *Draughtsman,* the man in the middle is always the loser. As Neville is soon to discover, he was constituted as such as soon as he agreed to play.

The Dutch

Returning to Compton-Anstey with a tribute of hothouse fruit, Neville finds Mrs. Talmann touring the grounds with a landscape designer. With Mr. Herbert's death, his wife and his daughter have set about redesigning the ground on which they stand. Sarah introduces Neville to her new advisor: "Mr. Van Hoyten is to consider for us a new management of the grounds, an entirely fresh approach."

The geometrical French-style garden was in effect the material statement of the social hierarchies endorsed by Mr. Herbert ("a house, a garden, a horse and a wife"). "Meant to be seen from the house," the garden

> was an extension of the house . . . ordered like a periodic sentence with all its members subordinated to one end. . . . The English contribution was to reject emphatically the rule of geometry, [to] replace geometrical symmetry and subordination as a structure of meaning with a much less regular or predictable one.[27]

As Mrs. Talmann states, Van Hoyten

> has come at our request to soften the geometry that my father found to his taste and to introduce a new ease and complexion.

"Mr. Van Hoyten has worked in The Hague," she notes, adding, "He is a draughtsman, too." In one of the film's rare close-ups, Van Hoyten speaks for some moments in Dutch, and the name Neville is heard.

A ruffled Neville scoffs, asking Mrs. Herbert when the others are out of earshot, "Why is this Dutchman waving his hands about? Is he homesick for windmills?" He hears from Mrs. Herbert that they plan to build an ornamental lake (or, as Sarah puts it, "to make a dam and flood the lower fields," terms redolent with possibilities). "Do you intend to join Anstey to the sea?" Neville asks.

The peculiar intensity associated with Van Hoyten marks a general unease with things Dutch, particularly insomuch as they are connected with water. In the second shot of the film, a lady tells a bawdy story as significant for the film's thematic weave as Noyes's story about plums:

> Some years ago, two gentlemen went back to Amsterdam saying Allheavinghay was just like home. There was so much water – so many ornamental ponds, so many canals, so many sinks and basins. There was even a waterpump.

Figure 10. Drawing #2: the formal garden. (Peter Greenaway)

Figure 11. Drawing #6: "the lower lawn of the garden by the statue of Hermes." (Peter Greenaway)

The purpose, it seems, was her father's fear of fire. With great amusement, she relates how she occasionally found need to relieve herself in the buckets of water stored under the stairs. Retiring decorously behind her fan, she notes, "I used to pee like a horse." After a pause she adds, "I still do," and bursts into peals of laughter.

While once again exposing the crassness of nouveau riche gentry, the vulgarity beneath the finery, this discourse on water also illustrates how women undo men's plans while mocking their greatest fears. Neville, for instance, is concerned with reputation. Hotly pursued by Mrs. Herbert and Mrs. Talmann when they originally commissioned him for the twelve drawings, he has now been replaced by a new draughtsman, one who has "worked in The Hague." When Noyes fixes on a scheme to sell Neville's drawings (allegedly to disperse evidence of Mrs. Talmann's infidelity), his crony touts Neville's stature by inventing a Dutch connection: "It is said Mr. Neville is to be invited to The Hague." The issue of European validation (especially by Holland or France) is sure to touch the insecurities of an English painter.

The Dutch are also uncomfortably close to water. In *The Embarrassment of Riches,* a study of seventeenth-century Dutch culture, Simon Schama refers to Holland as "an amphibious republic."[28] Mimicking the British attitude toward Holland in the seventeenth century, he writes:

> Was there not, after all, something conspiratorial about the Dutch actually wringing out their waters so the English would be left gasping on the dry mud flats?[29]

Schama's investigation of the values of the Dutch in this era reveals how deeply intertwined the concerns of the lowlands were with those of the sceptered isle ("this precious stone set in the silver sea").[30] Schama's very chapter titles evoke the precariousness of the world Greenaway's characters inhabit: "Trials by water," "Uncertain boundaries," "Between the windmill and the walker," "The mystery of the drowning cell." Some chapters suggest darker aspects verging on the occult: "Stygian fires and aqua fortis," "This indigested vomit of the sea."

One would do well to be careful around water in this part of England. We are also told in the film's opening about a "water mechanic" who built a high tower for his patron. When asked if he could build one higher (perhaps for another patron), the man said yes and was pushed off the tower to die "a watery death." Gazing dolefully at the algae-covered moat, Mr. Neville inquires whether or not the absent Mr. Herbert can swim. "I've never seen him swim," Mrs. Herbert casually remarks. As Mrs. Talmann proves, it is women who invite the Dutch in and who make terms with the possibility of watery death (see *Drowning by Numbers*).

Having invited him back to the house, the now widowed Mrs. Herbert notes that Neville is "full of hesitant pleasantries." He pleads, "That is because I am still unable to judge your present feelings as to past events." As he does with Van Hoyten's untranslated comments and indecipherable expression, Neville finds women unreadable – an insecurity fostered by the scenes where Neville is absent.

Throughout the film we have had brief glimpses of Mrs. Herbert and Mrs. Talmann in private. Usually silent, these scenes have great beauty, mystery, and stillness, their power confirmed by their essential ambiguity. Being washed by her maid, Virginia Herbert raises her foot to the maid's cheek. A playful touch or a caress? Awake in bed as her husband snores beside her, Mrs. Talmann sweeps her hair back with one hand as the other burrows beneath her nightdress. Shifting her weight onto her hidden hand, she closes her eyes and rests in a golden glow. Her face reveals nothing to us as we study it for signs of pleasure. Only once do the women speak privately. At one point early in her contract, Mrs. Herbert sits crying in front of her dressing table. Sarah sits nearby, holding her mother's hand. Summoning strength, Mrs. Herbert says with bitter irony, "I am grieving because Mr. Herbert is away." Knowing well the radical disconnectedness of words, Sarah replies, "Yes, Mother." As in *Drowning by Numbers*, women do not need words to understand each other.

But this does not mean women lack when it comes to playing games with language. Women must be quick-witted; like artists, they are valued only when they produce things to flatter or amuse those in power. Mrs. Talmann is particularly adept at sparring with Mr. Neville. Sitting under a tree, Neville makes a play on the word "significant," suggesting his arousal when he is with her.

MRS. TALMANN: Your significance, Mr. Neville, is attributable to both innocence and arrogance in equal parts.
NEVILLE: You can handle both with impunity, Mrs. Talmann. But you will find that they are not symmetrical. . . . One weighs heavier than the other. Which do you think is the heavier, Mrs. Talmann?
MRS. TALMANN: Your innocence, Mr. Neville, is always sinister, so I will say that the right one is the heaviest.

While Neville compliments her judgment (and her touch) – "Madam, your dexterity is admirable" – his double entendre may have a third dimension of which he is unaware. When Mrs. Talmann suggests it is his arrogance that weighs heaviest, she may be passing judgment on him. Playing with words' latent meanings, Neville misses what is manifest.[31]

When Neville returns to Compton-Anstey, he offers Mrs. Herbert a gift of three pomegranates "reared in English soil and under an English sun." As Mrs. Herbert says when she invites him to reconstitute their relationship ("to our – mutual – satisfaction") and do one last drawing: "It will be by way of returning your gift in kind." Later, lying disheveled opposite Neville on a couch, Mrs. Herbert covers her breast and carefully poses a pomegranate on Neville's bare chest. It wakes him up, in more ways than one.

Although fruit metaphors prove unflattering to women when wielded by men, women's discourse on fruit is, pardon the expression, masterful. They know too well what these linguistic maneuvers can mean. Mrs. Herbert explains how the "gift of Hades to Persephone" condemned Persephone to live half of the year underground.

> Persephone's mother, the goddess of fields, of gardens and of orchards, was distraught, heartbroken . . . [and since,] refuses to bless the world with fruitfulness.

She notes with some irony that gardeners "try hard to defeat the influence of the pomegranate" with things like hothouses, but when they do, "what do they grow? The pomegranate." Although Neville pleads his ignorance ("My scholarship is not profound. Maybe I am hesitant to acknowledge an unintended allusion"), he admits her story is "certainly a cautionary tale for gardeners." "– And for mothers with daughters," she adds as Sarah enters behind them.

Although hothouse fruits such as those provided by Mr. Neville are "seldom fertile," as Mrs. Talmann points out, they do produce many allusions. (Unmentioned, perhaps because it is of no great concern to the women, is an association that might weigh in the balance of Neville's "innocence" and "arrogance": in seventeenth-century Dutch sex manuals, Schama finds "the male testicles being nicely compared to pomegranates, full of seed.")[32] Splitting the pomegranate and squeezing out its juice, Mrs. Herbert notes its association with two things: "the blood of the newborn . . . and murder."

NEVILLE: Thanks to your botanical scholarship, you must find it cruelly apt that I was persuaded to bring such fruit.
MRS. HERBERT: Oh, Mr. Neville, I suspect that you were innocent of the insight – as you have been innocent of much else.

Taking offense at being thought innocent (gullible, naive) where he had planned to flaunt his daring "opportunism," craftiness, and wit, Neville finds that mother and daughter have been ahead of him all along. But Mrs. Herbert reassures him, "In our need of an heir you may very likely have served us well." "We had a contract, did we not?" Mrs. Talmann adds. Neville responds to the mother–daughter plot with the same words he used when Sarah first spoke to him about misadventure: "Madam, that was ingenious." (As he said to Mrs. Talmann when she interpreted his drawings, and repeated to Mrs. Herbert when she offered to renew their relationship, "Madam, it is as if you had planned it.")[33] Abandoning him in the frame, Sarah reveals her contempt: "Since when has adultery been ingenious, Mr. Neville. You are ridiculous."

Struggling to fasten his pants, Neville is framed by the two women, one on either side; framed in the dark center of the image by two windows, one behind each woman; and framed by the picture frame of a painting directly opposite. Trying vainly to argue points rendered irrelevant in this rout (that Mr. Talmann is *not* in Southampton, that Talmann's friend Mr. Seymour has *not* left town as implied), only Mr. Neville does not realize the position he is in: visually cut off at the knees and figuratively caught with his pants down. Mrs. Herbert suggests, by way of repayment in kind, that the gardener "bring Mr. Neville a pineapple" as he begins his last drawing. "A small one. They're sweeter."

In the "natural" English garden ("perhaps ultimately an extrapolation of the maze"), "the visitor lacks a sense of the whole and does not know exactly where he is in the total structure until he has reached the end."[34] The site of Neville's thirteenth commission is the moat. Backed by a wall, encountered by torchlight, this site presents a view almost completely without depth. In Greenaway's films "the outsider artist-figures fail to comprehend what they are observing until [it is] too late."[35] What Neville fails to see as he tries to order the world is that this world has already been ordered, elsewhere, and by the very people Neville optimistically banished from his field of view. As Neville sits quietly contemplating, a masked figure dressed in black enters the scene.

Asked whether he has completed his last drawing, Neville responds, "That is true. I am finished." The drawing, however, is only half done. Mr. Talmann (in the mask) suggests they find more light as a group of men in masks enter with torches and lanterns. Neville has dressed in white since his return, whereas Mrs. Herbert and her daughter, both in mourning, publicly wear black, as do members of the mob confronting Neville. Though he may be washed clean of his underhanded contractual dealings, it is already too late – he has already made his fatal mistake.

Blues and golds bounce off Neville's white clothing and plumed hat as he denounces the "curious observers" hemming him in. Talmann, he asserts, is "uninterested in painting or draughtsmanship," only money; Mr. Noyes, "a custodian of contracts" who asks what the late Mr. Herbert might have thought of the draughtsman's contract, probably showed it to him, Neville barks back. (Though Neville doubts Mr. Herbert would have known what he was seeing: "he was blind to so much, certainly blind to considerable unhappiness.") Accusing each member of the party in turn, Neville ends with the women, who, he suggests, are not above suspicion. "Is that why, Mr. Neville, you have just abused Mrs. Herbert further?" a voice asks, leaving Neville once again speechless.

Closing his eyes, blind to so much, Neville merely shakes his head. "Ah. What a pity. That was clever." Assuming Neville has returned to seduce and marry a rich widow (thus supplanting her son-in-law as heir), the men have come to secure their property. Knowing the men will act, brutally, to preserve their interests, the women need not be present as the witness (and accessory) to their "misadventures" is removed from the scene.

Undone, Neville is ordered to remove his hat. Attempting repartee suitable to a gentleman (Talmann once said he "dressed like a barber"), Neville replies, "My hat, gentleman, has no contractual obligations with anyone." Sweeping off his elaborately plumed headgear and bowing low, he is unceremoniously slugged in the back as Noyes begins to recite the final contract:

The contract's first condition – and there is no need to write it down for you will never see it – is to cancel your eyes.

Shoving a torch into his face, they burn his eyes out and replace his speech with screams. Tearing off his shirt, they pledge to spread its remains about the grounds as "ambiguous evidence of an obscure allegory." The last condition is his death, they say, as they beat him with heavy blows from their elegant walking sticks. As Neville's drawings curl in the flames, turning gold, blue, and charred black, Noyes, Talmann, and their associates remove their masks to watch. Dumping Neville's body in the moat, they file out.

The pineapple, small, potentially sweet, lies cloven in half, a knife handle at its heart. A servant whose job it is to decorate the garden by blending in with the grounds, takes this opportunity to sample the exotic fruit. He spits it out. The pineapple, time-honored symbol of hospitality, is sour.

3
A Zed and Two
Noughts (1985)

Taxonomy: 1. the study of the general principles of scientific classification: SYSTEMATICS.

"A is for . . . ?" "B is for . . . ?"

Unlike *The Draughtsman's Contract, A Zed and Two Noughts* feels like the true follow-up to *The Falls* and Greenaway's short films of the 1970s. Where *The Draughtsman's Contract* seemed miraculously full-blown, its self-contained coherence attributable, perhaps, to its period setting, *A Zed and Two Noughts* feels more transitional. Taking us back to the contemporary world of *The Falls, Zed* reexamines familiar preoccupations from Greenaway's earlier work (conspiracies, zoos, ornithology, anything Dutch, the failure of science, the comforts of art), while also pointing forward to elements that will become the foundations of Greenaway's style.

A Zed and Two Noughts is the film that first brings together the team of collaborators who were to remain steady contributors to Greenaway's work, beginning with producer Kees Kasander. Greenaway met his future producer when *The Falls* and *The Draughtsman's Contract* were presented at the Rotterdam film festival. Kasander was working as the assistant to Hubert Bals, the director of the festival. According to Greenaway, Kasander "was fed up with being an administrator and wanted to become a producer."

He actually came up to me, this young man. He must have been about twenty-five – I was at least eight years older than him – and he said he wanted to be my producer and anything I'd care to write, he would produce. I didn't believe him, couldn't possibly believe him, there was no credence there at all. He gave me a three-film, three-year contract. He reckoned he could find the money. It was quite an ebullient time in Europe at that time. There was a lot of tax-free money around the place. We agreed, anyway, to experiment with one film, *A Zed and Two Noughts.*[1]

A Zed and Two Noughts was also the beginning of Greenaway's collaboration with Sacha Vierny, whom he had also met in Rotterdam.

> He didn't speak very good English, my French is not brilliant [but] we understand each other. Very amiable, wry, very modest, self-effacing gentleman. Great quirkiness. He was Tulse Luper incarnate.[2]

With editor John Wilson, the production design team of Ben Van Os and Jan Roelfs, and Michael Nyman scoring the film, the creative team that would come to be identified with any Greenaway film was in place.

In both *A Zed and Two Noughts* and its companion, *Drowning by Numbers,* Greenaway tries with varying degrees of success to merge structuralist principles with narrative. In doing so, he reveals what was always implicit in his short films: that structuralism, or any attempt to subject the ineffable mystery of existence to a single, reductive explanatory system, renders a work, regardless of subject matter, inherently comic. Blinded by science, the characters in *A Zed and Two Noughts* systematically demonstrate the uselessness of reason when faced with the reality of death.

As becomes standard in Greenaway's features, the opening scene brilliantly condenses the film's chief concerns and the style in which they will be expressed. In Greenaway's early pseudodocumentary films, the outline of a narrative slowly emerges through the accretion of detail. In the dramatic films, Greenaway begins with a statement of the premise from which all else follows. With the opening presented as a kind of puzzle, the rest of the film patiently disassembles it, recombining the pieces in order to see how many stories and hypotheses they can generate.

As with the title sequence of *The Draughtsman's Contract, A Zed and Two Noughts* begins in fragments. Intercutting snippets of scenes with title cards, Greenaway elliptically introduces themes and characters so that by the time the title sequence has ended, the catastrophe that triggers the drama has occurred and we are well into the story proper. To a jaunty Michael Nyman score, a boy and a girl try to drag a dalmatian down a rain-soaked nighttime street lit by a giant blue neon sign that reads ZOO. The title of the film, *A Zed and Two Noughts*, is superimposed in red below them. Elsewhere, a blond man holds a stopwatch as a tiger paces in its cage. The head of a zebra lies on the floor in front of it. The man looks up briefly to the sound of a car crashing outside. As steam rises from the grill of the smashed car, a woman with flaming red hair screams in pain, her head poking incongruously out of the car window at the top of the frame. Another man, taking single-frame images of an ape with one leg, has also had his work interrupted by the noise. In a dramatic crane shot, the camera tracks across the crash site. A dead swan lies through the shattered windscreen as a man in red tries to cut the car open with a torch, a giant tiger on an ESSO billboard dominating the right side of the image. As the camera moves through the car's gaping windscreen to frame two women dead in the backseat, we hear the static-surrounded voice of a police dispatcher:

Leda? Who is Leda? Is she the injured woman? . . . Lay-da? Laid by whom? – Jupiter? . . .

In trying to determine the culprit's species ("A swan? How do you know it's not a goose? . . . Female? . . . Egg-bound?"), the one-sided miscommunication escalates until the voice demands, "Did it come from the zoo?" With a freeze-frame, the movement stops and the color bleeds out of the image, transforming it into a black-and-white newspaper photo. The headline establishes the victims as the wives of two doctors, as a flurry of superimposed credits (cinematographer, editor, composer, and writer/director) completes the title sequence.

The title sequence establishes death, the first shot following – grief. Oliver, the blond brother (Eric Deacon), kneels in the street under the Esso tiger. A stream of dark liquid flows by, speckled by feathers, as red and white streamers blow across the frame from the right. On the left the ZOO sign goes out letter by letter, leaving two "o"s, or two noughts. They, in turn, fade out one by one, as Oliver, sobbing, collects shards of broken glass into a piece of paper.

Following the deaths of their wives, Oliver and Oswald Deuce (Brian Deacon) turn to science for answers, using statistics as a way to conceptualize their grief. Walking toward us through a symmetrical colonnade reminiscent of a Roman temple, Oswald asks Oliver, "How fast does a woman decompose?" When Oliver muses, "Six months, a year," Oswald demands, "What is the first thing that happens?" Oliver coldly recounts how bacteria within the body begin to break it down: there are 130,000 bacterium "in each lick of the human tongue, 250,000 in a French kiss. The first exchange at the very beginning of creation when Adam kissed Eve."

OSWALD: Suppose Eve kissed Adam?
OLIVER: Unlikely. She used her first hundred thousand on the apple.

Oliver's casual delivery makes it hard to believe he has suffered a loss, and Oswald's momentary eruptions ("I cannot stand the idea of her rotting away") barely ripple the surface detachment the brothers maintain. Because of this ironic, distanced stance, the closer the film gets to the issue of grief, the more problematic it becomes.

Both brothers turn for answers to Alba Bewick (Andrea Ferreol), the woman who lost a leg in the accident that killed the brothers' wives. A Frenchwoman with a large appetite for life (she wants twenty-six children), Alba refuses to supply the brothers with a reason for their wives' deaths and instead tells them a story about a legless prostitute in Marseilles. Oliver and Oswald try to come to terms with their grief in different ways: Oliver holes up in an empty theatre and watches documentaries on the beginning of life on earth, Oswald sets up an apple in his lab so that he can photograph it as it begins to decay. Despite their research, they are compelled to return to Alba, together and separately.

The starkly stylized and symmetrical compositions outweigh feeling of any kind. As the brothers alternately comfort and interrogate Alba, she lies in the center of her white bed, a metal halo built into the headboard framing her bright red hair. Although displays of emotion are present – Oswald voices bitterness and anger toward fate for his wife's death, Oliver attempts suicide by eating broken glass from the car's windscreen, and Alba screams for the loss of her leg – from the beginning it seems certain that *A Zed and Two Noughts* will be the only Greenaway film where the actors are absorbed into the set design, there to provide symmetry for the compositions and nothing more.

"Why do we have to have two of everything?" Alba asks. "Symmetry is all," Oswald replies.

Symmetry versus Emotion

While *Zed* consolidates the switch from pseudodocumentary to fiction, just how far removed Greenaway is from psychologically based, traditional storytelling, can be seen if we compare *Zed* to a film with a strikingly similar subject made shortly after.

As with *Zed*, David Cronenberg's *Dead Ringers* (1988) concerns two doctors. Like Oliver and Oswald Deuce (played by brothers Eric and Brian Deacon), Beverley and Elliot Mantle are twins (played by Jeremy Irons). Beverley and Elliot have dreams of being linked like the original Siamese twins. Late in Greenaway's film, Oliver and Oswald reveal that they *were* originally Siamese twins, joined at the shoulder and the hip, but their mother

Figure 12. Oswald (Brian Deacon), Alba (Andrea Ferreol), and Oliver (Eric Deacon) in *A Zed and Two Noughts* (1985). (Museum of Modern Art/Film Stills Archive)

separated them so they wouldn't be "freaks," in other words, kept in a zoo. Both sets of twins are scientists. The research we see them do revolves around questions concerning sexual difference – both sets of brothers are obsessed with women's bodies. Oswald's work progresses from documenting Eve's rotting apple to charting dead and decaying female animals; "Bev" and "Ellie" are specialists in female infertility. At similar points in the films, the brothers' obsessions lead them to blur the line between science and art: Oswald and Oliver eventually come to star in their own film, while Beverley's designs are displayed in an art gallery under the heading "Gynecological Instruments for Working on Mutant Women."[3]

In each film, the brothers are involved with the same woman; in each case the woman is French, and defined as abnormal. Alba is "short a leg" when we meet her and loses the other in the course of the film, while Claire in *Dead Ringers* (Geneviève Bujold) is a "trifurcate," a woman with a three-part uterus. There are verbal attacks (some self-generated) on the women's bodies because of their difference. Claire is referred to as a mutant. She considers herself "not a real woman" because she can never have children. Alba reports that the surgeon Dr. van Meegeren wants to amputate her other leg because the remaining one "is dying – it's lonely." Speaking for herself as well as for the surgically separated brothers, she asks, "How much of your body can you lose and still recognize yourself?"

The women bring the brothers closer together. In *Zed*, Oliver and Oswald grow closer through sharing Alba (in a sexual way at first, consecutively, then concurrently but in a more platonic way) and through fathering her twin sons. In *Dead Ringers*, Beverley and Elliot take turns with Claire (unbeknownst to her) until Bev becomes emotionally involved and the fear of separation accentuates the brothers' desire to merge.

In both cases, merging results in the loss of identity and death. The brothers become more and more similar until people cannot tell them apart. Oliver's blond hair becomes the same dark shade as Oswald's. They visit the mysterious doctor Van Meegeren to see about being surgically joined, and later sport a specially made three-legged, two-man suit. While Oliver and Oswald do not want to be distinguishable from each other, Bev and Elliot lose the ability to tell the difference themselves. Confronted at one point by a patient, a distraught Beverley identifies himself as "one of the Mantle twins." Out of town on business, and away from Beverley, Elliot orders up twin girls from an escort service. He asks that, in order to help him tell *them* apart, one of them should call him Elliot, and the other, Beverley.

Prostitutes, or women whose only function in relation to the brothers is sexual, are also shared: Venus de Milo (Frances Barber) visits both brothers in *Zed* shortly after their wives' deaths, while in *Dead Ringers* Elliot tries to soothe Beverley's depression by bringing in a woman with whom they share a sensuous three-way dance. But in both films, it is the physically flawed woman who is psychologically compelling for the twins. (De Milo, by virtue of her namesake, recalls a woman without arms – but only via representation. Alba is the real thing.)

Both male couples end up in bed together. When Beverley has a drug-induced collapse, Elliot sleeps with him in his hospital bed. Seen from above, Elliot's gray suit pressing into the white sheet forms a pattern like yin and yang. (Or Chang and Ang. A moment before Beverley kills Elliot, they refer to each other by the pet names they have adopted, those of the original Siamese twins.) In bed with Alba, one on each side, Oliver and Oswald acknowledge their "true" identity as mirror reflections of each other, confirming as psychological taste something stated throughout the film visually. Oliver indicates that he has always liked being on the left, Oswald on the right, and we realize that that is how they are usually placed in the frame.

In each film the set design mitigates against realism. The brothers in both films live in spare, high-tech bachelor apartments. The surgery scenes stress the theatrical aspect of an operating theatre. The hospital settings are strikingly bare, focusing only on the swaths of color wrapping the male doctors and their prone female patients. In *Zed,* the surgeon Van Meegeren wears green (a sickly, dangerous color in Greenaway's film) and works in a room strikingly devoid of medical equipment or personnel. In *Dead Ringers,* the doctors wear robes with hoods like Eastern Orthodox priests, the color a jarringly intense red reminiscent of the Spanish Inquisition.

But the most striking thing in any comparison of *A Zed and Two Noughts* and *Dead Ringers* is how different they are. *Dead Ringers* is a psychological horror film, exploring the slow disintegration of characters. Despite its cumulative strangeness, the film attempts to establish a coherent psychological world and explanations for things that go unexplained in Greenaway. For instance, that Beverley and Elliot live together ("we both like Italian furniture") and how dependent they are on each other. By the time they meet Claire, we have been shown the development of their childhood interest in female anatomy (wondering why sex is necessary, experimenting on dolls), their collegiate success, and the establishment of their medical practice. Except for the story about their mother's having separated them at birth, Greenaway tells us nothing about Oliver's and Oswald's lives before the crash. We barely learn their wives' names (no photographs are displayed in the apartments the women supposedly shared with their husbands).

The emotional detachment of *A Zed and Two Noughts* is reinforced by Greenaway's visual style. Oliver and Oswald's relationship is spelled out through mise-en-scène. Using mostly long shots, Greenaway stresses the brothers' positions within the frame. The exaggerated symmetry when the brothers are in a shot together draws our attention to the relationship between the actors and the sets, encouraging us to read the scene intellectually, as visual composition, rather than emotionally.

In contrast, *Dead Ringers* demands emotional identification. The film is filled with long conversations and heart-to-heart talks, and its psychological realism rests heavily on the acting of Jeremy Irons. Most of his scenes as Beverley or Elliot are constructed around shot-reverse shot and done in close-ups. If Cronenberg were to use the symmetrical compositions and long shots of *Zed,* it would seem merely a primitive method to separate two halves of the screen so that two characters could be played by the same actor. It would also fatally distance us from the close-ups upon which psychological realism rests. It is the close-ups that make it possible for us to perceive the minute differences in facial expression by which we can read the shifts and changes in Beverley's and Elliot's emotional state. The close-ups also help us to tell them apart.

Although it may seem glib (and obvious) to say that Irons is a better actor than Greenaway's two leading players put together, the psychological complexity that is the hallmark of naturalistic film acting (see James Naremore's *Acting in the Cinema*) and the foundation on which *Dead Ringers* is built, is irrelevant to Greenaway's film. Detached, ironic, scientific, *A Zed and Two Noughts* is predominantly comic. Attempts to empathize with the brothers' grief are frustrated throughout by the distance from which they are filmed, by the symmetrical compositions that reduce them to paper cut-outs, and by the marked lack of affect in the performances. This frustration makes *A Zed and Two Noughts* one of Greenaway's more challenging (and least popular) films.

However, once the viewer gives up any hope for psychological depth from the characters or emotional engagement with their position, the film becomes more enjoyable – though even as a decidedly dry comedy, it pulls up short. Both Deacons are bland where a high-style, deadpan wit is called for. As Van Hoyten, Joss Ackland brings a welcome burst of energy to every scene he is in, and Frances Barber as Venus contributes a well-judged balance of artifice and warmth. But Andrea Ferreol's accent does not improve upon repeated viewings. Clarity is essential for comedy, as is timing; having to mentally decipher or reconstruct what Alba said afterward, spoils both. But the most notable lack in the film is that despite being constructed around the issue of how to deal with grief, the film never ventures close enough to the center. Unlike other Greenaway films where a strong emotional effect sneaks up on you, in *A Zed and Two Noughts* – where strong emotion is the subject – there is no aftereffect. Instead, grief is forestalled, infinitely displaced.

Taxonomy versus Plot

Trying to find out what the brothers are up to, the shadowy zoo authority Van Hoyten watches the documentary series on evolution that Oliver has been viewing. When his assistant suggests, "Maybe he's looking for an answer to his wife's death," Van Hoyten retorts,

> He'll not find it here. This is a straightforward account. . . . God, it's all such a dreary fiction.

Greenaway establishes from the first that *A Zed and Two Noughts* will not be *that* kind of movie – neither a documentary, nor straightforward, nor a good old-fashioned story. ("Darwin," we are told, "was a good story-teller.") So let us look at the film another way.

Examining the opening scene, in place of character we find a list of features whose development can be tracked through the course of the film. First: animals and related subheadings – alive or dead, male or female, black or white, physically present or present through representation. The swan alone represents the latter half of the first three subcategories, the Esso tiger the last. There is also the one-legged ape and a zebra.

We could watch how letters are literally signs, and how signs are separable from what they signify. Too fluid to stay attached to what they name, the letters slip from signifying one thing to another: as the "Z" in the "Zoo" sign slowly disappears, its two remaining letters are released from being part of a word and become two "O"s (for Oliver and Oswald), until there is only a single nothing. In this state the last "O" could be either a letter or a number, a zed or a zero. As a letter, the zed is what holds the two "O"s within one realm of representation. As the end of the alphabet, though, once it is gone, we have what is left after the end – nothing. All is for nought.

Cinematically, we could track the relationship between camera movement and production design. In the opening scene alone, Zed features camera movement of a kind rare in Greenaway as a crane shot swoops over the image then moves into the shot to close in on the backseat of the car. Designed by Ben Van Os and Jan Roelfs, photographed by Sacha Vierny, the symmetrical compositions are continually questioned, interrogated, and put under pressure by the dolly shots in and out of the frame. (This is quite different from the lateral tracking so common in every other Greenaway film, from The Draughtsman's Contract to Prospero's Books.)

The colors in this first scene evoke Godard, with the strong emphasis on primary colors – blue as the color of the zoo sign, red in the red and white streamers, in Alba's hair, and in the shirt of the man with the blowtorch throwing sparks into the corner of the composition. The vividly orange Esso tiger is itself a Godardian signature from around the period of Two or Three Things I Know About Her and La Chinoise (1967). (Though in Godard, of course, red, white, and blue is political – associated with France, the United States, and Vietnam – and the tiger an emblem of multinational capitalism.)

As in his structuralist-influenced short films, A Zed and Two Noughts returns again and again to the alphabet, evoking the ingenuousness of a child's primer. (Drowning by Numbers is the numerical companion piece to Zed's alphabetical play.)

The alphabetical code begins with the introduction of Alba and her daughter, Beta. As mother and daughter, one follows the other, the beginning that generates life and the new life that proceeds from it. The alphabet and motherhood are both about progression. Alba wants to have twenty-six children and name them all after the letters of the Greek alphabet. Oliver points out there are only twenty-three letters in the Greek alphabet. Later, when Alba proposes to name her twin boys Gamma and Delta, she's told "wrong sex," and asks, "Do Greek letters have a sex?"

Throughout the film, Greenaway intercuts scenes of Beta learning her alphabet by way of the zoo. Quizzed by adults, Beta combines the alphabet with the animal world. "A is for . . .?" "Angelfish." "B is for . . .?" "Butterfly." Proceeding in strict alphabetical order, these scenes provide transitions to Oliver and Oswald's relation to animals. When Beta associates B with Butterfly, we cut to Oliver freeing a cage of butterflies. When "R is for Rhinoceros" and "S is for Swan," we cut to Oswald's film of the rotting swan. (The rhino was freed earlier.) The only interruption comes when the animal world refuses to cooperate. When asked "X is for?" Beta snaps, "There aren't any animals that begin with X."

Taxonomy is defined as the "orderly classification of plants and animals according to their presumed natural relationships."[4] Although the series proceeds to its preordained end ("Y is for?" "Yak" "Z is for?" "Zebra"), what is lost in Greenaway, a loss momentarily held at bay by the presence of the little girl, is the presumption of innocence, of any "natural" relationship between animals and the world that names them. The whimsical arbitrariness of the connection between the letter and the animal it stands for is made explicit when de Milo asks Felipe, a figure in white, "What did they use for zed before they knew there were zebras?" Overturning the "natural" order, where language predates the thing named, Felipe suggests that "Zed was invented specially for zebras." But there is a darker side to taxonomy, represented by the zoo. Connected to Van Hoyten and Van Meegeren, the zoo is a place of institutionalized corruption. To be classified there is to be forcibly removed from the natural world.

One of the features most typical of Greenaway is precisely this fluidity of signifiers whose meaning is due entirely to the instability, the permeability, of categories. As with Borges's "Chinese encyclopedia" (see *The Falls*), just as we get the hang of what seem to be the master categories structuring a film, those categories begin to shift, combining and recombining, so that the signifiers that seemed to belong to one paradigm are suddenly cropping up in another, pointing us off in a new direction.

In Greenaway's collection of systems, taxonomies, encyclopedias, and classifications, categories refuse to hold. As the separate categories in *A Zed and Two Noughts* (animals, colors, letters, and names) begin to coalesce, dis-

tinctions collapse. The combinations of terms (or is it the original separa-
tions?) are shown to be logically impossible. For instance, when language
meets animal, instead of clarifying distinctions, it creates a series of nominal
hybrids: angelfish, elephant fish, zebra fish – each a logical impossibility.

Categories overlap as the color system is applied to the animal system.
In their first scene, Van Hoyten asks Venus, "How are the zebras?" and she
answers, "Black and white." Trying to negotiate a price for sex, he offers
her five pounds sterling and two pounds of zebra steak. She names her price
as the "tail feathers of a bald eagle." When he regrets he doesn't have one,
she responds, "I forgot. It's a black and white bird."

As the black and white animals (zebras, dalmatians, bald eagles, zebra
fish, pandas) are linked to the people who wear black and white, the color
system then becomes a key to a third category – Greek mythology. Besides
Venus, Greenaway identifies "the gatekeeper" (whom Oliver calls "everybody's pimp and messenger") as "a lightly disguised Mercury who wears
the zoo-colours, a silver hat with wings – the symbol and colour of Mercury."[5] Van Hoyten, striking in black, is "Pluto, God of the Underworld,
. . . the Keeper of Reptiles who makes an alternative animal collection of
black-and-white animals because there is no colour in Hell."[6] Associated
with night (he is also keeper of the owls), Van Hoyten is a figure of death;
he is accused by both brothers of systematically eliminating black-and-white
animals – a category that threatens to include Venus de Milo, who is always
shown wearing black and white (or nothing at all). As Van Hoyten's servant, Mercury is also dangerous. Alba relates that she lost her first child as
a result of mercury poisoning. Mercury is singled out as a method for procuring abortions. The car involved in the fatal crash was a Ford Mercury;
as Oliver tells Alba, by driving it she was "asking for trouble." As an archangel, Felipe Arc-en-Ciel, the man in white, is dazzlingly bright, but as an
arc in the heavens, he (like white light) contains all the colors of the rainbow. (The other pure white being, connected to Olympus through Zeus,
also comes from the sky, and like the archangel the swan is a messenger of
Fate.)

Through her name, Venus de Milo (who is herself a fount of references)
collapses the Greek pantheon with the history of Western art. Combining a
dizzying range of functions, she is a prostitute, seamstress, and storyteller.
Her stories concern bestiality, sexually collapsing the boundary between
species. (We are told Venus likes to meet her customers at the panda cage,
though there is a rumor the pandas are stuffed.) As Leda found out from
the swan, though, metamorphosis is the purview of the gods; Felipe and
Milo are both punished for their urge to copulate with animals. Milo is

metaphorically armless, and Felipe lost his legs when trampled by a white mare he lusted after.

As a prostitute, Venus blurs the distinction between everything she does and how much it costs. When she tells her clients sexy stories, Milo's every reference to literature concerns how much the author was paid: "Anaïs Nin was paid five pounds for her pornographic stories." Another tale is offered at "an eighth of what Pauline Reage got for *The Story of O.*" She offers to tell Alba "what Venus did to the unicorn in Beardsley's *Under the Hill.* He got paid sixty guineas. What do you think sixty guineas was worth?" For Venus, every kind of intercourse is an exchange – I'll give you this for that – and anything that can be exchanged is commodified. As such, art, literature, and sex become interchangeable as each becomes yet another way to make money. Negotiating with Van Hoyten or sewing special costumes for Van Meegeren, Milo also demonstrates how the failure to maintain distinct boundaries leaves one likely to be corrupted – though, like the gods, she's available to help or hinder anyone.

(Not quite anyone. One of the most succinctly funny scenes in the film consists of a single shot. Milo is in the cinema watching the documentary series [the flamingo episode]. Mercury leans over Milo's shoulder and whines, "Why not?")

The postmodern overload of off-the-wall references contributes to the film's deadpan comic brazenness. Sitting naked on Oliver's bed, Venus offers to tell him a story about an Eskimo and a polar bear, but when she starts talking about who got paid what, Oliver throws her into the hall. Naked, Milo casually dresses while walking down the stairs singing "The Teddy Bears' Picnic" ("Don't go into the woods tonight"). Uniting a children's song, an ultra high-tech apartment complex, and a nude descending a staircase (in static long shot this time), the scene ends as the original 1930s recording comes in on the soundtrack. A nonplussed nightwatchman in the foreground observes Venus's descent, a stuffed camel incongruously decorating the scene.[7]

The children's nightmare/fantasy of animals taking over when it is dark and no one is looking coincides with Milo's fantasy of a world of animals freed from human dominance. However, like every signifier in the film, once "The Teddy Bears' Picnic" is introduced, it slides away from its source, accumulating new meanings in relation to new situations and characters. Introduced by Milo, the song is next associated with Beta (Oliver and Oswald play it for her when they move Alba out of the hospital and into an apartment). When Alba is sewn to the piano stool in Van Meegeren's re-creation of Vermeer's *The Music Lesson,* she pounds the song out on the piano as she asks Oliver to get her out of there. Linked by genre and period, "An Elephant Never Forgets" becomes a companion piece to "The Teddy Bears"; Alba requests it be played as she dies. Oliver and Oswald take up "The Teddy Bears' Picnic" to accompany their last scene.

As the signifiers slip and slide across the text, the characters become progressively more adept at mixing their colors, fish, and birds. Watching a documentary series on the beginnings of life, Oliver tells the zookeeper Fallast, "It's cathartic, watching life begin. Because I know how it ends." "How?" "With a swan." Oliver is certain he "got it wrong before." This time he's out to "separate true clues from red herrings."

The adherence to logic, or systematic thinking, in the face of the fluidity of categories, reveals logic to be the foundation of nonsense. Trying to persuade Alba that having lost part of your body isn't so bad, Oliver cites Captain Hook ("It was his arm," Beta insists) and Long John Silver ("He was fictional," Alba counters). As the brothers' examples slide from fiction to reality, Alba rejects any connection to fiction as a taint. They point to Victor Hugo's father, whose leg was made of cork, to which Alba conclusively states, Hugo "wrote fiction so he doesn't count." Oliver and Oswald proceed regardless: listing examples of artificial legs ("Pinocchio's legs were wooden"), they alight on Toulouse-Lautrec. ("He *had* legs!" Alba interjects.)

OSWALD: Now *his* father kept horses.
OLIVER: Marie Antoinette's father kept pigs.
OSWALD: Marie Antoinette's father did *not* keep pigs –
OLIVER: Well, someone's father did.

When logic and narrative are joined, they are not only incompatible but inconclusive. Oliver and Oswald move Alba out of the hospital (and out of the reach of Van Meegeren) and into an apartment: "Now you'll be safe from art *and* medicine," they tell her. But Alba sees it as exchanging "one prison for another."

ALBA: So I'm to be a kept woman.
OLIVER: Not so you'd notice.
ALBA: You know they clip the wings of birds in the zoo.

When they counter that she is "free as a bird," she responds, "Just like Leda." Each reference, to birds, mythology, scientific practice, brings its own counterargument. So we go in a circle and make no progress. (Shortly after, the brothers note that the tiger and the zebra carry their own prison bars with them.)

The only logic that maintains its power, and one that is particularly addictive, is the logic of conspiracy. Feeding off facts but with the irrefutable, all-encompassing quality of myth, conspiracy logic has the tenacity of one's last hope. Oliver barges into Alba's room demanding answers: "Which way was the wind blowing? Was it blowing off the south buildings or the north buildings?" As Alba pleads with him to stop – "What difference does it make?" – he insists there must be an answer. But the more scientific the approach, the less comforting, as hypothesis generates counterhypothesis. Alba argues, "Another set of details from the same crash could produce something completely different." Oliver insists there must be some hidden logic that explains the accident.

> The wives of two zoologists die in a car driven by a woman called Bewick who's attacked by a swan on Swan's Way –

Alba retorts that he is "beginning to build a case for the supernatural. . . . Look. It was an accident," Alba insists. "Five thousand accidents happen every day." Besides providing little comfort, statistics can also cover up conspiracies. Accounting for the suspiciously convenient death of a crocodile, Van Hoyten's henchman points out, "In a zoo community of seven thousand animals, there are deaths every day." For Alba, ultimately, accidents are "acts of God, fit only to amaze the survivors and irritate the insurance companies." And so we are left with Fate and bureaucracy. In either case, nothing is explained.

For Greenaway, *A Zed and Two Noughts* began as a series of questions. Given the original premise of twin zoologists who have lost their wives, he asserts,

> We now have the beginnings of a plot to explore many things: the absence of meaning in gratuitous death; is death pre-determined; how do religion and science deal with the problem; is Genesis or Darwin the most likely myth; what other myth-systems try and answer the question?[8]

Not expecting answers, the questions proliferate and infect logic. As soon as one reaches the solid ground of fact, it evaporates into fiction or myth. Did I mention that Proust's Swann in *Swann's Way* is "working on a study of Ver Meer"?[9]

Vermeer

Crowded with references to outside texts, Greenaway's films often feel as if they have a centrifugal force, spinning us off into the world outside the film. If only we knew more about the connections between British and Dutch landscape architecture in the seventeenth century, or the resonances between Dutch painters like Hals and the thugs of British gangster culture in the 1980s. Many times, we need to know more simply to find out whether or not what we have just been told is true. Is that true about Webern in *The Falls*? Is there really such a person as Boullée? When Greenaway uses verifiable facts, they are more often than not as absurd as his fiction, leaving the viewer in doubt. In *A Zed and Two Noughts,* nearly every reference to Vermeer comes through the machinations of the criminally obsessed Van Meegeren, whom we are told is the cousin of a well-known forger of Vermeers and a Nazi collaborator. The actual existence of a Hans van Meegeren (discussed later in this chapter) anchors Greenaway's fiction in fact, but does that make it less fictitious? In this setting of forgery and fakes, it seems a Greenawavian irony to find, for instance, that Vermeer himself came from a line of counterfeiters.[10]

With Vermeer nearly everything is ambiguous, and this is what makes him an ideal figure for Greenaway. Experts (akin to those from the IRR in *Vertical Features Remake,* or the Bird Facilities Institute in *The Falls*) are perpetually confounded by Vermeer. In exasperation, one critic writes:

> Every approach has been tried, every conceivable theory put to the test – none seems acceptable, let alone convincing. As for the drawings of Vermeer, every art historian has discovered some, and he is usually the only one who believes in them.[11]

Forgeries are routinely exposed; long-acknowledged works abruptly dropped from the canon. In every book written on Vermeer's work, the expertise brought to the defense of one disputed painting dissolves before your eyes as allegedly definitive arguments mirror those floated earlier (by another expert) in defense of an obvious fraud. Unattractive paintings are deemed authentic on the basis of their connection to other unattractive paintings and the inclusion of details of the kind any forger would be sure to include. The arguments at times lean toward the absurd: the authenticity of *The Girl with a Red Hat,* for instance, is questioned on the grounds that it "looks too much like a Vermeer."[12]

The more scholarly the account of Vermeer's life and works, the slipperier things become, the language filled with qualifications and doubts. Things are "probable," "possible," "likely," "could be," "speculation." No one is certain how many Vermeers ever existed and how many exist now. Many of the best-known "Vermeers" were not even cited anywhere until the eighteenth century.[13] (Vermeer died in 1675.) Pierre Descargues notes that the more Vermeer is studied, the fewer Vermeers there are. Since Vermeer was "rediscovered" in 1866, when 76 paintings were attributed to him, the number of accepted works has grown progressively smaller: 56 in 1888, 34 in 1907, 38 in 1908.[14] In 1976 Christopher Wright counts 36 (though he admits *A Lady at the Virginals* "came to be rejected by most critics," and *The Girl with a Flute* is "controversial").[15] Arthur Wheelock, Jr.'s *Jan Vermeer*,[16] published in 1981, reproduces 34. By 1989 the number is down to 30, according to John Michael Montias's painstakingly researched *Vermeer and His Milieu*.[17] The dialogue in *Zed* is even more severe, stating there are now 23, down from 26.[18]

The confusion regarding how many Vermeers there are is exacerbated by the fact that most of the paintings do not have fixed names. Because the subject matter is often similar, the use of generic, descriptive titles only contributes to the confusion. For example, *The Music Lesson* may be called *Lady and Gentleman at the Virginals* or *Couple Standing at a Virginal* or *Interior with a Lady at the Virginals with a Gentleman*. (*Lady Seated at the Virginals* and *Lady Standing at the Virginals* are two different paintings, both "late" works and both dubious.) The woman in the ermine-trimmed yellow jacket who is interrupted at her letter writing by a maidservant delivering a note can be found under three different titles in three different sources. Because the generic description for one work would also fit several other paintings associated with Vermeer, it is easy to see how works can be confused in Vermeer's presumed oeuvre. *The Allegory of Painting* (re-created in *A Zed and Two Noughts* in Van Meegeren's studio) is also known (in English) as *The Art of Painting, Interior with an Artist Painting a Model*, and *Artist in His Studio*. Even though it is the only painting of its kind in Vermeer's work and thus unlikely to be confused with any other, the profusion of titles creates an illusion of subterfuge typical of too many aliases. Each title in its way tries to locate this painting within an accepted genre (allegory, studio scene, eccentric self-portrait), but the fact that none of the titles succeeds in capturing everything within the painting speaks again to the enigmatic quality at the heart of Vermeer.[19]

The closer one looks at Vermeer himself, the more *he* begins to seem a fiction (much like Tulse Luper, Louis-Etienne Boullée, or William Shakespeare). One study of Vermeer opens with the question "Did Vermeer really exist?" "Accounts of him," we're told, "are contradictory, and meager at best." Depicting Vermeer as an "elusive and shadowy figure," this writer continues:

We catch fitful glimpses of him and that is all. The lights of history play on him in sudden flashes, like a beacon turning in the night. We see him for a moment in the glare of celebrity. Then we lose sight of him altogether.[20]

In the most exhaustively detailed study of the information that exists relating to Vermeer, Montias's *Vermeer and His Milieu*, Vermeer himself seems a void surrounded by the better-documented relatives of his litigious family-by-marriage.

Yet at the same time it feels as though Greenaway wants there to be a "real" Vermeer. But like all art for Greenaway (and perhaps like all artists), the best work generates more questions than can be answered and we are left with the pleasure of mystery. Art withholds an essential part of itself, preserving, in the face of intense study, a sense of something ineffable, intensely private but at the same time open – qualities most often associated with Vermeer.

The mysteries of art are far from the cheap conspiracies of men like Van Meegeren who obsess over details while missing the essence – and still get the details wrong. Van Meegeren is cloaked in fiction. Glimpsed in surgery, and later laughing in the shadows as Oliver and Oswald show Alba their film of decaying prawns, the mysterious doctor is introduced with a question: "Who is that man?" Oswald asks. Alba replies he is her surgeon but that "he wants to be a painter, a Dutch painter – the Dutch painter Vermeer, no less." Oliver notes that Vermeer "only painted 26 paintings, and three of those are dubious." When Alba suggests twenty-three is sufficient, Oswald replies "evidently not" because Van Meegeren came along and painted some more. "That's his name!" Alba interjects, "He's the cousin of the faker of the fake Vermeers."

Caught up in this flurry of fiction and questionable fact, Van Meegeren's work, both medical and artistic, is equally dubious. His reenactments of the scenes in various Vermeers are riddled with mistakes. His elaborate re-creation of *The Music Lesson* is built on the lie that the woman at the virginal (unwillingly portrayed by Alba) is sitting down, sewn to her piano stool, when the painting itself, intercut with the scene, clearly shows her standing.

According to Van Meegeren, Alba tells us, she "looks like *The Lady Standing at the Virginal*; I suspect it's because you never see her legs." Some reviews of Greenaway's film repeat as a fact the idea that "Vermeer's domestic paintings never show their subjects' legs."[21] However, a cursory glance at Vermeer's work contradicts this: because the women wear skirts, of course, we cannot see their legs directly, but they are clearly modeled under the fabric (see, for example, *The Glass of Wine*).[22]

Even so, the staging of *The Music Lesson* (*A Lady at the Virginals with a Gentleman,* c. 1662–65) is hopelessly confused in *A Zed and Two Noughts* with Vermeer's *The Concert.* In the latter painting, the woman whose dress Alba wears *is* seated. The triangular composition of the Vermeer is doubled in Greenaway and inverted: where Vermeer has two women flanking a man, Greenaway changes angle and has Oliver and Oswald flanking Alba on the left and Van Meegeren, Venus de Milo, and Catharina Bolnes (Van Meegeren's assistant) on the far right. The three pseudonymous characters (Catharina Bolnes was Vermeer's wife's name) stand under a copy of Dirck van Baburen's *The Procuress* (another triangle) – a copy of which occupies a similar spot in the Vermeer. (The original was owned by Vermeer's mother-in-law.)[23]

When Van Meegeren stages *The Artist in His Studio,* he casts himself in the role of the artist. But instead of holding a brush, he stands before a tripod, snapping single images as Oswald does. Some critics suggest that Greenaway, by making Van Meegeren a photographer, is drawing a comparison between himself and Van Meegeren. "In a sense, Greenaway, like Van Meegeren, is a 'faker' of Vermeers."[24] While Greenaway's films frequently sport artist figures with connections to the filmmaker (Kracklite, Madgett, Tulse Luper), even considering those of whom Greenaway is critical (Mr. Neville, Prospero), Van Meegeren is hardly a compatible soul.

Van Meegeren's uses of Vermeer are progressively more obscene. He uses his re-creation of *The Music Lesson* as an excuse to grope Alba and measure her breasts when she comes to be fitted for an artificial leg. He makes a mockery of *The Artist in His Studio* by putting a nude Catharina Bolnes smack in the middle of it. (Vermeer did not do nudes.) He also mixes his references by having Bolnes wear the red hat from *The Lady with the Red Hat.* (In this pose, she evokes the nineteenth-century *Pornocrates* by Félicien Rops, a citation Greenaway will use again in *Prospero's Books.*)[25]

Above all, Van Meegeren uses Vermeer as an excuse for abuse. He made his assistant (who does bear a remarkable resemblance to the Lady in the Red Hat) legally change her name to Catharina Bolnes so that she would be a suitable wife for a would-be Vermeer. Regrettably, he tells Alba, Catharina (like Van Meegeren) falls short of her Dutch ideal. She cannot have children; the real Catharina Bolnes had eleven.

If Van Meegeren falls short of being either Vermeer or Greenaway, we could ask, "Is he even a good imitation Van Meegeren?" The actual Van Meegeren's story is as improbable as that of any Greenaway character. Wheelock relates:

Every Vermeer invites us to create a story. (Of the critics on Vermeer available in English, Edward Snow tells the best stories.)[29] In Vermeer, the same woman appears time and again. She is blond, usually pregnant, her hair tightly tied in a bun. The tone is always very quiet, the woman glowing, private, serene. Looking at these images and making up our own stories about Vermeer, we can say he loved his wife. Above all, he loved his wife.[30]

While the plot of Greenaway's film grows out of a similar feeling (the brothers' love for their wives), the powerful emotions held so close in the Vermeer paintings seem to be utterly absent from *A Zed and Two Noughts*. Perhaps Vermeer can tell us why. In an article speculating on Vermeer's seeming detachment from the wars and upheaval of Europe in the late seventeenth century, Lawrence Weschler argues that "the pressure of all that violence (remembered, imagined, foreseen) is what those paintings are all about."[31] Emotional chaos is "held at bay, but conspicuously so."[32] In describing how *A Zed and Two Noughts* came about, Greenaway said he was thinking about how animal behaviorists "relate their anxieties to their subjects." Pursuing the thought, he added, "The greatest loss I could imagine would be the death of my wife."[33] (The blond woman with pearls in her hair from Vermeer's *Mistress and Maidservant* bears a strong resemblance to Prospero's deceased wife in *Prospero's Books*.) Watching *A Zed and Two Noughts*, one gets the feeling that when faced with a loss of such magnitude, Greenaway cannot allow himself to really imagine it. Consequently, feeling itself is passionately held at bay.

Zoo-Cinema-Zed

If Greenaway identifies with Vermeer, it is through Vermeer's implicit connection to cinema. For Greenaway, in this his most cinematically self-reflexive work,

> the overall master-of-ceremonies of the film was to be Vermeer – adroit and prophetic manipulator of the two essentials of cinema – the split-second of action, and drama revealed by light.[34]

While there is hardly any overt action to be captured in *A Zed and Two Noughts* (most of the major action occurs offscreen), Greenaway is very sensitive throughout the film to the use of light. In place of Vermeer's consistency (according to Greenaway, "always from the left of frame, coming from a source four and a half feet off the ground"),[35] Greenaway revels in the exhilarating variety of lighting techniques made possible by cinematographer Sacha Vierny:

There is a deliberate catalogue of the various ways to light a set in *ZOO* – by daylight, dawn-light, twilight, candle-light, fire-light, moonlight, starlight, search-light, by cathode-tube, arc-lamp, neon-lamp, projector-beam, car headlamps, fog-lamps, and many others.[36]

But light is not the only cinematic register important in Greenaway's *ZOO;* cinema itself becomes a major trope for exploring the film's central themes. Because of Greenaway's taste for "sending out many messages simultaneously" to ensure a "diversity of multiple meanings," by the end of *A Zed and Two Noughts* two of the film's most important themes/categories/taxonomies begin to collapse into each other, intensifying the film's "overall sense of metaphor."[37] Cinema and zoos are best understood as metaphors for each other; exploring one tells you interesting things about the other.

To begin with, cinema is a kind of zoo. Greenaway remarks,

> I have always been fascinated by zoos – three-dimensional encyclopaedias, living dictionaries of animals, yet a continuation of man's reprehensible relationship with animals. The first animal prison was the Ark where animals went in two by two. Berlin Zoo – an animal prison inside a human prison – gave me the idea of putting these and other speculations into a film.[38]

In this brief statement, zoos progress from being about life ("living dictionaries") to being prisons ("reprehensible"). In *Zed,* it is even worse. Seen mostly at night, the zoo is a location associated with death. The first image we see inside the zoo is of the rotting head of a zebra as another zebra (both behind bars) paces in the background. The line that freezes cinema on the image of death (the wives in the backseat of the shattered car) is "Did it come from the zoo?"

Greenaway's ambivalence toward zoos is divided according to gender in the film. Women do not like zoos. Alba mentions that Oliver's and Oswald's wives did not like zoos. Venus's contempt is evident. If the mythical beast, half woman, half zebra, existed, she says, "they'd only put it in a zoo."[39] Alba does not like zoos either. When taken from the hospital to an apartment (which she characterizes as being transferred from one prison to another), she notes, "It's certainly convenient to the zoo." Zoos are the artificial, arbitrary bringing together of incompatible species – holding in one place what was meant to be separate. Beta, on the other hand, is intent on making a new kind of zoo. Surveying her collection, Oliver deems it "the old story with a new taxonomy – only an innocent would put a spider in the same jar as a fly because they're both brown." Death in Beta's child-like system is part of nature's daily life, as it is with Smut, her male counterpart in *Drowning by Numbers*.

Where women are associated with sexuality and life, it is the men who are associated with cinema and zoos. Except for Felipe Arc-en-Ciel, every man in the film is connected to the zoo. Men's obsession with taking a scientific approach to life and death weaves together the relationship between zoos ("three-dimensional encyclopaedias") and cinema. The men in *A Zed and Two Noughts* (which Greenaway abbreviates as ZOO) are obsessed with watching films as well as making them. Oliver watches a pseudo-BBC film series called *Life on Earth*; Oswald makes a companion series on death. Oswald's films are a zoo of death, the daily process of animals decaying made visible, viewable, by cinema. If zoos are anti-life, and if cinema is associated with zoos, is there then an essential connection between cinema and death?

To address the relationship of film and death, we need to look at the films made by the two noughts. The films-within-the-film become, like the alphabet, another organizational system. Complaining about how tedious it would be to watch the BBC series about life on earth, Van Hoyten worries: "There are eight parts. This is only the third." And *A Zed and Two Noughts* can be broken down into eight sections: a prelude, an ending, and six sections bracketed by "decay" films. At first these do not seem to be in order because although they start with A for apple and end with Z for zebra, for the most part they are not alphabetical: (1) apple, (2) prawn, (3) fish, (4) crocodile, (5) swan, (6) dog, (7) zebra. Instead, there is a different system at work. Death has an evolution, too, as we move up the Darwinian ladder from vegetable (apple) to crustacean (prawn), fish (angelfish) to amphibious reptile (crocodile), birds (which came from reptiles) (the swan) to small mammals (dog), and from small mammals to large mammals (zebra).[40]

In Oswald's films we see the metaphorical array of reference of which Greenaway is so fond. The first "decay film" is of an apple. Associated with Eve (not only the first woman but the first woman to die), the apple calls to mind the brothers' dead wives. Oswald takes the apple, originally, from Alba's bedside. Its color is the same sickly green associated in *The Belly of an Architect* with figs, photocopiers, sickness, and death.

The second inset film focuses on prawns. Questioning Alba, Oliver and Oswald want to know what their wives were shopping for the day of the crash. She tells them the women bought china and prawns. Oliver saves the shards of china found at the crash site (blue and white, the kind associated with Delft, the home of Vermeer, also known as the Master of Delft) and

Figure 14. Women and sexuality, men and cinema (Frances Barber and Brian Deacon). (Museum of Modern Art/Film Stills Archive)

watches the documentary episode on prawns. Oswald puts the prawns in a blue-and-white china bowl and films them going bad. Insisting on the grosser truth about physical decay, Greenaway inserts a scene where Van Hoyten and his associates peer intently at the prawns, looking for a clue to the brothers' behavior. Speculating on what the connection might be between apples and prawns, they crudely joke that the prawns probably smell the way Oswald's dead wife now smells.

Unlike the zoo, in the "decay" films all the subjects are dead. The question becomes "Are their deaths *necessary* for cinema?" Are their deaths caused by

94

and for cinema? Van Hoyten and his henchman electrocute a crocodile and give it to Oswald after inquiring how much he would pay for such a thing. Mercury dumps a dead swan on the table when the brothers are playing poker. Jogging in the two-man suit they had Milo make for them, Oliver and Oswald come upon the children from the first shot, their dead dalmatian lying in the street in a zebra crossing. Evidently, death by misadventure. As Oswald and Oliver's now joint project nears its end, their cinema begins to demand fresh bodies in order to construct a climax and a kind of closure.

Cinema's artificial relation to life becomes clear in the crocodile film. As the corpse repeatedly bloats and collapses, it appears to be breathing, given a pseudo life only possible on film. Stop-motion photography is a form of animation, a term that, with cruel and morbid irony, literally means breathing life into something. Dramatically condensing time, stop-motion allows us to see changes that would be imperceptible in real time, in effect making a kind of narrative out of thousands of single-frame images (what are essentially still photographs). Applied to nature, this process has a pronounced alienation effect. Corpses act out a macabre "living" death, one that seems grotesquely unnatural.[41]

As the animals become larger and easier to identify with, the scenes of decay become progressively more difficult to watch. At one point, when Oswald's collection seems complete, the camera, starting on a close shot of the dead dalmatian, begins to pull back, slowly revealing the entire laboratory with lights flashing a frame at a time to chronicle the stages of disintegration of the swan, the crocodile, the prawns, and so on. While Nyman's lively score and the vivid visual complexity of the image add a certain exhilaration to the shot as a shot, the camera movement is literally pulling away. The fascination/repulsion toward the dead animals stated in the camera movement calls to mind experimental films, particularly *Sirius Remembered* (1959), where Stan Brakhage charts the decomposition of a dog, its corpse left exposed in the woods as it returns to nature.[42] While there is a personal relationship between Brakhage and his pet (so that Brakhage, in a sense, can't help looking), the outdoor setting stresses the natural process of decay, a very different experience than that resulting from the corpse's decay within a laboratory, before a scientific grid, and under artificial light.

As Oliver and Oswald find, the problem with any film, or series of films, is how to end it. Despite (or perhaps because) of the scientific rigor of Oswald and Oliver's cinematic research, the experiment turns deadly. Van Meegeren notes that all Oswald's subjects have been female, and he and Van Hoyten darkly hint that they can supply a dead woman for the final film subject, one who is pregnant.

How much would you pay, do you think, for a human corpse? Milo is about your wife's build and age and weight and she is ten weeks pregnant with my child.

(Van Meegeren in the previous scene makes an identical claim about paternity.) Van Hoyten suggests Milo "could be persuaded to visit the zebras." Although it is dangerous to be black and white in Van Hoyten's world, it is worse to take the place of the dead wives. Oswald has also been implicated, early on, in the abuse of women. When Milo visits him shortly after his wife's death, he orders her to dress in his wife's clothes and to sit and speak on command, in much the same way Van Meegeren tries to dictate dress and behavior to Alba. With a projector aimed almost directly at the camera showing the apple film from the other room, the cinema is not far away.

The cinematic apparatus itself, prominent throughout the film in the form of cameras, tripods, projectors, and television sets, is presented in a progressively more complex way, with television and cinematic projection often deployed simultaneously and commenting on each other. As Oliver and Oswald go deeper and deeper into Plato's cave, they sit a few feet from a wall, "watching" the film of the decaying zebra even though the image is projected over their heads and onto their backs. When the film is over they rise to look at their own shadow, and through a cut to a matching movement, assume their place on the small screen. African tribesmen rise up too as the fake-BBC *Life on Earth* series also nears completion, the footage shown on a television in Alba's room.

The plot ends symmetrically when Alba decides to commit suicide (having given birth to twin sons, fathered by Oswald and Oliver, and leaving Beta and the babies in the care of her new husband, Felipe Arc-en-Ciel). Oliver and Oswald ask her to, in a sense, leave her body to science.

ALBA: You want my corpse?
OSWALD: We need the use of the garden at L'Escargot for nine months.
ALBA: A significant period.

At her deathbed, the brothers go down a checklist, as they did after the death of their wives. Oswald asks, "What are the signs?" Oliver recites, "No pulse, no eye movement, no heartbeat, the skin pales and turns stiff." They sit, symmetrically, until "An Elephant Never Forgets" finishes. "Now what?" When the family won't let them take Alba's corpse to L'Escargot, they substitute themselves. Wanting to merge with each other, they become their own cinematic subjects.

L'Escargot is Alba's country estate, a watery world where canals cut through deep grass, a Dutch landscape in an English film called by the French name of a snail too literally present. As references proliferate and categories are inverted and collapse, the question at L'Escargot (as it does in *The Cook, The Thief, His Wife and Her Lover*) turns out to be who is the diner and who is the dish.

The brothers attend their last picture show alfresco. Their makeshift cinema is distinctly Fellini-esque, made up of a string of lights, a sheet for a screen, and a platform in the middle of an empty countryside. Shedding their three-legged suit, they lie down on an inclined grid (symmetrically, with Oliver on the left, Oswald on the right), start the phonograph record of "The Teddy Bears' Picnic," and inject themselves with something neatly lethal. The camera stands before them on its tripod, and as the record ends, lights flash to begin the single-frame recording of the last animal to decay.

Where Oliver began by watching films on what happens before life begins, Oswald focused on what happened after death. They end with a cinema poised precisely between – at the exact moment between life and death.

However, the zoologists fail because they forget to take nature into account. As daylight dawns and dew covers the fields, the snails move in. Covering the camera, the record player, the bodies, and the fuse box for the lights, they cause an electrical short and the experiment shuts down, taking the film with it. At the end, the sound of crickets is all we hear.[43]

The defeat of cinema at the hands of nature is also the defeat of technology, equipment failure a metaphor for the inadequacy of science. The apparatus is flawed – not only the physical machine, but the rational system on which it rests. The entire conception – of zoos, science, art, alphabet, numbers, language – fails to account for something as simple as a slug.

Greenaway's use of systems is not systematic because all knowledge, technology, and expertise eventually fails. For Greenaway, structural systems are a thing of delight. If another way of organizing the material catches your eye, follow it. In the end whether the Vermeers are real or fake does not matter because in *A Zed and Two Noughts,* all systems are red herrings.

4

Drowning by
Numbers (1988)

Water may be Peter Greenaway's natural element, though typically it is his ambivalence about it, his sense of its myriad associations and contradictions, that makes water for Greenaway a perpetual lure. When asked about its ubiquity in his films, he rhapsodizes:

> Water is fantastically photogenic. But of course, the world is four-fifths water, we're all born in amniotic fluid, water is a big cleansing medium whether it's literal or metaphorical. On another, pragmatic level, water provides almost a legitimate opportunity for people to be seen nude. . . . But it literally is the oil of life, it is the blood of life, which splashes, dribbles, washes, roars – it's a great friend and a terrifying enemy, it has all those significances.[1]

Admitting "there is a way in which somehow water is the unguent, the balm, the cooling agent of a lot of the dramas of all the films," he concludes: "And I suspect I should go on using it, too."[2]

The subject of some of his earliest shorts (*Water* [1974], *Water Wrackets* [1975]) and a constant theme in *The Falls* and *The Draughtsman's Contract,* water evokes a trace of longing in Greenaway's work, something of the rootlessness of the amphibian, caught between land and sea, or the island dweller's sense that land is a temporary foothold and we animals exist under constant threat of being swallowed up by the sea. In *Drowning by Numbers* the combination of fear and yearning in relation to water becomes enmeshed in attitudes toward women. Opening with a shot of the stars, *Drowning by Numbers* suggests that all women are born under the sign of water, while men are left to fend as best they can.

A Zed and Two Noughts and *Drowning by Numbers* are companion pieces in Greenaway's work, one urban, the other pastoral, each restating the alliance of women with nature, men with the inadequate comforts of reason. Both films revolve around death, but differ dramatically in tone. *Drowning by Numbers* nestles firmly into the tradition of British black comedy, where murder is a familiar, if regrettable, eccentricity common to the idyllic countryside. As British as the Empire, this tradition extends from De Quincey's "Murder as a Fine Art," through Oscar Wilde on the precipitous moral decline from murder to lying, to Ealing films where the laurel rests on *Kind Hearts and Coronets* (1949). In these works, wit excuses anything, the heroes and heroines blissfully cool when faced with the void. The key to success in this genre is a sprightly screenplay and pitch-perfect casting. In a 1990 interview, Greenaway suggested that when it came to working with actors, he still had not "discovered how to have both the artifice and the performance – both the self-consciousness and the suspension of disbelief."[3] However, the uniform excellence of the acting in *Drowning by Numbers*, made two years earlier, brings it very close to the ideal.

In place of *Zed's* multiplicity of organizational systems, *Drowning by Numbers* supplies a simple counting game a child can follow. The film, in fact, begins with a child counting. In one of the most ravishing images in Greenaway, a little girl dressed like a Velázquez Infanta skips rope on a village street at night while counting the stars. Of course, they aren't real stars. They have Greenaway names like "Twenty-five: Luper," "Thirty-seven: Zed," "Fifty-eight: Kracklite." When she reaches one hundred ("Elektra"), she stops. A grandmotherly figure (Joan Plowright), walking by, pauses to inquire, "How many did you count?" When told one hundred, she asks, "Why did you stop?" "A hundred is enough. Once you've counted a hundred, all the other hundreds are the same."

Scattered throughout every succeeding scene are numbers that proceed from one to a hundred, the latter coinciding with the end of the narrative and the film. In a film filled with games, the numbers are presented in an appropriately playful manner. Sometimes they are scattered throughout the image, sometimes mentioned in passing on the soundtrack. The numbers do not appear in every shot or even, it seems, every scene. Nor are they presented in strict chronological order. Trying to outsmart the film, you find that as soon as you are convinced a number has been left out or skipped over, it suddenly appears, proving you wrong. As one slowly becomes more engrossed in the story, it is easy to lose track of the numbers until a particularly brazen display reminds the viewer that they are there – and counting.[4]

As we have seen in Greenaway's earlier films, numbers always count. In *A Zed and Two Noughts* classification can be a matter of life and death; in an early film like *Windows,* everything is measurable in numbers, each statistic relating to death. For Greenaway, *Drowning by Numbers'* narrative and its number count "are often interchangeable – the narrative indicating the characters' so-called 'free choice' and the numbers representing some sense of destiny."[5] Trapped in an irrefutable web of numbers, the characters in *Drowning by Numbers* are caught in a terminal system: to be counted is to die.

Drowning concerns the marital dissatisfactions of three women named Cissie Colpitts.[6] The oldest and first Cissie is played by Joan Plowright. Walking home in the dark after questioning the girl skipping rope, she discovers her drunken middle-aged husband, Jake (Brian Pringle), in a debauch with a local woman named Nancy, passed out next to him in a metal tub (#2) used for washing apples. (Although it is not mentioned in the film, A is for Apple and they are everywhere in this first scene. It is harvest time.) Tired of Jake's vulgarity, Cissie neatly pushes up her sleeve and drowns him in his tub. Counting "one" for the first time he goes under ("I've had a wash already, Cissie. Nancy gave it to me") "two" (". . . not play games . . .") and "three," she firmly holds his head under until he does not come up again. Kissing him gently on the forehead, she takes off the wall a ceremonial pitchfork presented to him for his work as a gardener and throws it on the bonfire. (The pitchfork has four prominent shiny tines.)

Needing help to transport the still unconscious Nancy back home in a wheelbarrow, Cissie enlists the aid of a second Cissie, played by Juliet Stevenson. Hearing that Cissie #1 has drowned her husband (though not terribly upset by the news), Cissie #2 tells her mother they should call the youngest Cissie (#3, played by Joely Richardson). At one point the third Cissie asks a man if he thinks they are all the same woman because they have the same name. (He demurs that they seem like one unit because of their camaraderie.) Related as mother and daughters, the three represent the greater category Woman, involved in a prehistoric struggle with men called the battle of the sexes. All women, however (even in the film), are not Cissie Colpitts – there is Nancy (who calls herself Nell) and the other women who ally with the men to expose the Colpitts' crimes. The true Cissies are those who recognize, through the act of murdering their husbands, a deeper form of kinship. In doing so, they discover a primordial affinity with water.

In killing her husband, each woman realizes how to make water her friend. All of the women named Cissie Colpitts use water to help free themselves from the adulterous (husband number one), insensitive (number two), or merely unnecessary (number three) men in their lives. When asked by the other two why she killed Jake (her second husband, not their father),

Cissie/Plowright asserts, "He was unfaithful." When her daughters point out that this was not a new state of affairs, Cissie relents and admits the truer, more mundane reasons: "Because he'd stopped washing his feet, because his nose was too red, because he had a hairy backside, because . . ." She concludes, simply, "I didn't like him."

Cissie/Stevenson's husband, Hardy (Trevor Cooper), has also let himself go. When Cissie/Plowright first appears in their room, she points out to her daughter how much weight the sleeping, naked Hardy has put on. "He looks pregnant," she asserts. "He doesn't smell very fresh, does he? . . . Do all fat men have little penises?" her mother asks. "I don't like the beard." "Neither do I," Stevenson replies, "I tried to persuade him to shave it off." She has even less success trying to get some sign of affection from her disdainful husband.

Attempting to seduce him later, Cissie/Stevenson finds her Hardy hardly worth it. A priggish businessman, Hardy spends most of his time typing ("65 Vesuvius, 66 Amsterdam Rd."). Bringing him a popsicle, Cissie/Stevenson opens her robe and poses provocatively on a divan. When this has no effect, she asks him how *he* asks for what he wants. She follows his instructions: saying "please," calling emergency services (police, ambulance, fire brigade), and writing a memo. (Attacking his typewriter later, she spells out "Kiss me Hard," and the numbers 67 68 69.) When he does come over to her on the couch, instead of making love he shocks her by inserting the cold popsicle into her vagina. When she asks for some "warming up," he snaps "I'm not that thirsty" and goes out for his (final) swim.

All the men drown, in keeping with the title. Hardy drowns in the sea, having gotten cramps from eating too much. Cissie/Stevenson resolutely strides out to save him, but announces that she shall drown him instead. "I just ruined your very best typewriter [drowning it in lemonade and sugar] and now I'm going to do my best to drown you." Contemptuous to the end, he tells her she hasn't got a chance. But she succeeds – and has witnesses to prove it. An athletic team running along the beach – in shots unfailingly reminiscent of *Chariots of Fire* (1981) – pauses to watch as Hardy's cries for help turn into Cissie's choking pleas for assistance (now that it is too late). When the runners with the numbers 70 and 71 ask if she needs help as she kneels by Hardy's body, she insists, "you must let *me* phone the police . . . or the ambulance . . . or the fire brigade. Or the coroner."

The third Cissie has the most powerful connection to things aquatic. She is training to be an Olympic swimmer and is frequently found in rivers or pools. Like a water sprite, she cannot be treated like other women. When her boyfriend Bellamy asks, "When are you gonna break away from that bunch and come live with me?" she replies, "I'll marry you on two conditions – that you learn to swim and never ever take me from the front." As she tells him this, she reclines provocatively against a tree, like a dryad about to become one with nature. Usually found making love outdoors, Cissie #3 and Bellamy at one point bicycle past two cows with 76 and 77 prominently displayed on their rumps. As they pass behind a tree where Sid the gravedigger sits, we hear the exaggerated sounds of a crash (reminiscent of a scene from Godard's *Weekend* [1967]). They have run into two dead cows splashed with red paint (as in Godard), the numbers on the dead cows (78 and 79) preserving the numerical series. Content to demonstrate her power over the increasingly suspicious Bellamy, Cissie asks him to kiss her behind and they begin to make love on the roadside as the camera pans away.

Despite their evenly matched appetites, we know this Cissie and Bellamy can never be well matched because he doesn't swim and is well advised to be afraid of water. "Fancy a plumber not being able to swim," Cissie/Richardson teases him. "What's water for?" She marries him anyway because, as she tells her mother and sister, "Championship women swimmers always have their sons early." Once pregnant, Cissie/Richardson tires of Bellamy and lures him into the deep end of the pool. After his death she tosses his radio in as well, the words "eighty-six" the last we hear before the sound submits to its watery grave.

As the men die, people become suspicious. As the coroner, Madgett, warns the women, "One is just possible, two is very unlikely." Nancy complains about Jake's death being declared "accidental." Jake's cousins Jonah and Moses Bognor pop up in the pool where Cissie/Richardson is in training, asking questions and insisting the deaths were suspicious. As the number of doubters grows, they are most frequently seen standing near bonfires under the water tower. The Colpitts women dub it "The Water Tower Conspiracy."[7]

His most self-referential work outside of *The Falls*, *Drowning by Numbers* expands stories and characters mentioned in earlier Greenaway films. The original Cissie Colpitts, for instance, first appears in *Vertical Features Remake* as a close friend of Tulse Luper and Gang Lion. In *The Falls*, she has changed her name to Propine Fallax #27, "in order to make a clean break with her past reputation." During the heyday of British documentary filmmaking in the 1930s, *The Falls'* Cissie Colpitts stored film in a nearby water tower for the "Goole Experimental Film Society," a fact illustrated by many low-angle shots of a water tower reminiscent of the one sheltering the Water Tower Conspiracy here.[8]

Figure 15. Cissie #3 (Joely Richardson) and Cissie #2 (Juliet Stevenson) in
Drowning by Numbers (1988). (Museum of Modern Art/Film Stills Archive)

Drowning by Numbers takes the enigmas circulating around Cissie Colpitts and other Greenaway characters and elaborates upon them. At times
it seems as if the women in the later film have almost supernatural powers.
Cissie/Plowright, for instance, tends to appear in rooms without formally
entering them. In the opening scene, the camera tracks right to follow
Nancy as she looks for an apple tub to bathe in; tracking back, it discovers
Cissie/Plowright overseeing a blaze outside the scene of her husband's debauch. As Cissie/Stevenson rises to dress the next morning, her mother's
image in black appears in a mirror. Cissie/Stevenson is surprisingly unper-
turbed by the quiet, but sudden, apparition. At another point, a flash from
a camera summons the first Cissie, suddenly present in glowing red on the
far side of the screen, carrying her familiar bouquet of autumn flora.

But the women have external help as well. When Cissie/Plowright needs
to make sure Jake's death is deemed accidental, she phones the local coroner, a man her late husband leeringly called her *"friend* – Madgett." Madgett (Bernard Hill) has a yen for Cissie and offers to write out a death
certificate in exchange for "a little bodily comfort." When she protests,
"This is blackmail," he agrees – "Yes." They go riding in his car into the

woods, where he propositions her again, asking her to take her clothes off. Blushing at the thought but highly amused, Cissie placates him by telling him he'll have to wait awhile, "to stop tongues wagging." Besides, she notes, "Cissie's more your age" and his "prospects [there] might improve."

When Cissie/Stevenson's husband does indeed suffer an untimely death, Madgett grumbles, "You women are getting too proficient at this. . . . You've got to stop." Again, he takes the recently bereaved for a car ride. Less courtly with a woman closer to his age, he proposes at once, but Cissie refuses. ("I could never marry a coroner. How could I be sure you'd washed your hands?") She points out the advantages of necrophilia (corpses would be less likely to reject him) and offers herself to him when she is dead. ("I wouldn't mind if you took a few liberties.")

The car rides are presented in a fairy-tale manner. Sacha Vierny's lighting of the scene emphasizes this in a charming, childlike way. The car is lit from within in a way that makes the people seem far too large for the mini-conveyance. In one shot, where the car follows a runner setting a paper trail, the car seems much smaller than the man. Driving into the deep, dark forest becomes a mythical journey, as if one is entering troll country. The women explicitly refer to Madgett as a gnome when they warn Cissie/Richardson that, having drowned Bellamy, she's due for her ride with Madgett – but, they assure her, "he's harmless." "He's really only interested in games and chocolate pudding."

However, the third car ride proves rougher. Madgett is getting frustrated. Cissie/Richardson lacks the social skills of the more experienced women who parried Madgett's thrusts with little effort. Attracted to him ("I like his hands"), the youngest Cissie invites him to touch her breast and kiss her, but reacts with shock when he asks her to take her clothes off. "No, Madgett! I'm a widow of 48 hours." He roughly grabs her despite her screaming, "Is this attempted rape? You're supposed to be harmless." Even though – as he knows better than anyone – the women do not tolerate misuse by men, he tries to tear her blouse off, insisting, "You Colpitts women have used me – You women have destroyed me." Cissie tumbles out of the car and runs across a field of sheep, blood on her forehead.

Up until this point Madgett has been an honorary member of the Cissies' circle. And indeed he forms the fourth in a series of "imaginary beings" thought to inhabit "the four elements once believed to make up the physical world."[9] The Sylph lives in the air (when Cissie #2 emerges from her airy beachhouse, intent on drowning Hardy, a stormy wind howls around her, whipping up the surf). The Salamander dwells in fire (Cissie #1 attends the bonfire raging outside as Jake and Nancy fornicate in a world littered with rotting fruit scrutinized by scores of patient insects). The Undine (also called a nymph) is a water spirit (Cissie #3, the Olympic-hopeful swimmer). When her husband has drowned and the police arrive to question her and Madgett, Cissie #3's main concern is whether or not there will be swimming pools in prison.

The first three elemental spirits are female, but the fourth is always male. Madgett is the Gnome, a species of "little old men or dwarfs dwelling in the earth." Walking on a quayside littered with dead fish ("Look, a herring," Cissie/Plowright announces), the older women tell Cissie/Richardson she should expect an invitation to accompany this fairy-tale-like figure to his haunt in the woods. At home in the forest, Madgett nevertheless does not have much power there. "This field is synonymous with my failure," he tells Cissie/Richardson. "Three rebuffs in the same place."

Useful and (for the most part) unthreatening, Madgett is also welcomed into the Cissies' homes as the master of games. At Jake's wake they play Dead Man's Catch as Jake's coffin is carried away. Tossing skittles in a circle, anyone who drops one must play with a handicap. Drop too many and you must lie on a sheet in the center of the circle. All the men (Hardy, Bellamy, Madgett, and even the boy Smut) end up "in the winding sheet." The women never miss a trick. When one of the women assures the losers "it's only a game," Hardy cracks, "The way Madgett plays it, you'd think it meant something."

At Cissie/Stevenson's big house party on the beach (a giant yellow 50 marks the site with white streamers blowing in the wind, reminiscent of *A Zed and Two Noughts*), Madgett supervises a game of Hangman's Cricket, a virtually unwinnable game with endless rules in which everyone must dress up as a prescribed character. Hardy's mother, cast in the game as the Mother-in-Law, complains to Madgett, "this game has everything in it except the kitchen sink," to which he replies, "Thank you." Hardy and Bellamy again refuse to play along, Hardy fuming, "I do not run a pathetic Punch and Judy show for lonely bachelors." ("The Businessman," we're told, "can be saved if he submits to the Red Queen." For once, Hardy turns for comfort to Cissie/Stevenson in her red beret and wrap, asking her to cut his hair.) Bellamy insists he wants to play a "proper game" of cricket, but Madgett begins to regale him with lists of famous cricket deaths (possibly fictitious but heavily documented nonetheless). "Games," he tells Bellamy, "can be very dangerous." The game of Hangman's Cricket, Smut tells us, can only be appreciated after people have played it for several hours. Only then do they know which characters they want to be permanently. A loser eventually emerges "and presents himself to the Hangman who is always merciless."

As the coroner, Madgett is comfortable with the phases of life avoided by most people. When Cissie/Stevenson asks if he has ever fallen in love with one of his corpses, he tells her, "I once kissed an old lady of 82 on the forehead. She was twice my age." There was also a young woman trampled by cows ("there wasn't a mark on her"); he sat up with her all night, holding her hand, and couldn't bring himself to close her blue eyes. For the Colpitts women, death is an integral part of life and Madgett is the man who understands this. His son, Smut (Jason Edwards), celebrates it.

Smut (like Greenaway himself) demonstrates what Michael Walsh calls "the obsessional's love of death."[10] A serious young boy with glasses, wandering through the fields and woods of rural England in short pants and chunky boots, Smut comes across death everywhere – mutilated cow's heads in the forests, dead birds hanging from trees, animals killed in traffic by the roadside. More systematic than his father, Smut paints numbers in bright colors by the corpses he finds, tags each according to his own hierarchies of death, and sets off fireworks to mark the occasion. Shoveling up a dead bird on the roadside while Madgett consults a map, the water tower looming in the distance, Smut tells us in voice-over the rules to this game.

> A great many things are dying very violently all the time. The best days for violent deaths are Tuesdays. They are the yellow paint days. Saturdays are second best – or worst. Saturdays are red paint days. The Great Death game is therefore a contest between red paint days and yellow paint days. So far, yellow paint days are winning by 31 corpses to 29.

We see a close-up of two matchboxes, each with the word "corpses" and the numbers 31 and 29 on them, as Smut lights a fuse. "Whatever the color," Smut adds, "a violent death is always celebrated by a firework."

A kind of self-portrait, Smut re-creates facets of Greenaway's own childhood. Greenaway once told an interviewer,

> When I was nine or ten I started to collect insects. Trying to identify them and sticking them neatly in boxes was, I think, as important to me as finding and catching them.[11]

In Smut's room above the barn, there are endless shadow boxes of preserved insects, each neatly catalogued and pinned. Insects and their identification provide unlimited opportunities for introducing numbers into the image. In the original murder, a butterfly flaps its wings on a bar of soap while a snail crawls over a "Number 3" printed on a sack. When Cissie/Plowright hands Smut his towel at the pool, two bees drop out, but Smut tells the women not to worry – "These have been counted" – and in a close-up we see the bees resting in his hand, a 45 and a 46 neatly painted on their backs. Whenever Smut ventures into the forest at night, we see his book under a bush, lit by a torch. The etchings of bugs (numbered, of course) are enlivened by actual creatures crawling across the page.

There is something dark and growling and frightening in the woods, but only we and Smut know it. When Madgett takes Smut along on one of his evening drives, Smut hears terrible sounds while poring over his insect book out in the dark. (A roach crawls over illustrations 61 and 62.) Running for his life, Smut pops up back in the car, breathlessly pretending everything is fine. The grown-ups are too preoccupied to notice that the dark surrounds them, too.

One of the most charming aspects of *Drowning by Numbers,* and one unprecedented in Greenaway's work, is the depiction of the relationship between Madgett and Smut. There are other little boys in Greenaway's films – Pup in *The Cook, The Thief, His Wife and Her Lover,* for instance – and other inquisitive children of nine or ten (Beta in *A Zed and Two Noughts*), but there is no other sustained focus on a father–son relationship. Madgett includes Smut in his researches (using masking tape to mark on Smut's body the sites of all the fatal blows in the history of cricketing) and in his games.[12] Smut coordinates the game of Sheep and Tides and keeps track of the rules for Hangman's Cricket. He even corrects Madgett at one point when Madgett says that Sheep and Tides is "an Old Testament game." "No, it's not," remarks Smut (though no one notices).

It is Smut's job, or possibly his vocation, to document each game. It is Smut's voice on the soundtrack telling us the rules of the games. He structures his day around them. He awakens, for instance, to "the game of Dawn Card Castles," where one can predict the next night's dreams by stacking fifty-two playing cards into a pyramid and waking before it collapses. Smut awakens, turns on a light, and smiles at his pyramid – which promptly falls apart in slow motion. He gets dressed each day by counting very quickly from one to ten and jumping out the window of a barn into a haystack.

After each successful jump [in "the game Flights of Fancy or Reverse Strip Jump"], the competitor is allowed to put on an article of clothing.

He takes Polaroid snapshots of himself during each jump (number 11 marks the photo collage). Number 13 is on the side of the barn, and an incongruously large 14 is propped next to the phone Smut fails to answer because he is busy with his game. Asked why he didn't answer, he replies, "I never answer the phone until the cock crows three times." (Smut seems to know all the best numbers. At one point Smut's friend Sid, the Gravedigger in Hangman's Cricket, tells Smut "I haven't found 54 yet." Smut tells him it's in the woods under a tree – "near a water hydrant.")

Smut is in love with the girl who counts the stars. She lives on Amsterdam Road. Like Smut, she knows something about death; she confidently recites the last words of Prime Minister Pitt and King Charles II. Sweetly befuddled about what it is women want, Smut follows up on her query as to whether he is circumcised. "My mother," she tells him, "says it's better that way." (Her mother, it seems, occupies the red-light district of Amsterdam Road; we only see her when she looks out her window, having received her regular visit from a local policeman. Her daughter says her mother would like to have been Nell Gwynne so she could have "serviced Charles II.")

Not knowing what circumcision means, Smut asks Madgett, who is up late one night reading in bed. A good parent who takes all of Smut's questions seriously, Madgett casually holds back the covers so Smut can see what it looks like. "Was Samson circumcised?" Smut asks, and presents a picture showing Samson asleep with his head in Delilah's lap.[13] As Delilah with bare breasts plays with Samson's hair, another woman approaches from behind with a pair of scissors at the ready. "Do they circumcise women?" he asks. "Sort of," Madgett tells him. "In hot countries." Madgett tells him to go to bed, "And anything unanswered about man's barbarity to women, you can ask Cissie in the morning. She's an authority."

But the adults underestimate the seriousness of children, as is clear when Smut tries to circumcise himself with a pair of scissors. This and the Polaroids taken of Smut in his "cricket fatalities" pose are used to malign Madgett's ability to raise the boy. Smut's only other friend is the elderly Sid, the Gravedigger. Cissie/Stevenson points out that Sid follows Smut around "like a black shadow." Although he is innocent as a male, the darkness waiting out in the woods will eventually get Smut too.

Smut and the skipping girl form a couple at odds with the others in the film. Unlike Madgett's attempts at sexual blackmail, Smut's love is romantic, naive, unselfish, "pure." He brings her the stars, telling her the names of three more he has found "over by Cissie's house." Smut urges her to jump in the street so her rope won't catch on the doorstep. Even though she says her mother told her to stay out of the street (where evil men are), he tells her it will be all right because "the safest time of all is Friday night – tonight, in fact." But in Greenaway's world true love can't survive, so true lovers must leave it together. In *Windows* they jumped into a plum tree.

Throughout the film, the numbers and the drownings keep pace. Greenaway notes that "at the end, narrative and number count complement one another, the action has been completed and the film is over."[14] There are three women, three propositions in the woods, three funerals. Madgett knows Bellamy is dead before the women can tell him because, he says, "drownings come in threes." Drunk in the woods, blackberrying with Smut, Madgett refuses to go on helping the women at this point, while behind him the fields are on fire.

Fire, the realm of the first Cissie, is associated with destruction, specifically of men's lives. Against the burning fields, Madgett tells the women he has been avoiding water ("I haven't had a bath since Monday") and asks if Bellamy drank enough water to put out the fire raging behind them.

But water inevitably triumphs. At Jake's funeral, Cissie/Stevenson distracts her mother and sister by telling them why there is a crematorium there. "The ground is too waterlogged to dig a proper grave." Any hole becomes a pond. Even so, she continues, they have the funerals at low tide so the water doesn't come and put the fire out. At Bellamy's funeral, Smut can't light the fireworks because the ceremony is held under the water tower and the atmosphere is "too damp." "It's not surprising," he comments, "Bellamy was pretty wet out of the water." All the husbands are cremated after they drown, the ashes consigned to water. The women tell Madgett (lolling in a hammock under a tree with a large #91 on it), "On Saturday we'll put the ashes out in the sea. You, Madgett, can be a witness." "Isn't that illegal?" he asks rhetorically. (Saturday is a red paint day.)

Madgett arranges one last game in honor of bringing game playing to an end. Summoned to the docks, Cissie/Plowright asks, "What's the game today?" Madgett tells her, "Tug of War." "Who's going to play this game?" she asks, and he replies, "Good and evil." They are playing, he adds, for "me and what's left of my reputation."

> Since there are obviously no rewards for me helping you, I thought enough was enough. . . . I've had enough of game-playing. This is serious. Besides, you're better at playing games than I am.

When the water tower conspirators arrive ("There are seven of them!"), Madgett announces his intention to tell them everything if they win the tug-of-war. Cissie/Stevenson warns him that the game he is playing is dangerous. "Haven't I told you?" he asks. "All games are dangerous."

In the end Madgett's taste for games, used against him throughout the film, proves fatal. Earlier, in the car with Cissie/Plowright, he assures her he is not playing games. "Aren't you? It's impossible to tell with you." Cissie/Stevenson rejects him for the same reason: "How could I trust a game player?" The snapshots he takes of Smut when documenting where cricket

Figure 16. Madgett in the burning fields (Bernard Hill, Joan Plowright, Juliet Stevenson, and Jason Edwards). (Museum of Modern Art/Film Stills Archive)

balls struck their mortal blows, are confiscated by the police. "To a casual eye, they could be suspicious," he is told. Combined with Smut's trip to the hospital after his circumcision ("sexual mutilation"), the photos can be seen as evidence of "procuring pornography, maybe child abuse." Cissie/Stevenson throws in possible necrophilia for good measure.

When the police arrive at the tug-of-war and call Smut aside, Madgett's last game is lost. Smut releases the rope on the women's side and the conspirators win. (As Cissie/Stevenson said to Madgett when the police were questioning him, "I told you Smut would get you in the end.") As the women hurry Madgett into a boat, no one notices that Smut has been handed his late girlfriend's jump rope. It becomes a noose in his last game.

Like the other road-kill in the film, the skipping girl is killed in a hit-and-run – moments after Smut urged her again to jump farther out in the road. While Madgett's (would-be) relations with the Cissies draw toward their inevitable end, the adults are too busy to notice Smut's loss. Reciting the rules, he climbs the nearest tree.

The object of this game is to dare to fall with a noose around your neck from a place sufficiently high enough off the ground such that the fall will hang you. . . . The object of the game is to punish those who have caused great unhappiness by their selfish actions. . . . This is the best game of all because the winner is also the loser and the judge's decision is always final.

To mark his death, the film "celebrates" with an eruption of fireworks that goes on for minutes. As the sky, land, and sea are lit by the shooting candles, and blue-lit smoke radiates around the silhouetted tree, the fireworks (misread by Madgett as "a spectacle [Smut] arranged for the scattering of the ashes") provide a transition from day to night.

Alone in a boat with the three women who rejected him, the three women he loves, Madgett can't swim. The women (Cissies #1, #2, and #3) are the numbers who drown men who disappoint them. Explaining to Madgett that *they* have not lost, they urge him to accept the judge's final decision. It will make for "a neater ending," Cissie/Richardson assures him.

One by one they ceremoniously throw mementos of their late husbands into the drink: the charred pitchfork "in loving memory of a gardener," the typewriter "in loving memory of a businessman," and the still-working radio "in loving memory of an unemployed non-swimmer." One by one they take the urns out of a cardboard box and in a single gesture drop them overboard. One by one each woman approaches Madgett resignedly removing his clothes in preparation for the end. Cissie #1 kisses him with affection, Cissie #2 lingers on his lips, Cissie #3 presses her body against his for the longest kiss as his hands tightly grip the sides of the boat. One by one the women slip into the water. A storm is coming. As Walsh points out, Madgett "is friendly with death; putting his shoes away as the rowboat sinks, he is the unemotional obsessional to the end."[15] Neatly packing his clothes into the cardboard box, he takes off his watch as a last thought and tosses it in too.

With a flash of light and the rockets' last boom, we see the last shot in the film – the prow of the boat, low in the water, marked with the number 100.[16]

In *Dead Ringers* (see Chapter 3 on *A Zed and Two Noughts*), two little boys, curious about sexual reproduction, compare humans to fish. Fish don't need two sexes, one explains, because the water spreads the sperm magically from one fish to another. Sharply rebuffed when they ask a neighborhood girl to have sex in a bathtub as an experiment, they turn sadly homeward. "They're so different from us," they ruefully conclude. "And all because we don't live under water."

Figure 17. "The End": Greenaway's drawing of #100. (Peter Greenaway)

5
An Englishman Abroad
The Belly of an Architect
(1986)

Traveling full-speed through the Italian countryside, a man and a woman make love in a train, horizontal against the passing landscape. They are going to Rome, identified by the man as the "home of the dome, the arch, good food and high ideals." The woman argues that her father was from Italy (*padre/patria*), that he was thin (the man is fat) and had no ideals except the desire to make money. Her father took his money to Chicago, identified by the woman as the city of "blood, meat, and money," and by the man as "the home of some of the best carnivorous architecture in the Western world – that is, outside of Rome." With a cut, we are in Rome, the camera sweeping past classic monuments, gazing up at the statuary, until we arrive at a full stop before twin domes and the title appears, bright red.[1]

Stourley Kracklite is an American architect come to Rome to prepare an exhibition. He is being welcomed with a dinner at an open-air restaurant in front of the Pantheon. The film's principal characters are arranged symmetrically along a long table, the obelisk before the Pantheon visually cutting the building in two, separating Kracklite from his wife, Louisa.

The subject of Kracklite's exhibition is the French architect Etienne-Louis Boullée (1728–99), his name proclaimed on a banner opposite. The centerpiece of the meal is a cake in the shape of a dome, a confectionery model of one of Boullée's unrealized works, what Stourley declares "Boullée's crowning achievement," a memorial to Sir Isaac Newton.

As is typical of Greenaway, the opening scenes of *The Belly of an Architect* are crammed with so much detail, it is difficult to process it all. Within the excess of signification lies an exhilarating proliferation of possible metaphors collapsing architecture, food, capitalism, death, and the body as each term becomes substitutable for the others. Carnivorous buildings are said

Figure 18. Greenaway on the set of *The Belly of an Architect* (1986). (Peter Greenaway)

to "suffer from excess cholesterol." Domes appear as buildings, breasts, bellies, and cakes. The cake alone points to French architect, artist, and theorist Boullée, the English scientist and philosopher Isaac Newton, and Augustus Caesar, whose tomb served as Boullée's inspiration. The system by which this excess is organized is less overt than in *A Zed and Two Noughts*, *The Draughtsman's Contract*, or *Drowning by Numbers*, as Greenaway moves away from exposing specific systems of organization toward a more traditional style of interweaving thematic elements – which I will break down in an arbitrarily systematic (in this case, alphabetical) way.

Architecture
Belly
Consumption
A is for Architecture, solid, spanning time, man's permanent mark on the physical world. And you can eat it. In the opening dining scene, Boullée's revolutionary heavenly spheres let the characters eat cake.

B is for Belly, the expansive American gorging himself on architecture.

But as he grows bigger so do the seeds of his destruction. Pax Americana: like the Caesars, what he eats consumes him.

C is for Caesar, consumption, and carnivores. The tragedy of late stage capitalism (consumer society and its atavistic impulse to make itself greater by eating what it loves – the consumption of culture[s] on a global scale), is that in the West everything is available. It is just impossible to consume it all.

Artists
Actors
Americans Abroad
Despite his loss of faith in explanatory systems, in *Belly*, Greenaway finds two things worth holding on to, each utterly compromised in the late twentieth century: the artist and remnants of Western culture. *The Belly of an Architect* (1986) and *Prospero's Books* (1991) situate the artist amid the rubble of a postmodern consciousness. Both films are dominated by central male figures, artists and scholars whose would-be mastery of culture exposes them to the threat of usurpation at home and abroad. As a father, each man struggles to fulfill his role as guarantor of patriarchal succession. But the fear of failure surrounds each man, inhabiting every fragment of patriarchy's ever-present cultural past.

Not since *Intervals* (1973), shot in Venice in 1969, had Greenaway set a film abroad. *A Zed and Two Noughts* was originally conceived for a divided Berlin.[2] Despite being shot in Holland, *Zed* is defined mostly by its symmetrical sets; its exteriors remain unreal and place-less, an unidentified landscape that is either shrouded in fog or seen at night.

In *The Belly of an Architect*, Greenaway uses an American protagonist to illustrate the tensions and risks of his own ventures into multinational coproduction. In a way, *The Belly of an Architect* mirrors Greenaway's struggle not to *be* Stourley Kracklite. Like his character, Greenaway found himself surrounded by intrigue and attempts to undermine his authority. "It was a horrendous experience," Greenaway recounts. There was considerable tension between Greenaway and the film's producer, Colin Callender. "I think he wanted to direct the film."

> We had arguments on the steps of the Vittoriana, shouting at one another in front of the whole crew. The crew were very, very loyal though. He tried to sack me and Sacha [Vierny] said "If Greenaway goes, I go too and the whole crew goes as well."[3]

Greenaway completed the film.

Despite Greenaway's personal victory, in *The Belly of an Architect* Europe is seen from the point of view of an outsider – and one who feels his status keenly. Like Mr. Neville in *The Draughtsman's Contract*, the Irishman's son going to work up at the manor house, Stourley Kracklite is out of his depth, in over his head, conspired against by those whose claim to belong is slightly greater. Only his arrogant conviction of his own merit buoys up the artist figure. But not for long.

Artistic and intellectual in equal measure, the artists in Greenaway's films find that neither quality is sufficient or holds sway for long, each trait undone by the other. Riven by this contradiction, the artist-intellectual falls apart. Under the constant pressure of his culturally reinforced self-doubt, he cannot hold.

For Neville and Kracklite, Greenaway's primary artist figures, the artist's own world is too dependent on the opinions of others – he needs approval from above, not merely for financial survival, but deep inside. Behind each character is the excitement and pathos of the motto "Poor Boy Makes Good." In class terms, both suffer a petit bourgeois crisis – outstripping your parents with talent or skill, you find yourself isolated, caught alone outside the gates, dependent on the goodwill of strangers, a position uncertain and unsafe. In these terms, the English painter is as disadvantaged in regard to Europe as the American tourist.

In cultural terms it is not surprising that Greenaway chose an American to play his architect. Burly Brian Dennehy plays Stourley Kracklite, whose provenance (Chicago, Sandburg's "city of broad shoulders") is physically inscribed in the actor's imposing physical presence. The figure of the American abroad as cultural innocent points directly to Henry James, whose Daisy Miller braved specifically Roman charms only to catch her death.[4] The danger of travel is reiterated when Kracklite is warned that his hero Boullée "stayed at home for fear of embarrassment abroad."

Greenaway's cinema is seldom seen as an actor's cinema, yet Greenaway has a consistently good eye for casting. The choice of Dennehy is probably the one piece of casting most remarked upon by Greenaway himself.

Brian Dennehy taught me much. I have tended to use English actors with a theatrical background to sustain the long scenes without cut-aways, to use stylized language and be very familiar with artifice and multiple-layered language. I was frustrated that some of those things had to be jettisoned in working with Brian, but was much rewarded by many things he demonstrated that I had been denying. He demonstrated the self-evident truth that complex ideas needed as much help as possible from the actors.[5]

Dennehy's performance provides a tension between the director's style and the vividness of the character as an individual. The American actor gives the film not only energy but also a subtle psychological realism – both hallmarks of American film acting and both atypical for a Greenaway film.[6] "The film is just as layered" as the other films, Greenaway asserts, "but, by his approach, he made it seem less consciously so."[7] The psychological complexity in the acting also adds to the tension between a Romantic vision of the artist as individual and Greenaway's ever-present postmodern irony.

The other major shift in *The Belly of an Architect* is the move away from the pastoral settings characteristic of Greenaway's earlier work. In fact, except for sections of *The Falls, Belly* is Greenaway's only truly urban film. Before it, the films were predominantly pastoral (the short films, *The Draughtsman's Contract*), and the ones that follow (except *Drowning by Numbers,* a chronological throwback) become more and more about interior spaces (*Cook, Thief*). In *Belly* the view of the countryside as seen from the train is a preamble; the film does not really start until we enter Rome. Then we see what the countryside lacks: architecture.

Boullée

Who is Boullée? Kracklite describes him as "this visionary architect whom I've admired since I was a child." He also identifies with Boullée and defines himself in relation to him. As with Kracklite, Boullée "admire[d] antiquity, favoring the Romans over the Greeks, whose temples seemed monotonous to him."[8] And, as is quite possibly true of Kracklite, Boullée's "creative power far exceeded the economic feasibility of his buildings."[9] Dominique de Menil asserts that "historians and architects look[ing] at Boullée's drawings with an eye trained by modern architecture . . . find in them innovations that anticipate modern design."[10] Kracklite's wife, Louisa (Chloe Webb), describes the house Stourley built for her as "two marble cubes and a brick sphere on stilts. Boullée would have loved it."

According to de Menil, Boullée "found little opportunity to practice architecture."[11] As with his contemporary Piranesi, Boullée's reputation as an architect is partly imaginary, based on drawings of things that might have been. ("Boullée regard[ed] the art of architecture as far superior to the mere technique of building.")[12]

> His fame rests mainly on some one hundred unpublished drawings he donated to the Bibliothèque Nationale, along with a manuscript containing his philosophical and practical views on his profession. . . . Outlined and brushed with precision and elegance, [the drawings]

Figure 19. Kracklite at the opening reception. (Peter Greenaway)

Figure 20. Applauding architecture (Brian Dennehy). (Peter Greenaway)

mostly represent imaginary buildings of geometric simplicity and co-lossal proportions, cast against romantic skies. They have an eerie quality of immensity.[13]

Of course, there is always the chance that Boullée could be fictitious. Louisa tells Kracklite's rival Caspasian Speckler (Christopher Lambert), "In Texas, Kracklite was accused of inventing him." Caspasian suggests, "Per-haps Boullée is the ideal architect for your husband to invent?" He adds that the exhibit has "nearly a million dollars to persuade the Italian public that Boullée is not a fiction." (Having convinced the investors, Greenaway had around £850,000 to persuade everyone else.)

Belly
Caesar
Death

Boullée's monument to Newton is defined as a cenotaph, "an empty tomb; a sepulchral monument erected in honour of a deceased person whose body is elsewhere."[14]

> The sphere [of Boullée's cenotaph] is lodged in its base as if in a gigan-tic eggcup. The terraced base is reminiscent of imperial Roman tombs. . . . Boullée may have derived the tiered base with cypresses from reconstructions of the tomb of Augustus in Rome.[15]

The first sight-seeing trip Kracklite takes, one he takes alone, is to see the tomb of Augustus. A green mound of earth, it too is empty. A man playing a violin outside tells him, "It is closed. There is nothing much inside any-way." Stourley reiterates, "This *is* the tomb of Augustus," but is told in reply, "He is not at home." Seemingly erected in the center of an amphithe-ater so that an audience could gather to look at the grave, the scene at Au-gustus's tomb is also where we find that Stourley is being watched.

As soon as Boullée's cenotaph for Newton appears as a cake, it is clear that the characters are consuming the past and that even something as solid as architecture can be eaten. (After dinner, Signor Speckler leads the gath-ering in "applauding great architecture," as they arrange their seats to face the Pantheon and literally applaud.) What the formal beauty of the ceno-taph disguises (in addition to the obscurity of the term) is the fact that the characters are eating the representation of an empty monument to the dead, (a sign of a sign, a signifier emptied of its signified).

Discussing Boullée's fame, Louisa asks Stourley if he thinks "they'll put on an exhibit . . . [dedicated to you] 180 years after your death?" Trying to make love to her, he asks "Death? Who's talking about death?" "Everyone in Rome talks about death." An art historian notes,

> The eighteenth century, toward[s] its close, was haunted by the funerary, even the macabre. Boullée, in his grandiose and dramatic fashion, has captured just that aspect of the Romantic imagination.[16]

Caspasian, who holds the purse strings for the exhibition, stages a death as a publicity stunt at the party announcing the exhibition. At lunch, later, Caspasian relates with great relish how Augustus was poisoned by his wife, Livia, expanding on the gory details until Stourley rushes to the bathroom and vomits – not for the last time. When his sister Flavia (Stefania Casini) scolds Caspasian, he dismisses it as "just a history lesson for foreigners."

Exhibition
Work on the exhibition starts, as the film did, in bed. Stourley flips through pages of Boullée's drawings: the cenotaph, a lighthouse, spheres, pyramids, domes, and phallic towers. The camera tracks along multi-tiered tables covered with drawings, books, and models in Stourley's hotel room, and in an answering scene, slowly sweeps around the cavernous room where Stourley works, an unearthly space seemingly situated in the bowels of the Victor Emmanuel monument.

The major accoutrement in the "office" is a photocopying machine. Telling Louisa to go sight-seeing with the Specklers, a preoccupied Stourley takes two postcards of a statue of Augustus and runs them through the copier, enlarging them until a huge detail of Augustus's stomach comes out from under the sickly green light.

Barking orders that no one follows as he tries to assess the models being made for the exhibition, Stourley keeps losing Caspasian – "Where is he?" When told Caspasian wants to paint the buildings and use lasers to link the sites, Kracklite rails against the color scheme: there will be no blues or greens in his exhibit – Boullée hated them. The film around Kracklite is designed in reds and earth tones. Shooting in the Roman heat, even the sky is white.[17] Yet despite the ban, green persists, highlighted against beige and black, and always linked with decay.

Figs
Fascists
During lunch on the terrace of the Vittoriana, site of the exhibit, Stourley grows increasingly irritable behind a large plate of decoratively stacked green figs as Caspasian and Flavia Speckler make barbed remarks about

Boullée's work, aligning it with fascist architecture. "Do you think Mussolini would have liked Boullée?" Caspasian asks. "Albert Speer did," Flavia asserts, "and he was Hitler's architect." Augustus would have admired Boullée. Flavia points out that copies of Boullée's works appear in every totalitarian capital, "Moscow, East Berlin – " "And Rome," Stourley adds.

Fascist rhetoric is echoed in Boullée's writings on architecture. Regularity and symmetry "represent order, and order is clarity."[18] "Symmetrical compositions are true and pure. The slightest disorder, the slightest confusion becomes intolerable."[19] Only "smooth masses produce virile effects."[20] Boullée scholar Helen Rosenau confirms Speer's fondness for Boullée.[21] Another writer identifies the "Lenin Mausoleum by Shchusev . . . Tatlin's projected monument for the Third International, and Albert Speer's building projects for Berlin" as direct descendants of Boullée's work. "It is not until the twentieth century, with the rise of the totalitarian regimes, that we find a renewed concern with the symbolic implications of architectural designs."[22]

Flavia's list of fascist and totalitarian admirers of Boullée implicates Stourley, who identifies and is identified by everyone else with Boullée. At home that evening Stourley and Louisa trade insults over who is a fascist, Caspasian or Stourley, framed in terms of carnivores and vegetarians. Stourley, having stomach trouble, sides with the vegetarians, not realizing that such a stance does not absolve him of the charge.

When Louisa disparages Stourley's productivity (in bed, in Rome) he experiences his first pain. Her attack takes the form of associating him with Boullée: in a discussion after their welcome dinner, Louisa notes, "You've built six-and-a-half buildings, and now you're spending nine months putting on an exhibit in memory of another architect who also built practically nothing – " She stops only when he gasps in pain. She dismisses the second attack (when she begins talking about death as he tries to make love to her) as the result of over-consumption: "You're always stuffing yourself." Disgusted, she questions his manhood and turns away. "Don't start what you can't finish."

Their next night together, Stourley is more forceful. After a day of being bated by the Specklers, he becomes suspicious and asks Louisa to taste one of the figs displayed beside their bed. Cajoling turns to aggression as he tries to force her to eat one. Fleeing the bed, she insists he see a doctor.

As Louisa retreats to the bathroom, Stourley contemplates a haphazard photomontage in the clutter on his desk – newspaper photos with Stourley alone before the Pantheon opposite a shot of Caspasian and Louisa together, one postcard of Augustus, one of his tomb. He begins to write a postcard to Boullée. "Monsieur Boullée. I hope you don't mind my writing you like this. I think my wife is poisoning me. You can laugh, but I'm serious."

As Stourley begins to confide his deepest feelings to Boullée, he initiates the separation from his wife. From this moment, Louisa exists mostly separate from Stourley, offscreen (as in this scene), absent or distant. He watches her moving away, at the Villa Hadrian, and from the lit foyer of their apartment to the darkened bedroom as seen through a keyhole. He does not intercede. They have only two real scenes together after this: when she tells him she's pregnant [see **Postcards**] and when she leaves [**Newton**]. As they move on their parallel but opposite trajectories, she toward birth and completion, he toward death, each becomes absorbed and defined by what is growing inside his or her body.

Hadrian
Identification
The first doctor Kracklite consults asks him about his symptoms. Stourley says, "I've made some notes," and hands the doctor several photo enlargements of Augustus's belly with red and yellow figs drawn over it. The doctor asks, "Do you have such an heroic abdomen?" His diagnosis of Kracklite is succinct: "Mr. Architect, I can assure you you are not being poisoned. I would suggest that you are suffering from dyspepsia, fatigue, over-excitement, excess, and unfamiliar food, lack of exercise, too much coffee and maybe also – too much *egotism.*"

The egotism that leads Stourley to identify with his idols also destroys him. In identifying with the great, he is also identifying with the dead – a reminder that all biographies end badly. In a postcard to Boullée, discussing his symptoms, he notes, "The Emperor Hadrian died of a perforated ulcer. Did the Pharaohs suffer from stomach cramps?" [See **Rome, Reproduction**]

Kracklite's main identification is with his architect-hero. When Caspasian visits the apartment to seduce Louisa, he sees the photocopies of the postcards of Augustus and asks, "Does he think he's Augustus?" Louisa responds, "No, he thinks he's Boullée." Being so closely associated with Boullée has its drawbacks. It is very easy to turn discussions of Boullée into insults directed at Kracklite. During the negotiations to secure accurate architectural models for the exhibit, it is mentioned that Boullée's unit of measurement was his own body. A "boullée" was the distance from his nose to his navel. "He wasn't a prude," someone notes. "Are you a prude?" they ask Kracklite. "Ask my wife." "Ask Caspasian to ask his wife," someone murmurs, and gets a punch in the nose.

As Stourley begins to suspect Caspasian of stealing not only his wife but money from the exhibit, Caspasian and his rude friend try to make amends by hurriedly presenting Kracklite with a picture of Boullée, an engraving of a figure standing on a pedestal labeled "Architecte Visionaire, 1782." As in Resnais's *Last Year at Marienbad,* the pseudoclassical figure becomes the object of debate and interpretation. Caspasian allegedly found the print at the Bibliothèque Nationale. (Boullée donated his papers and drawings to the Bibliothèque Nationale.) Stourley argues that that does not make this a reliable likeness, sourly noting that the picture "looks suspiciously like Piranesi." As with the statues in *Marienbad,* the use of classical costume is dismissed as a conceit as Flavia intercedes. "Let me look. He's wearing a toga Romana and I do believe lace-up shoes." Caspasian says that by the look on his face the shoes must be pinching him, but Flavia thinks it is much worse. "He's eaten something nasty." Their friend adds, "I'm afraid it is worse than that." Flavia: "Disease of the pancreas." "Pancreatic carcinoma." Stourley snaps to attention: "Boullée died of cancer?" Flavia assures him they are joking.

Having been confronted with Louisa's infidelity, Stourley accompanies the Specklers to a Roman bath where anonymous men needle Stourley by presenting spurious "facts" about Boullée. "Monsieur Boullée was a French hypochondriac. Did you know that?" Stourley: "No." "He was a little lame. Are you a little lame?" Stourley limps away – "No." "He suffered from gout. He was afraid of thunderstorms. They made him incontinent. Why do you think he built so little? His illness incapacitated him. He stayed at home for fear of embarrassment abroad."

Infectious insecurities eat at Stourley as friends use his illness to suggest he should step aside, take a vacation, let Caspasian handle things. In a postcard Stourley questions Boullée: "I wonder why you never came to Rome. Did travelling make you ill? Were you suspicious of foreigners?"

To some extent it is Kracklite's egotism (on behalf of Boullée) that prevents him from completing his work as his life, his wife, and his exhibition slip away from him. At one point Caspasian tells a friend that Kracklite's a wreck ("He won't last til August") and lists all the reasons the exhibit is bound to fail: " – *and* the catalogue won't be completed because he wants it all in color." Switching to American accents, they mock Kracklite with wicked accuracy: "*My* architect knew more about color than Leonardo da Vinci," " – and more about publicity than Michelangelo Buonarroti," " – and more about love-making than Casanova."

Greenaway points out that the names in *The Belly of an Architect* "carry Ben Jonson-like connotations of character if not job-description, i.e., Caspasian – the imperial-sounding, parvenu pretensions of an out-of-town Roman 'foreign' Emperor."[23] "Krack-lite" evokes "the sudden sound of thunder followed by a flash of lightning, to rhyme with 'anthracite' – black shiny coal capable of bursting into flames," while "Stourley" identifies Kracklite with the "tired old man up from the sea" Flavia finds sitting by a fountain [**Mussolini**]. "Stourley" is

> an old Yorkshire/Lincolnshire masculine Christian name pertaining to "river-language" – perhaps referring to the several rivers in England called The Stour – slow, meandering, bank-scouring rivers. In Quaker/Pilgrim-Father/Boston Lincolnshire "to be stourley" is to be "thick in the mind," "as of a pudding," suggestions of stirring and scouring, pertaining to nursery-food, and therefore child-like if not simple-minded – a characteristic of the somewhat naive and sweet/bad-tempered Stourley Kracklite.[24]

Keyhole, Kracklite
Livia, Louisa

Louisa's father is a sausage king. Louisa notes that Stourley's major construction in Chicago is known as the slaughterhouse. "It suffers, like Stourley, from excess cholesterol." Her mother is from Umbria, "a fine fig growing area." When Caspasian first sees Louisa, he can tell she is "looking for a romantic experience" by "the way she eats cake." At one point, discussing figs and perfidy, Kracklite compares Louisa to Augustus's wife, Livia. She does not understand the reference.

Kracklite confirms Louisa's infidelity one day when he comes home early. Hearing laughter, he bends over to look through the keyhole and sees Caspasian and Louisa frolicking naked in the long, narrow apartment. As with other powerfully voyeuristic moments (*Blue Velvet* was a particular favorite of Greenaway's at this time), what we see through Kracklite's eyes has the effect of a primal scene while being marked strongly with the unreality of fantasy.[25] Stourley blindly grabs a chair so he can sit and watch, but his vision is revealed as inadequate. The lovers have removed to the far end of the room, voices and laughter emerging from impenetrable darkness as a white model of Boullée's lighthouse stands incongruously on the table in the foreground.[26] When Caspasian brings Boullée into it, heading toward the dark holding Boullée's lighthouse in front of him as a huge fake phallus, Stourley's chair collapses.

A little boy who has been watching Kracklite watching, comes forward and gives the badly shaken Kracklite an orange. Kracklite trades him a gyroscope and leaves. Climbing on the doors to look for himself, the little boy (wrapped in a toga-like sheet) sees only the mystery of a white obelisk against the darkness of a black arch.

Mussolini, Monuments

Having seen his wife with Caspasian, Kracklite reciprocates, halfheartedly allowing himself to be (symmetrically) seduced by Caspasian's sister. Taking pictures of Bernini's Fountain of Four Rivers in the Piazza Navona, he winces as Flavia inquires after his health ("Have you eaten?") and misinterprets his narcissism as sexual. "Are you interested just in the cocks?" she asks. "I'm interested just in the bellies." "A new erogenous zone," she suggests, and asks, "Why don't you photograph women?" "Different metabolism," he responds, "different organs, different complaints."

Flavia compares him to the figure of Neptune behind him. "You look like a tired old man who's just come up out of the sea." When he tells her he has "tried a little drowning," she invites him to "try some more," and they go to her place to take a shower. There she poses him as Andrea Doria, another figure associated with the sea. Flavia points out that, like Stourley, "*He* had a belly and he wasn't shy about showing it." The line of representations proliferates as Stourley is photographed in fake beard and towel, resembling a photocopy of a painting of the fifteenth-century statesman dressed in ancient Roman style.

For the second time in the film, Stourley comes upon a collage of photographs of himself, Caspasian, and Louisa, but this time what he sees captured by others, objectified and external, is wrenching. An entire wall of Flavia's apartment is lined with photographs summing up the film so far. A red tape leads him across the series: the opening dinner, Augustus's tomb, Caspasian and Louisa at the Villa Hadriana, Caspasian and Louisa sight-seeing, Stourley pocketing postcards, in pain, alone. The last entries are a shot of Stourley's face tacked above the belly of a stone dwarf (never identified in the film).[27] Devastated, Stourley leans against the wall, the image split between the black-and-white close-up of his face, the belly below, and Kracklite in tears on the right. The emotional impact is similar to the moment in *The Draughtsman's Contract* when the artist simultaneously finds that he is part of someone else's story and that he has been outwitted from the beginning. (When Flavia tells him, "It's been noticed you steal postcards," she fails to mention that the "noticing" has been done by Flavia, Caspasian, and friend, who have been trailing Stourley since the beginning.)

What this collage most resembles is a storyboard made up of production stills from the film so far. Because the photographs are often taken from angles that exactly reproduce the position of the camera, angles it would have been impossible for the character to occupy, they collapse Flavia's position with that of the filmmaker. Greenaway seems to identify with her most when they combine to destroy their central character emotionally.

Finding Kracklite collapsed against the wall, Flavia winds the red tape around his throat as if conferring an honor, opens her robe, and leads him behind a billowing curtain where they embrace as silhouettes. Almost blindly he is led to make love to her as if the genetic urge to go on is all he has left.

The modernist architecture associated with Flavia is shown to be directly descended from fascism. Outside her window Kracklite sees a building with an exceptionally flat facade made up of story after story of arches. Commissioned by Mussolini and built in the late 1930s, the Palazzo della Civiltà Italiana was part of a program to present fascism as the culmination of Italian culture, as its nickname, the "Square Coliseum," suggests. As Kracklite looks out the window, we see a single figure entering the building far below, a shot reminiscent in its eerie quietness of Giorgio De Chirico's underpopulated cityscapes, their empty plazas lined by colonnaded arcades. (One of the articles Greenaway wrote as a would-be critic was on De Chirico and Resnais.)[28]

Indoors, Flavia's spare modernist apartment is reminiscent of another artist abroad, this time an Italian filmmaker working in England – Michelangelo Antonioni – and the definitive film on the photographer as predator, *Blowup* (1966). Flavia's apartment is a studio, white on white with red accents, the balcony above glowing a sickly but attractive green. Three classical heads lie on her coffee table in the foreground. The only clutter is photographic. As she sits on Kracklite's lap to make love, a camera on a tripod (ironically) blocks our view. Caspasian makes a casual attempt at blackmail when he comes in and snaps a picture of them together, but Flavia reveals that her camera has no film.

Navels, Noses
[See **Postmodernism**]

Newton
When Stourley introduces the Newton monument as "Boullée's crowning achievement," he mentions that "Boullée had great reverence" for Newton. Boullée himself has been quoted on Newton thus:

> Sublime mind! Prodigious and profound genius! Divine being! Newton! Deign to accept the homage of my feeble talents. . . . O Newton![29]

Why Newton? For Boullée, Newton "defined the shape of the earth," and its placement in the enveloping universe besides.[30] Kracklite describes Newton within a slightly different set of parameters.

Sir Isaac Newton, the subject of tonight's cake, appears in every Englishman's wallet. A man who discovers gravity must be a very good companion. In fixing us firmly on the earth, he enables us with equanimity to keep our heads in the clouds.

As the film abandons the narrative for a short visual disquisition built around Newton's picture on the English one-pound note, Kracklite's voice-over guides us through an interpretation of the image.

If you look carefully you can spot a reference to gravity. See if you can find it. It's an English note so of course it's laconic. It's there – the apple blossom.

Although Boullée's cylinders, pyramids, and spheres evoke art and architecture as pure formalism (not forgetting Kracklite's house as "two cubes and a sphere"),[31] Boullée was not altogether apolitical; he saw himself as building for people who were citizens both of the state and of the cosmos. Despite the various political contexts into which one may insert Boullée (revolutionary France, twentieth-century totalitarianism) or the association of Newton with capitalism and imperialism through the English pound sterling, for Kracklite and for Greenaway, Boullée serves as the individual par excellence, the visionary artist centuries ahead of his time. And the Boullée structure Greenaway celebrates most is the one devoted to another singular individual, Sir Isaac Newton.

Yet even the kind of fame that comes from reenvisioning the cosmos is fleeting. After Stourley's discourse on Newton, the last we see of the pound note that bears his image is it lying in the remains of the half-eaten cake, a candle burning its edge. In the distance we hear Kracklite say he has lost his pound note. When someone reassures him he can always get another, he says, "No, they're dropping out of circulation." Near the end of the film, when he has been barred from the opening of the exhibit, he tries to bribe a guard. The guard returns the pound note – it is useless to him. When Stourley dies, the pound note slips out of his hand and blows away.

For Greenaway, *The Belly of an Architect* deals with "very, very sensitive material." "The film makes lots of personal references to myself and my family and my offspring and my next of kin." (Both Greenaway's parents died of stomach cancer.)[32] "But also, it does really examine this question of 'Can art make you immortal?'"[33] Yet, as the cake and the pound note each in their own way make clear, all human endeavor is transitory. For Greenaway the only real immortality is genetic.

The question then would be, "Did Newton have children?"

The first scene Kracklite has with Louisa after she has told him she is going to have a baby is when she comes to tell him she is leaving. In wine-red pajamas, the green light of the photocopier flashing in the corner, Stourley stands on a chair on the bed staring intently at the floor. Instead of hanging himself, he descends from the chair to the bed, then to the floor lined with row after row of photographs of bellies, like the arches on the Palazzo della Civiltà Italiana. Rows of Augustus, of the contested etching of Boullée, of Andrea Doria, and of Kracklite as Andrea Doria. Louisa walks in, stepping on the photos, and announces she is leaving. Over eight months pregnant, knowing about Stourley and Flavia, Louisa has had her picture taken too. She makes a last attempt to get Stourley's attention by presenting herself to him in the genre that obsesses him, as a photo of a belly – hers.

That too fails. When Stourley declares nude photos of the pregnant Louisa "obscene – how could you display yourself like that?", she counters with a scathing attack on his Romantic egotism.

> It's for Art, Kracklite. Everything's permissible for Art. Look at our marriage. Art first, Kracklite second, and the rest a long way down the line.

Louisa has had several miscarriages, something she sees as parallel to Kracklite's failure to complete projects. "I get anxious." Standing up to Kracklite, she refuses to risk losing the baby. "You're not gonna ruin my child's future for the sake of another unfinished Kracklite fiasco." "Our child," he insists, "*our* child."

Piranesi

Most writers on Boullée find it useful to contrast him with Giambattista Piranesi (1720–78), an exact contemporary of Boullée's. According to Helen Rosenau:

> The style of Boullée is by no means related to that of Piranesi. It stands aesthetically for the very opposite valuations, austerity against richness, moral inference instead of emphasis on formal character, clarity and rationalism in contrast to the romantic and picturesque.[34]

Compared to the regularities Boullée found in classical form and in Newton, Piranesi "treasured the instabilities that plagued him and the Rome of

Figure 21. Stourley alone. (Museum of Modern Art/Film Stills Archive)

his era."[35] In Piranesi's work, the present is built literally on layers of the past, Renaissance buildings top medieval fortresses that rest on foundations built in ancient Rome. Piranesi's world is populated by peasants, dilettantes, scholars, thieves (the last two usually identified as "antiquarians" who may be scholars *and* thieves; see the character of the Nose-picker), the human figures showing what it means to be forever in the shadow of the past. In one engraving, tiny groups loiter around the feet of a crippled viaduct, its colossal arches supporting an expanse broken in midair. Like Boullée's, Piranesi's proportions give the impression of immensity, but instead of pointing toward a future, the arches, submerged in the past, lead nowhere.

The greatest insult a Boullée devotee can lob at Piranesi is that the Italian was content with the two-dimensional products of his imagination and seemed not to care whether the structures could actually be built. With Piranesi

> imagination reigned supreme. . . . The architectural drawing took on the value of a finished work, for now there was increasingly less to distinguish the plan of a fine piece of architecture, the inventions of an ornamentalist, or elaborate perspective drawings from the works of a landscape painter or a painter of ruins.[36]

Conceding the imaginary quality involved, Piranesi's pictures are nevertheless filled with the vivid detail of a living world, including the by-product of life Greenaway is most frequently drawn to, decay (*Zed, Drowning by Numbers*) – something nowhere to be found in Boullée's clean, neoclassical, futuristic spaces, emptied of people.

Greenaway's artists seldom fit comfortably into one single medium, and in this they reflect not only Piranesi and Boullée but their creator. Piranesi is said to have "aspired" to be an architect while earning his living as a "professional printmaker."[37] Boullée, on the other hand, "had never ceased to regret that he had not become a painter" and "headed his *Essai sur l'art* with a famous quotation from Correggio" ("I too am a painter").[38] Greenaway went to art school and has said repeatedly, "Sometimes I think I'm not really a filmmaker but a painter working in cinema, or a writer working in cinema."[39] Kracklite is caught between being an architect and an exhibitionist. [See **Restaurant**].

Throughout the film Kracklite seems oppressed by references to Piranesi. Early on we are told that one of the Italian gentlemen, Signor Caspetti, is not only the exhibit's "most important benefactor" but "a great authority on Piranesi." He suggests that after having an American exhibit on a French architect in Rome, it would be polite to reciprocate with a Piranesi exhibit in Chicago. Caspetti tells Kracklite that when he first saw Boullée's drawings as a child they reminded him of hell. Stourley countered that they reminded him of heaven. "Caspetti was against Boullée from the start," Stourley grumbles later.

Although Piranesi is set up as the antithesis of Boullée for Kracklite, many of the film's compositions seem more indebted to his work than to Boullée's. Stourley's workspace is reminiscent of Piranesi's drawings of imaginary prisons, the *Carceri d'Invenzione*.[40] (Rosenau notes that "Boullée may well have known Piranesi's *Carceri* and his volume devoted to Roman Ruins.")[41] Seeing Kracklite at work in a dark world of archways and shadows calls to mind this description of Piranesi: working on

> effects of perspective and scale, Piranesi extends his images endlessly to demonstrate their inexhaustible power to imprison him, to block his path to spiritual wholeness.[42]

All the Piranesi references are unmistakably translated to conform to Greenaway's interests. The shot under the main title, when we arrive in Rome, seems based on Piranesi's "Piazza del Popolo" which has an obelisk dividing two identical domed buildings.[43] In Greenaway's version, the diagonal composition has been rendered symmetrical to such an extreme it seems nearly stereoscopic.

Today Piranesi is best known for his views of Rome in the late eighteenth century. These *vedute*, or "scenes," are upscale eighteenth-century versions of what we would now call postcards.

Postcards

When Flavia mentions to Stourley, "It's been noticed you steal postcards," he casually asserts, "They're part of a city's publicity campaign. I'm just helping to distribute the advertising." A central structuring device, Kracklite's postcards serve a much more multifaceted purpose than his cynical answer suggests.

I. Content. There are seven postcards.[44] The postcards form a narrative within the narrative:

- The first follows Kracklite's fight with Louisa. Respecting proper form, he addresses Boullée as "Monsieur."

   Monday, May 20th, Monsieur Boullée, I hope you don't mind me writing to you like this. I feel I know you well enough to talk to you. I think my wife is poisoning me. You can laugh, but I'm serious. I'm sure it's part of her general animosity towards you. Yours with respect, St. Kracklite, (Architect).

- The second briefly informs Boullée that the planning stages for the exhibition are under way, despite difficulties with the Italians (Caspasian).
- The third is written in sections at Hadrian's Villa. As Stourley vomits in a cool corridor, he describes in voice-over the lump in his stomach ("some days it's spherical, somedays it feels like a cube. Most days it feels like a sharp-cornered pyramid"). Outdoors in the grassy ruins populated by columns, Caspasian and Louisa are visible in the distance as Stourley sits and writes about his emotional state. "When you're 54, . . . eat badly and pee like a fire engine, what do you do if you suspect your wife no longer cares for your company?" Adding parenthetically, "Sorry, Etienne, since you never had a wife that was never your problem."
- The fourth becomes more personal as Stourley shares his good news. "Dear Etienne-Louis: Apparently I'm to be a father!" The pleasure is momentary as Stourley moves to comparisons – "Were you ever a father?"

– then doubts. "If your wife is unfaithful how can you ever be sure that the child is really yours?"

- The fifth: Kracklite sits outdoors, musing in voice-over after seeing Caspasian and Louisa together. "I wonder why you never came to Rome." Eating the orange given him by the little boy: "Did you ever eat an orange?"
- The sixth: "January 10th. Dear Etienne-Louis, I don't like doctors, they always see you at a disadvantage." Plopped on a gurney, Stourley sits in an ill-fitting hospital gown, awaiting medical tests. Measuring out red tubing to mimic his intestines, he uses his arm as a rough yardstick. For Boullée, it was nose to navel.
- The seventh postcard: Stourley's last. "Monday, February 10. Dear Etienne-Louis. Well, it's no good, Etienne. I've been fired." Having finally lost control of the exhibition and about to hear the verdict from the doctors, Stourley turns and walks away, into the depth of the hospital's garden. A close-up of words provides a transition; Kracklite sits at a table, writing. "I've got an idea. Suppose you come to open the exhibit with me? . . . How about that? That would show them." Deep in the background the doctor appears to summon him. Stourley motions for him to wait. "Come and stay in my apartment. Louisa's not there anymore. I don't sleep too well but I'm sure we could manage." He signs the card one last time, in close-up, "Yours with respect, St. Kracklite (Architect)."

II. Form. Using the postcards as a forum through which Kracklite can express his deepest feelings – fears, pain, paranoia, and desire – to establish a personal relationship with Boullée, Greenaway makes room for a greater degree of insight into a character's feelings than can be found in any of his films so far. This device also calls attention to formal and thematic issues unique to the postcard.

As a style of communication, postcards are associated with tourists, emblematic of the way their lives and wanderings are inserted into preset patterns and an already established economy of "sight-seeing." Time and again a scene in *The Belly of an Architect* begins with the comparison between a postcard and a cinematic image of the same subject. When Stourley first visits Augustus's tomb, he checks the postcard in his hand to see if he is in the right place. In this world, postcards function as maps; they tell you if you are there or not.

Postcards promise a cheap, readily available kind of ownership, "possession" of the view. More often, though, Kracklite is possessed by the postcard – or displaced. At the Piazza Navona, Kracklite sorts through postcard after postcard, each showing the fountains from a different angle, in different seasons and different light, and at different times of day, and he is dissatisfied with them all. The space is not as depicted because he is in none of them. Kracklite fulfills the function addressed by the postcard, the role of tourist, yet that function can be fulfilled by numberless others. As an individual, Stourley is disposable. In "helping to distribute the city's advertising," Kracklite becomes a means of distribution, just as his propagation of the species through fatherhood simultaneously fulfills his role in a larger biological scheme and renders his further existence irrelevant.

The scene of the fourth postcard ("I'm to be a father") begins in a square so empty, it could pass for a postcard until Stourley enters the shot. In their role as maps, postcards invite you to do exactly this – to enter the space of the image and stand in it. Thus they pose not only a relationship to history (stand in the same place where so-and-so once stood), but a relationship to representation. Kracklite's presence makes the "flat" images "real."

Again and again postcards call attention to the "flatness" of a still photograph versus the seemingly three-dimensional cinematic image. Kracklite lowers the postcard of the tomb of Augustus to reveal the real thing in three dimensions. In the introduction to the second postcard, discussing the exhibition, we see the Victor Emmanuel monument three times: a shot of it "live," a nearly identical shot of the facade in postcard form, then an architect's scale model surrounded by actors.

Greenaway's self-reflexive irony, however, undermines any simple privileging of the cinematic image as "real" or as more "present." All three representations of the Vittoriana are reproductions; any perceived increase in depth is pure sleight-of-hand. Everything within cinema is two-dimensional. As with postcards, it is cinema's job to give you the illusion that you can enter the image, occupy that "space." In this way, Greenaway himself can be seen as a maker of "scenes" or *vedute,* a tourist promoting tourism. His Rome is a promotional ideal, beautifully lit, empty of other tourists. The whole place is an exhibit, on display.

The other formal device Greenaway uses to break the traditionally seamless narrative concerns the graphic power of writing. The striking closeups of writing point to several things: Greenaway's taste for calligraphy; the small discrepancies between the spoken and the written word, especially with regard to Kracklite's signature. Most of all, these shots recall the dynamics of *Dear Phone* in which pastoral images are contrasted with vibrant, messy close-ups of the highly fictitious letters of various would-be communicators.

What served as a structural conceit in *Dear Phone* is an almost vertiginous shift in perspective when it occurs in the middle of a narrative feature.

Usually, the postcard is seen as "a 'two-sided' discourse – [made up of] the imagistic and the linguistic signifier" – radically split from each other.[45] But in Greenaway there can be three sides to every postcard: a voice-over; the written word as it is inscribed on blank paper; and an actor performing the scene of writing. The resulting fragmentation of traditional cinematic representation, coupled with the starkness of the images of writing, emphasizes the painful fragmenting of the main character, able to express his most painful emotions only as his controlled surface cracks.

III. Communication. In *The Post Card,* Jacques Derrida argues that the act of writing and sending letters is based on "repeated attempts of *l'ecriture* to affirm our sense" of being, of existing as subjects constituted by language.[46] The "failure of communication" inherent in the project of writing postcards is thus based on the inability of writing to achieve what it promises. It doesn't "deliver."

As in *Dear Phone,* Derrida deconstructs the assumption that a message sent will arrive. "The promise of the letter/postcard is renewed with each act of affixing an address, or of writing one's signature." When Kracklite signs his name – "yours with respect, St. Kracklite (Architect)" – it signals "an intent to channel meaning," to communicate with another.[47] However, communication from writer to recipient is always deferred, open-ended. Once sent, there is no guarantee that the card will arrive, be read, or be understood as intended.

For Derrida, "the act of writing assumes (at least structurally) that writer and reader are involved in a [missed rendezvous]: they will not both be present at the same time, now or in the future, or there would be no need for writing."[48] As such, any act of writing takes place in an imaginary realm: the writer engages in an imaginary conversation with an imagined reader. The logical recipient for such a missive, then, would be an imaginary one. As Kracklite's imaginary friend, Boullée is the only figure Kracklite can trust. (Imaginary friends are usually inventions of childhood; Kracklite discovered Boullée at age ten.)

As Stourley's relationship with Boullée intensifies, the boundaries between them – centuries, life and death – blur and dissolve. ("I hope you don't mind my writing you like this," "I feel I know you," "Suppose you come and open the exhibit with me.") Stourley is not "mad," but his paranoia is at its most pronounced in the postcards ("I believe my wife is poisoning me").[49]

Derrida is particularly interested in "transgressive uses of the postal," especially in those "messages disseminated and a-destined."[50] When Kracklite tries to post one of the cards (the fourth: "I'm to be a father"), a disheveled man casually blocks the postbox until Kracklite pays him off – one of the smaller costs of any attempt to communicate. Posting these cards is not only an act of faith (or delusion) but illustrates again the corruption in which life embroils Kracklite. Of course, this card like the others would be impossible to deliver. Once they are posted, the only possible destination for Stourley's postcards to Boullée must be the "dead letter" office (where, presumably, one can contact the dead).

Postmodernism

Piranesi is a connoisseur of fragments, which he finds everywhere. Retrieved from the classical past, they are [like Boullée's spheres] emblems of unities so far distant they can hardly be imagined. Even his most accurate archeological rendering is charged with an early-modern sense of exile from fully lived history.[51]

The petrified, frozen, or obsolete inventory of cultural fragments spoke to him.[52]

At first the literal fragments of classical Rome scattered throughout *The Belly of an Architect* seem "discarded fetish[es] . . . so hollowed out of life that only the imprint of the material shell remains."[53] But once hollowed out, a new meaning can be "artificially" inserted, then removed in favor of another. When a culture is reduced to fragments, those fragments can be put into circulation in many different ways.

As fragments, culture can be made portable: hearing a faint tapping noise, Kracklite finds a man nonchalantly chipping the noses off classical statues and dropping them into a sack.[54] Culture can be labeled: when Kracklite returns to the exhibit from which he has been barred, he finds that the view of Rome has now been divided up, framed by plastic cones that limit the view to small rectangular images, each singling out one famous building, further limiting the viewer's interpretation of what there is to see.

Culture can be reused: in Flavia's apartment the stone heads on the coffee table serve as accents in the modern decor. Culture can become part of entrepreneurial capitalism, either for sale (the Nose-picker divides statues into smaller and smaller pieces to sell), or to be seen (as "culture" in museums). Whole statues become sites for contested culture: at one point we see statues covered with graffiti (swastikas, profanity), objects upon which one can literally write on the past. Culture is also available to supply "symbolism" in European art cinema (see the giant head, torso, and hand on the walls of the police station, site of Kracklite's interrogation).

This slippage – as fluid as definitions of postmodernism itself – threatens the cohesiveness of identity as the individual abroad (displaced from his own historical, cultural moment) struggles to establish himself as present *in* a present separable from a clearly defined past. This postmodern dilemma is tied directly to reproduction.

Reproduction

In an interview, Greenaway asserts that

> the film is about the way that man reproduces himself. At the beginning we see a lot of three-dimensional sculpture. . . . A little later on we begin to examine painted representations . . . and then there's that representation of man through photography, and finally the most banal of all, through photocopying.[55]

"New technologies" such as photocopying are not an advance because they "imitated precisely the old forms they were destined to overcome."[56]

When Louisa leaves him, Stourley's rows of photocopies (Augustus, Boullée, Andrea Doria, and himself as Andrea Doria) are also pictures of, respectively, sculpture, etching, painting, and photography. Regardless of the method, all are attempts at immortality and all fail. For Greenaway the only true form of immortality comes from genetically reproducing yourself through having children.

Yet it is a paradoxical kind of immortality as Man lives while all men die. Receiving the verdict, the results of his medical tests, Kracklite accompanies his doctor down a long corridor lined on the left by archways, on the right with a series of busts. The young doctor stops opposite each bust and provides a brief lesson in metaphysics for foreigners.

> Cato. He died screaming.

> Titus. Started out well enough, soon became greedy. He was disembowelled on the Tiber steps. He died screaming.

> Hadrian. As you know, an architect of some repute. He put a lot of faith in stones. He died peacefully – still, he's dead.

> Nero. It's best not to talk about him, eh? Caused untold damage, burnt Rome – he deserved to die. He died screaming in a summer house.

As he comes to the last, he turns to Stourley: "He's unknown. Suppose he's you." Every choice for identification offers the chance to identify with death. The doctor admits that he has taken others on this walk before, and he assures Stourley that "there's comfort in contemplating the folly of so many dead. And more comfort still in contemplating the continuity."

Restaurant

In an example of narrative symmetry, Kracklite returns to the restaurant outside the Pantheon where the film began. Drunk, he accosts two women diners. Pulling up his shirt, he shows them his belly: "I'll show you mine if you show me yours." He jokes that while they eat to fill their stomachs, his is "being eaten from inside," and starts shouting at them, "Jesus Christ himself would have died of stomach cancer if you people hadn't crucified him." Intruder instead of honored guest ("What happened to the place? Where's my sign?"), he tries to applaud the Pantheon while evading solicitous waiters and security guards. Seized by pain, he collapses.

Rome

One must remember [Greenaway suggests] that Rome, both in the ancient empire and certainly in the Second World War, was the home of fascism. Ultimate power, ultimate narcissism . . . taken to extremes. And Rome is full of monuments to death and glory, ruins, enormous pyramids to Sestius, triumphal arches representing slavery, representing colonization of the rest of Europe. So Rome itself is the most extraordinary image of all these power crises: it has kings, it has republics, it has democracies, it has Garibaldi, it has emperors like Napoleon, it has oligarchies, it has the most extraordinary range of political systems. And that Roman power and glory and might and narcissism . . . were all part of what was represented by Storely [sic] Kracklite.[57]

Taken to the police station after his drunken exhibition, Kracklite, surrounded by mute fragments, answers a series of existential questions. Squarely facing the camera (though not looking directly at it), he answers the following: name, nationality, place of birth, present address. "Age at next birthday?"

"I'm not gonna have another birthday."
"Pardon?" – "55."
"Married?" – "Yeah."
"Children?" – (pauses) "Yeah."
"Occupation?" – "I'm an architect."
"That's all. Thank you. You may go."

137

KRACKLITE: "You mean that's really all?"
VOICE: "What else would there be?"

He laughs, but doesn't leave.

Surveillance
[see **Mussolini**]

Urban
Vedovelli, Ludovica
Vierny, Sacha
The film ends with the opening of the exhibit. Stourley returns to the Victor Emmanuel monument, bribing his way in through the back. Opening the exhibit (in Italian) and bathed in a blue light, Louisa collapses and begins to give birth as Stourley climbs onto a high balcony and gazes on the formalities below. As his child begins to cry, Kracklite puts his arms out against the sides of the window frame, like a crucified Christ, and falls backward into the empty blue sky.

Though Greenaway calls the conjunction of birth and death "rather clichéd, rather contrived, how the actual birth of his child happens at the self-same moment as the artist himself . . . throws himself out the window,"[58] the ending does underline that the exhibit is in honor of the birthday of someone long since dead. Birth can be seen as a traumatic leaving of the dome. (Helen Rosenau refers to Boullée's buildings as "*enceinte.*")[59] For centuries the Pantheon was the world's largest dome. When Stourley lets go of architecture, all that is left is open sky.

At the end, Stourley has been flattened. Three shots show the exterior of the exhibition, looking as flat and still as postcards. The only movement comes from the one-pound note with its tribute to gravity; it flutters in Kracklite's hand then blows away.

Victor Emmanuel Monument
Built of "glaring white botticino marble," "Rome's monstrously conspicuous landmark . . . quite overpowers the lovely grays and browns, oranges and reds of the surrounding buildings."[60] Ludovica Vedovella's production design for the film stresses warm tones, reds, creams, browns, and black. Although Kracklite proclaims that there will be "no blues or greens in my exhibition," green persistently leaks in, from the figs at lunch and in the Kracklites' bedroom, to the grass of Augustus's tomb and the repeated sweeps of the light of the photocopier.

Signor Speckler tells Kracklite that Romans have mixed feelings about the Vittoriana: "They call it the typewriter or the wedding cake. It's like a box in a theatre, Rome is the play." But from these seats the urban scene is unusually bereft of people. In order to avoid crowds, cinematographer Sacha Vierny appears to have shot many scenes in the early morning. Romans traditionally go on holiday, abandoning the city to tourists, in late summer.

The film, it happens, was shot in August.

Voice-Over: See *Prospero's Books*

6

Daddy Dearest

Patriarchy and the Artist
Prospero's Books (1991)

Like *The Belly of an Architect*, *Prospero's Books* (1991) tells the story of
an artist-scholar, a dominating central figure played by a commanding male
star. However, this time Greenaway has no ambivalence about adjusting to
his star's technique. In fact, more than any other Greenaway film, *Prospero's Books* is from the first a star vehicle.

> The proposition to make a film of *The Tempest* came from Sir John
> Gielgud and this film-script was devised for his playing of Prospero.[1]

"A particular wish of mine," Greenaway states, "was to take maximum advantage of his powerful and authoritative ability to speak text – verse and
prose."[2] Gielgud's stardom is due in large part to his voice. His presence
makes *Prospero's Books,* despite its literary title, as much about the spoken
word as the written – or more precisely, about the relationship between
them.

In the beginning was the Word. In all of Greenaway's early work there is a
distinct separation between sound and image, a legacy perhaps of Greenaway's work as an editor placing soundtrack against random image. The
first two shots follow the old order: (1) a close-up of a drop of water, (2) a
close-up of a text being written as Prospero reads aloud ("Knowing I loved
my books . . ."). However, by the third shot (which is discussed later in the
chapter) image, sound, writing, and speaking are combined layer upon
layer, frame within frame, with a density that makes it difficult to speak of
"an" image.

As *Prospero's Books* opens, the word calls the world into being. Like
God, Prospero creates the world not out of a drop of water, but with a
word. As a pen completes the word "Boatswain," its writing is superim-

Figure 22. Greenaway with Michel Blanc on the set of *Prospero's Books* (1991).

posed over Prospero's forehead. Almost as an experiment ("ruminatively . . . curiously . . . interrogatively"),[3] Gielgud voices it: "Boatswain?" Refusing to privilege either the written or spoken, Greenaway stages an extended interaction between the two. As the word is written again, a chorus of voices joins in. Gielgud playfully echoes the reprise with a series of alternative readings. Instructing the sailors in how to command a ship in a storm, Prospero makes a boatswain, his mariners, their ship, and the storm appear in a mirror – by saying so.

In the book *How to Do Things with Words*, J. L. Austin describes performative speech as the kind of speech where uttering the appropriate words constitutes an action in and of itself.[4] Saying "I do" can make you officially married, or saying you will abide by certain conditions can constitute an oral contract. With performative speech you have not merely said something, you have *done* something. Because Prospero is a sorcerer-magician, when he calls out the words that start the tempest and wreck a ship, the events happen. His describing them makes them real. In this sense, casting a spell is an act of performative speech.

For Walter Ong, in an oral culture spoken words are themselves "occurrences, events."[5]

The Hebrew term *dabar* means "word" and "event." . . . [A]mong "primitive" (oral) peoples generally language is a mode of action and not simply a countersign of thought.[6]

Ong identifies Shakespeare's period as "a culture with a still massive oral residue."[7] And in *Prospero* we can see the lingering marks of "the highly polarized, agonistic, oral world of good and evil, virtue and vice, villains and heroes."[8]

Instead of privileging one or the other, Greenaway explores the interaction between oral and written, image and sound. "The shift from oral to written speech is essentially a shift from sound to visual space" and the pre-credit sequence is an idyllic moment where words-as-sound and words-as-image coexist, the image playfully intertwined with the word, the voice with music.[9] In a preliterate culture, words can only be spoken and as such have no "visible presence," "no focus and no trace (a visual metaphor, showing dependency on writing)."[10] It is Greenaway's goal to provide the spoken word with oral *and* visual life while at the same time initiating a subtle, cumulatively devastating critique of the power of language.

> The first word of the play is "Bosun," which is a very interesting word because it is one that is never written down. It was used by seamen who were basically illiterate, so that when they came to write the word down it was "boatswain." It's a nice opening point about the topsy-turvy use of oral and written language.[11]

From the opening on, the world thus summoned is artificial, the word a thing to be played with. Yet despite this playfulness, Greenaway's opening is leading us directly toward issues of authorship/authority, in other words, power. Ong points out that

> the fact that oral peoples commonly and in all likelihood universally consider words to have magical potency is clearly tied in, at least unconsciously, with their sense of the word as necessarily spoken, sounded, and hence power-driven.[12]

But Prospero also wields the power to write.

> Writing fosters abstractions that disengage knowledge from the arena where human beings struggle with one another. It separates the knower from the known.[13]

Writing makes possible the categorization of the world into encyclopedia, of people into races and types, of colonization and slavery, Ariel and Caliban.

This kind of "text-formed thought" (which embraces categories, logic, causal relations) is but one of the ways literacy changes the way people think.[14] Another is seen in the relationship of the teller to the tale. Instead of the storyteller's being a participant in a communal act, the written text "introduces . . . the concept of a text as controlling the narrative."[15] In other words, the teller is subject to a higher authority – the written text that will outlast his personal ability to speak. A third change is the influence, pressure, or sheer availability of other texts, the idea that one's knowledge is not restricted to what is in his head but springs from everything that is in his library.[16] Of all of Greenaway's characters, Prospero is the one most formed by preexisting texts; with them, he creates a new text and thus re-forms the world.

Unlike the vivid evanescence of the oral, written words can be stored, locked away, reduced to "things":

> Such "things" are not so readily associated with magic, for they are not actions, but are in a radical sense dead, though subject to dynamic resurrection.[17]

Thus we see how truly powerful Prospero's magic is when at the very beginning Gielgud's clarion voice resurrects the word from the dead.

However, one of the film's greatest strengths (the casting of Sir John Gielgud) might also be the root of its greatest failing – Greenaway's decision to have Prospero vocally play all the parts, turning the film for all practical purposes into one long monologue. Greenaway justifies his choice in the "Introduction" to the published screenplay of *Prospero's Books*: "The legitimacy of this approach is to see Prospero not just as the master manipulator of people and events but as their prime originator" (p. 9). He literalizes Prospero's position as author.

> On his island of exile, Prospero *plans a drama* to right the wrongs done to him. He *invents* characters to flesh out his imaginary fantasy . . . *writes* their dialogue, and having written it, he speaks the lines aloud, *shaping the characters* so powerfully through the words that they are conjured before us. (p. 9)

Prospero's control of language is so great none of his creations can talk back except in the words he gives them – "Their lands, their lives, and all are Bolingbroke's" (*Richard II*). Given these terms, Prospero's role might be seen not as simply that of dramatist but as ventriloquist. It is only when Ariel persuades Prospero to abandon his plans that the characters that his passion for revenge had created out of words now speak for the first time with their own voices, brought to a full life by his act of compassion. (p. 9)

– that of an allegedly compassionate author-father.

Prospero's ever-present voice underscores the possessive apostrophe "s" in the title. *Prospero's* stresses that the film's focus will be about the issue of possession, Prospero's authorship conceived of in terms of control of the plot and of the world, and how his authority (authorization) stems from his position as both generator of the word and its heir.

I. Prospero

"For he is listening to speech invested with desire, crediting itself – for its greater exultation or for its greater anguish – with terrible powers."[18]

In addition to considering the spoken word in theory, and its relation to power and magic, we should examine the spoken word in practice – what it means when Gielgud speaks in *Prospero's Books*.

At first glance, Peter Greenaway's *Prospero's Books* seems a straightforward act of Bloomian filial chutzpah where the younger male artist brazenly tests himself against the works of the artistic father-figure in order to see just who measures up.[19] In most respects Greenaway's adaptation of Shakespeare's *The Tempest* can be seen as the usual postmodernist shuffle through the rubble of Western culture, a leisurely stroll beneath the calves of England's literary colossus.

Yet even Shakespeare can be encompassed by star discourse and by a director's vision of his star. Greenaway insists:

It is intended that there should be much deliberate cross-identification between Prospero, Shakespeare and Gielgud. At times they are indivisibly one person.[20]

Gielgud's position within the film evokes an earlier film by one of Greenaway's few acknowledged cinematic forebears, Alain Resnais's *Providence* (1977).[21] Each film examines the ethics of authorship, probing the intersection between language and the power of the father. Consider this summary of the plots of two films made fifteen years apart. An aging writer's re-creation of the world is peopled by fictionalized members of his family and events from his life. As author, his power is absolute, not only constraining the lives of his children within his limited, even clichéd, view of them, but

Figure 23. Sir John Gielgud as Prospero.

dictating the body of the film itself. Two-thirds of the film takes place in his imagination; scenes are triggered by his memory; his narration intrudes in the middle of scenes to change their course if an errant detail displeases him; his voice speaks the lines of "characters" within his fictitious world. In both films the spoken word becomes the word made flesh, and that flesh is John Gielgud.

For both Resnais and Greenaway, Gielgud epitomizes the grand tradition of British acting. Each conceived his film with Gielgud in mind, and it was his voice that garnered their praise. Gielgud's reputation as one of the best English actors of the twentieth century centers on his use of language. Knighted in 1953, Gielgud is traditionally compared with Laurence Olivier, the latter assaying a naturalistic approach to the Shakespearean text while Gielgud is described as being more sensitive to the music of the poetic meter. The musical metaphor is quite common in descriptions of Gielgud. For instance, James Naremore asserts that "Gielgud virtually sings the blank verse" as Henry IV in Orson Welles's *Chimes at Midnight* (1967).[22] In his memoirs, Dirk Bogarde notes that "Resnais was passionate about John's voice, indeed . . . he was determined to immortalize the splendour of the voice and the actor on film."[23]

Greenaway shared this desire to preserve Gielgud's gift on film. The valedictory aspect of Greenaway's attitude toward Gielgud is accentuated by the actor's age.[24] In an interview after the film's release, Greenaway noted that

> Gielgud at eighty-seven is obviously near the end of his life, and he has had an incredibly long theatrical career.[25]

Ong notes that "oral cultures encourage fluency, fulsomeness, volubility"[26] – all characteristics in ample supply in Gielgud's vocal performance as Prospero. While Greenaway recognizes a certain excessiveness, once Gielgud is draped in his mantle as greatest living actor, he becomes a monument before which Greenaway can only yield: "He is giving in some ways a purple performance; he is a virtuoso actor and we allow him that space."[27]

As Clive Langham in *Providence* and as Prospero in Greenaway's film, Gielgud's physical performance is restricted almost exclusively to talking; the only excess is vocal. In questioning the ethics of authorship, both *Providence* and *Prospero's Books* show us how the author's power is linked to his voice. These writers do not write texts as much as speak them. In each, authorial subjectivity is figured as a vocal performance. Clive Langham's "book" is all in his head – we see no books on shelves, no typewriters or manuscripts, not so much as a notepad. It is working it out that matters, not writing it down.

Writing as thinking it out – as speaking it – goes hand in hand with each film's presentation of the fluidity of the image. The image exists only momentarily and always in response to the soundtrack. When Clive Langham says in voice-over, "I think we'll try this one again," we return to a scene we have seen earlier though the setting has been altered, the costumes changed. Images pass through the mind unbidden; at one point a footballer jogs through a love scene and Langham blurts out, "What's he doing here?"

Langham's voice usually comes from offscreen, directing the characters – "A little more venom, children. A little more violence." As a voice "off," Langham comments on his work as it progresses and loses his temper when characters resist him. "Christ, he's intractable. I'll never get the hang of him," he blurts out. Memory and imagination mix, occasionally bringing the fiction to a halt. Thoughts of his late wife intrude, causing Langham to stop and muse: "Will you kindly get out of my mind, Molly? Will you please stop interfering with my last feeble efforts."

The images summoned by Prospero are equally mutable, though unlike Clive, Prospero frequently walks among them. Seemingly real scenes are revealed to be images in mirrors held up before Prospero at Miranda's bedside or in his writing cell. Prospero's words are literally fluid – "All the images come out of Prospero's inkwell, as though the inkwell were a top hat, with the magician pulling out the scarves, image after image."[28] When Prospero speaks, it is more than simple voice-over. Unlike Langham, Prospero *never* loses control of his characters.

> The characters walk and gesture, act and react, but still they do not speak. Their life-giving words are not their own, they continue to be the mouthpiece of Prospero, the master dramatist. (p. 9)

Each film balances its valedictory for the star with a critique of the author figures he plays. Both authors use people for their own ends. Langham's characters are based on his family. He names the main character, Claude, after his son and explains the character's psychology in terms of his son's childhood. "What a thin, owlish little sod you were at school. . . . Eyes like marbles." Claude's mistress Helen is played by the same actress who plays his mother, Molly. ("I fear the boy must have an unconscious mind.") As fiction and memory blur, Langham's characters turn on him, questioning the autobiographical roots of his artistic method. At one point his son asks, "Did you create hell all these years just to have something to write about?"

Prospero's "characters" are not fictional variations but the actual figures upon whom Prospero wants revenge. Under constant surveillance and subject to his spells, they cannot speak. In place of the playful give-and-take between author and recalcitrant characters in *Providence, Prospero* presents the author as omnipotent despot, exemplified by the ubiquitousness of his voice. When the illusion slips for a moment in *Providence* and Gielgud's voice comes out of an actress's mouth, it is for comic effect early in the film. In *Prospero's Books* whenever the characters "speak," Gielgud's voice is heard (sometimes electronically altered). When Prospero first confronts Caliban, for instance, the "dialogue" seeming to take place in memory or as an aural flashback – the actor playing Caliban does not move his lips. When Ferdinand courts Miranda, Prospero "plays" both parts. Most of Prospero's arguments thus seem to be with himself. Everyone else is allowed to exist only as he sees them. He hears only what *he* wants – as do we.

There are a few cracks in the system. Caliban is portrayed by a dancer (Michael Clark). If he cannot speak directly, he gives the impression that he can strike out at any moment. Uncoiling his body, unwinding, balancing, he seems outside of language. Such a physical, *material* body seems painfully difficult to communicate through while at the same time establishing Caliban as a different order of being than the others contained by Prospero's words. Accepting for the time being that he is trapped by Prospero's power,

Caliban bides his time as Prospero "speaks" for him. Anything he or anyone else might say is mediated by Prospero's language; it is literally *his* language.

In addition to the dancers, whose physicality puts them outside of speech, the singers use their own voices and not Gielgud's. Ute Lemper sings the role of Ceres and others sing for the various Ariels. Only Miranda (Isabelle Pasco) has some kind of speaking voice, though it is limited for most of the film. As Gielgud reads her dialogue, we hear a woman's voice in the background, "shadowing" him. Like the others, she is not heard clearly as herself until the end.

Both films have a final section where the characters "come to life," occupying the same reality as the author figure. In *Providence* the last half hour reveals the distance between Langham's fictional versions of his adult children and their "real" selves. Psychological interiority is signaled by a more naturalistic acting style: subtle facial expressions indicate hurt feelings and the suppression of things left unsaid. Langham's limitations as an author are stressed as we see all the things he has missed, noting in particular the discrepancy between his arch fictional characters and the complex, loving adults his children actually are.

As a flawed man with many blind spots, Langham is doomed to miss much of the richness around him. The limits of the man are necessarily the limits of his work. As the film steps out from Langham's perspective, moving beyond its "author's" view, Gielgud's voice-over ends and traditional synchronized dialogue takes its place.

The switch from monologue to dialogue happens much later in Greenaway's film. In the script, the captives, released from the spell, speak for themselves in scene 89 (out of 91). The result, though, does not so much liberate the characters, allowing them to speak as equals to Prospero, as it enables them to acknowledge his power more fully. In *Providence*, the introduction of the other characters reveals the author's limits. In *Prospero's Books*, Prospero only allows others to speak once they cannot challenge him. He removes the chains when the beasts have been tamed.

In confronting the spoken word, each film must also confront the word's material source; even "the most beautiful English-speaking voice in the world" is connected to a body.[29] And each film's attitude toward the author, exemplified by his voice, is underscored or undermined, respectively, by its revelation or exposure of the body.

Providence's attitude toward the body precludes nostalgia for the author. Early in the film we see a grim autopsy. Resnais prevents us from reading the (apparently actual) autopsy of a desiccated old man as tragic by having

Gielgud in gleeful voice-over turn the gruesome scene into an extended metaphor on criticism and the much-vaunted theoretical "death of the author."[30] "I get it. He wants to cut me up. Shall we let him try?" While humor is frequently a prominent feature (even a saving grace) in Greenaway's films, it is more surprising coming from Resnais.[31]

In *Providence,* the death of the author is a messy thing, located exclusively around "another one of those stabbing pains right up the ass – "

> Noticed some reddish brown stains on the underpants yesterday. . . . slip a suppository into position. Slow, squalid, messy thing. Live by the guts and die by the guts. Now let science soothe the troubled rectum.

Hardly a respectful valedictory.

As Langham, Gielgud plays a man whose body is filled with corruption as he faces death. In Greenaway's film, Gielgud is treated with extravagant respect. As Gielgud emerges nude from the pool in *Prospero's Books'* opening scene, he is literally pink. To quote four other British icons on a dubious father figure: "He's very clean" (*A Hard Day's Night,* 1964). Although the nudity may be surprising, the ritual and ceremony that attend Prospero's dressing utterly resist any urge toward irreverence. Looking much healthier at eighty-seven in Greenaway's film than at seventy-five in Resnais's, the nudity of Prospero insists that Gielgud is in the pink of health. This authorial figure is not going anywhere soon. In his deference toward Gielgud, Greenaway upholds Prospero's authority in all its aspects.

In their critiques of the author, both Resnais and Greenaway stress his position as father. While both films show these male figures living predominantly in imaginary worlds, to dismiss these "worlds" as merely fiction trivializes both authors and their "texts." Making choices, organizing signs into a text or a framework, is a discursive act. As a term, "discourse" reinserts power into relations between authors and texts and between authors and readers (e.g., the struggle over who has the authority to define the world according to their values). The power of the patriarch is one that sons – and would-be auteurs – have a stake in.

The question, then, becomes that of the relationship between fatherhood and the word, between the Father and the Law, the phallocentric and the logocentric, power and language. Both Langham and Prospero establish their dominion over their children through their power over language. Both explicitly locate control of the word (Logos as language and Law) within the domain of the Father, thus demanding a critique both of patriarchy and of logocentrism as central to patriarchal power.

It is important to remember that in both films the character of the author is Janus-faced, pointing back toward the written word of the screenplay (Logos) and outward toward the auteur of the image, the film's director. Thus, the celebrated "auteurs," Resnais and Greenaway, implicate themselves in a long line of authorial despotism.

It is interesting that although Resnais exposes Langham's limits, moral and physical, he would not change a word of David Mercer's screenplay. Dirk Bogarde recounts that "the script as far as Resnais was concerned, was as sacred as the Turin Shroud" – Resnais would not "permit an alteration unless I telephoned Mr. Mercer himself and got his personal approval."[32] Greenaway also seems to defer to Shakespeare: "The script follows the play, act by act and scene by scene, with few transpositions and none of any substance to alter the chronology of the original" (p. 12). This, however, does not stop him from putting his own words on a par with Shakespeare's when it comes time to describe Prospero's books.

II. Books

The title "Prospero's Books" refers not to books Prospero, the author figure, has written, but to those he owns – his library. Having structured itself around books ("words making text, text making pages, pages making books"),[33] the film nevertheless lacks faith in them. To begin with, there is no single ideal book, one that explains everything and has all the answers. This is not surprising considering the many needs Greenaway sees as having to be met. Prospero's books would have to keep "Prospero and Miranda alive, well and sane" while making Prospero "so powerful he could command the dead and make Neptune his servant" (p. 12).

> There would need perhaps to be books on navigation and survival . . .
> books for an elderly scholar to learn how to rear and educate a young
> daughter, how to colonise an island, farm it, subjugate its inhabitants,
> identify its plants and husband its wild beasts. . . . There would need
> to be books to encourage revenge. (p. 9)

Perhaps a collection of books then? Greenaway picks a number ("Twenty-four volumes might be enough") and begins to elaborate on the kinds of books that might fulfill such broad requirements (p. 9).

As Greenaway notes, "the starting point for these strategies" is the passage where Prospero tells of having been overthrown and Gonzalo's escorting him as he is sent into exile.[34]

> Knowing I lov'd my books,
> he furnished me from mine
> own library with volumes
> that I prize above my
> Dukedom. (p. 8)

Sited in the published screenplay between a watercolored architectural sketch of Prospero's island and Greenaway's "Introduction," this line is singled out and reproduced on a full page in calligraphy imitating that of folio editions of Shakespeare. Calligraphy once again serves as a starting point for Greenaway, in whose work language is best appreciated as an image and images are seldom unaccompanied by language.[35] Even the first image in the book (architectural drawing as map – A *Walk Through H* meets *The Belly of an Architect*) has important sites identified in neat blue penmanship and a caption that reads, "Prospero's island, rebuilt in all it's [*sic*] many parts to fit the requirements of an exiled scholar far from home, dreaming of Italy," signed "P.G. April 89. Prospero's Books" (p. 6).

Having no faith in books per se, Greenaway has an endless fascination with the infinity that can reside within them. The books he creates for Prospero hover blissfully beyond the reach of logic. As intersections of argument, superstition, art and research, each is, in its own way, impossible. For instance, some books exceed the infinite. Take "The Book of Universal Cosmography," Book #19. (As with maps, everything must be numbered even if the key is lost.) "Full of printed diagrams of great complexity, this book attempts to place all universal phenomena in one system" (p. 24). Some books are simply declared to have done so. In #18, "The Book of Utopias," "every known and every imagined political and social community is described and evaluated" (pp. 21–24). "An Alphabetical Inventory of the Dead" (#9) "contains all the names of the dead who have lived on earth" up to the present, and, as a book, existed "before the death of Adam" (p. 20).

Apparatuses of organization are everywhere, organization being not only a guarantor of serious scholarship but part of the fun. "The Book of Utopias" has "twenty-five pages . . . devoted to tables where the characteristics of all societies can be isolated, permitting a reader to sort and match his own utopian ideal" (pp. 21–24). It also sports an index ("six hundred and sixty-six . . . entries") and "a preface by Sir Thomas More" (pp. 21–24). "Full of printed diagrams of great complexity," "The Book of Universal Cosmography" offers "disciplined geometrical figures, concentric rings that circle and countercircle, tables and lists organized in spirals, catalogues," and so on (p. 24). (Of course, it goes without saying that Greenaway has organized the film as well; in the published screenplay he points out that *Prospero* is divided into three parts: Past, Present, and Future. "But," he assures us, "it is most strongly structured into 91 sections" [p. 13].)

Maps provide guidance in "A Primer of Small Stars," "An Atlas Belonging to Orpheus," "Love of Ruins," and "The Book of Games," while diagrams are thoughtfully supplied in "A Harsh Book of Geometry," "The Vesalius Anatomy of Birth," and "The Book of Universal Cosmography" (pp. 17–25).

Lists abound. "The Alphabetical Inventory of the Dead" contains "a collection of designs for tombs and columbariums, elaborate headstones, graves, sarcophagi, and other architectural follies" (p. 20) – although it must be noted that the veracity of what is listed is oftentimes questionable. With "A Bestiary of Past, Present and Future Animals" (#17), we are told that "Prospero can recognise cougars and marmosets and fruitbats and manticores and dromersels, the cameleopard, the chimera and the cattamorrain" (p. 21).

The books are a miniaturized collection of Greenawavian obsessions. Recalling *The Belly of an Architect*, #20, "The Love of Ruins," contains "a checklist of the ancient world for the Renaissance humanist interested in antiquity" and is considered "an essential volume for the melancholic historian who knows that nothing endures" (p. 24). Number 13, "The Ninety-Two Conceits of the Minotaur," evokes *The Falls* numerically, while *Drowning by Numbers* could be parsed with a quick consultation of "The Book of Games" (#23). Its description is itself a collection of lists. There are board games "to be played with counters and dice, with cards and flags and miniature pyramids," as well as those played with "Roman busts, the oceans of the world, exotic animals, pieces of coral, gold putti, silver coins and pieces of liver." The boards these games are played on come "in the shape of the constellations, animals, maps, journeys to Hell and journeys to Heaven," and are designed out of "pages of text, diagrams of the brain, [and] Arabic carpets." Covering "games of infinite supply," this book includes "games of death, resurrection, love, peace, famine, sexual cruelty, astronomy, the cabala, . . . magic, retribution, semantics, [and] evolution" (pp. 24–25).

The literary descriptions of Prospero's books find Greenaway caught between the written and the cinematic. Many of his descriptions contain things that cannot be visualized. In "The Book of the Earth" (#11), the "pages are impregnated with minerals, acids, alkalis, elements, gums, poisons, balms and aphrodisiacs." Its effects are also invisible, requiring dramatic action to demonstrate cause and effect. One page cures anthrax; "lick a grey paste from another page to bring poisonous death" (pp. 20–21).

There are facets of a book that we can only be told about: its material history, its effect on the reader, how it feels in your hand. Number 15, "End-plants," has "varnished wooden covers," which "have been at one time, and probably still are, inhabited by minute tunnelling insects" (p. 21). "The Book of Colours" "when opened at a double spread . . . so strongly evokes a place, an object, a location or a situation that the associated sensory sensation is directly experienced" (p. 20). "The Autobiographies of Pasiphae and Semiramis," being pornographic, "is always warm" (p. 24).

What cannot be visualized or enacted must be explained, as are "A Book of Mirrors" (#2) and "A Book of Love" (#16).

> Some mirrors simply reflect the reader, some reflect the reader as he was three minutes previously, some reflect the reader as he will be in a year's time, as he would be if he were a child, a woman, a monster, an idea, a text or an angel.

"One mirror," we are told, "constantly lies, one mirror sees the world backwards, another upside down. One mirror holds on to its reflections as frozen moments infinitely recalled," and one "simply reflects another mirror across the page" (p. 17). Of course, some things should not be explained but held close. In "A Book of Love," we are told "these things were once spotted, briefly, in a mirror, and that mirror was in another book. Everything else is conjecture" (p. 21).

Much of the information in these books is unreliable or unknown (even to its authors). The creatures in the Lewis Carroll–like "Bestiary of Past, Present and Future Animals" (#17) are "real, imaginary and apocryphal" (p. 21). In "A Book of Mirrors" "there are ten mirrors whose purpose Prospero has yet to define" (p. 17).

The properties that *can* be visualized are described in vivid detail. When one opens Orpheus's Atlas (#5), "the maps bubble with pitch. Avalanches of hot, loose gravel and molten sand fall out of the book to scorch the library floor" (p. 20). The pages of the "Primer of Small Stars" "twinkle with travelling planets, flashing meteors and spinning comets. The black skies pulsate with red numbers" (p. 17). "A Book of Motion" (#22) "is always bursting open of its own volition. . . . At night, it drums against the bookcase shelf and has to be held down with a brass weight" (p. 24).

The film is bounded by the first book and the last. While the order in which the books appear in the film has been changed from their order in the screenplay, thus altering their numbering, the first remains "The Book of Water." Water makes possible the tempest, the pool where it is plotted, and the ink with which it is written. It also makes possible the inelegant figuring of Greenaway's encounter with Shakespeare as a pissing contest; the littlest Ariel pees on the toy ship to create the tempest, but because he cheats (with a hose tucked under him), he can't lose. When Prospero, having succeeded in all his plans, decides to relinquish "this rough magic," his vow brings the water imagery full circle: "I'll drown my books" (p. 152).

The twenty-fourth book out of twenty-four described by Greenaway is entitled "Thirty-Six Plays."

> A thick, printed volume of plays dated 1623. All thirty-six plays are there save one – the first. Nineteen pages are left blank for its inclusion. It is called *The Tempest*. The folio collection is modestly bound in dull green linen with cardboard covers and the author's initials are embossed in gold on the cover – W.S.

However, in the screenplay Greenaway keeps *The Tempest* – the one that has just been written by Prospero – separate from the collected works of W. S. As both *The Tempest* and the collected works of Shakespeare drop into the water, Greenaway adds a last bit of narration regarding the title objects –

> Whilst all the other volumes have been drowned and destroyed, we still do have these last two books, safely fished from the sea –

Caliban swims by and retrieves them.

In order to adhere to his system of twenty-four books in the film (with "A Play Called *The Tempest*" the twenty-fourth), Greenaway must abandon one, a *Through the Looking Glass* kind of book that would seem particularly difficult to visualize given its highly conceptual and literary nature – #14, "The Book of Languages." "More a box than a book," it has "a door in its front cover."

> Inside is a collection of eight smaller books arranged like bottles in a medicine case. Behind these eight books are another eight books, and so on. To open the smaller books is to let loose many languages. Words and sentences, paragraphs and chapters gather like tadpoles in a pond in April or starlings in a November evening sky. (p. 21)

Although Greenaway has sacrificed "The Book of Languages," words, sentences, and paragraphs have already escaped their context and dart across the image throughout the film through the use of a computer animation program called The Graphic Paintbox.

Animated Books

Prospero's books are brought vividly to life through the use of high-definition video technology and computer animation. Greenaway's use of HDTV (with the cooperation of Sony) drew much attention to the film. The contribution of computer animation to the depiction of the books provides many of the film's highlights. Most importantly, the computer imagery makes it possible to see the books not as a string of words but as a constant interplay between image and text.

In an illustration from "A Harsh Book of Geometry" (reproduced in the published screenplay) we can see the way the layering of images, made possible by the new technology, works with Greenaway's characteristic style as a graphic artist: the presence of maps, nude bodies covered with numbers, arrows and unintelligible diagrams, pseudomathematical lines, with various parts of the image identified by letters and numbers – the significance of which remains unknown (pp. 14–15).[36] In this two-page illustration, two images of a young boy, naked except for a neck ruff and feathers, flank a block of numbers (some circled, some crossed out) and a large diagram. The faded right-hand side of the image is a mirror version of the left, as if the paper had been folded leaving its trace on the other side; the diagrams do not obey this logic, suggesting that they were added later. The paper on which the image is printed (a surface on which the boy is superimposed) contains writing in Greek, parts of the diagrams have Latin names, and the red-lettered English title is printed over its own shadow – spelled backward.[37]

For the portrait of the Juggler (which may or may not be in the film),[38] Greenaway describes in great detail how the image was produced and the thought that went into its creation. As he did with the books, Greenaway first provides an extremely complex background story about a female prostitute/juggler/Fool. (This character does not have a parallel in Shakespeare's *The Tempest* and seems entirely Greenaway's creation.)[39] Greenaway spends two pages describing how the image condenses references to the character's background; artistic, architectural, and cultural references; and Shakespeare himself. (The "printed text itself – with its distressed font – is a direct quotation photographed and enlarged from a facsimile edition of the 1623 folio of Shakespeare's plays" [p. 32].)

Greenaway's use of sources is no surprise, though the breadth of his knowledge is. He models the youngest Ariel after a "curly-headed child" in Bronzino's *Allegory with Venus and Cupid* (p. 43), "Prospero's 'poor cell'" from da Messina's *St. Jerome in his Study* (50), and Prospero's "Palace of Libraries" on "an exact copy" of Michelangelo's Laurenziana Library (p. 59). Among those represented by direct reference or as illustrations are Piranesi, De La Tour, Botticelli, Bernini, Leonardo da Vinci, Velázquez, Géricault, Rembrandt, Breughel, Rubens, Titian, Veronese, Raphael, Poussin, Fuseli, Giorgione, and Mantegna. Particular images in the film are based on

Figure 24. Greenaway configures a mythological past via Eadweard Muybridge. Paintbox Image #14: Allegorical Figures. (Paintbox Images by Peter Greenaway and Eve Ramboz)

Figure 25. The interplay of image and text. Paintbox Image #8: Autobiographies of Semiramis and Pasiphae: Standing Woman. (Paintbox Images by Peter Greenaway and Eve Ramboz)

specific works by lesser-known figures, such as the engraver John White, an "English Draughtsman" whose fancifully Europeanized depictions of American Indians "about the time Shakespeare was writing" serve as models for the original inhabitants of the island (p. 66); Félicien Rops, whose "Pornocrates" appears wandering through the library and later on in male *and* female guises as part of the Allegories of Autumn (pp. 83, 157); and Robert Fludd, who "manufactured metaphysical graphics to stimulate belief in a single universal order," and whose diagram "trying to connect angels to stones, lead to gold and mankind to everything" bears a resemblance to the designs for the more mathematical books such as "The Book of Universal Cosmography" (p. 123).

As he did with Boullée in *The Belly of an Architect*, Greenaway gives particular prominence (if primarily in the screenplay) to an obscure figure for whom he has a special fondness. In this case it is Athanasius Kircher,

> scientist and humanist, whose enquiry covered every aspect of knowledge – the architecture of the Tower of Babel, the construction of the Ark, the exploration of China, manipulative acoustics, linguistics, seismology, medicine, magic, resurrection, Islam, the education of children, Egyptian hieroglyphics and much else. (pp. 50–51)[40]

Greenaway explicitly links Prospero with scientist-artists like Kircher and Da Vinci, asserting that Prospero

> has the enquiring, scholastic imagination which recognized no boundary between art and science or literature and natural history and, open-minded and unprejudiced, looked forward to the first century of science – the seventeenth. (p. 50)

Greenaway's confidence in his use of sources is so strong, he can even mix and match as he does when he stages Antonio's plotting as "a pretext to see Veronese through Dutch eyes" (p. 68) and points out how Rembrandt can provide a legitimate "model for the effete shipwrecked Neapolitans" because they "had strong dynastic connections with the Spanish Netherlands" (p. 108). He justifies this fearless approach in the Introduction:

> The history of painting is one of borrowing and reprising, homage and quotation. All image-makers who have wished to contribute to it have eagerly examined what painters have done before and – openly acknowledged or not – this huge body of pictorial work has become the legitimate and unavoidable encyclopedia for all to study and use. (pp. 12–13)

Of all Greenaway's films, *Prospero*'s most captures the postmodern sense of art history as a giant storeroom in which one can play.

An example of the way Greenaway incorporates his love for references with modern technology occurs as Prospero warns Ferdinand to respect Miranda's virginity until the wedding. A series of books appear, embodying references to Greek mythology in images borrowed from motion studies conducted by the nineteenth-century photographer Eadweard Muybridge. Greenaway recombines photographs from Muybridge's eleven-volume study *Animal Locomotion* (1885) to evoke what the narrator tells us are pornographic scenes from antiquity. For the rape of Europa, a buffalo charges a woman bending over as blood splatters across the page. Muybridge wrestlers repeatedly fall to the ground in a perpetual struggle as a seemingly indifferent woman undresses to the left. Against unreadable pages of manuscript, stained and dirtied with tangles of hair, a naked male pugilist on the left side of the screen throws a punch toward a nude woman hiding her face in shame on the right.

Images like those just described go by so quickly in the film, it is unlikely we would register all of the sources, let alone all of the visual and verbal information condensed into nearly any given image in the film. Without the book of *Prospero's Books,* we certainly would not know the fictitious backgrounds Greenaway has created for his books and characters. Greenaway himself seems to have realized, after writing the screenplay, that the literary form of much of his most inventive work was incompatible with a visual approach. The way he rectified this is clearest in the images whose existence is most exclusively dependent on Paintbox techniques.

The presentation of the books in the film was clearly done last as a form of postproduction. The script's description of when and how the books were to appear in the film indicates that much of Greenaway's thoughts on this evolved after he wrote the script. For example, in the script Greenaway describes the books in characters' hands or lying on desks. As the characters open the books and read, "we see" the books' titles and most prominent characteristics. For instance, when telling the sleeping Miranda the story of their exile, Prospero was supposed to pause originally, "taking one of the heavier volumes."

> It is Vesalius's "Anatomy of Birth." . . . As he turns the pages . . . Prospero's fingers appear to become covered in blood. (pp. 69–70)

However, based on images alone, it is not always possible to know which particular book a character is reading. For example, when we first see "A Book of Mythologies" under the titles (identified as such in the script), it is merely a large book whose pages are turned by two adults. The obscurity of complex images necessitates Greenaway's major deviation from Shakespeare, from his conception of Gielgud reciting all the parts – and from his own screenplay.

Greenaway did so love his books, he added another voice, a narrator, never identified, who brings into the film what otherwise would have been lost – verbal descriptions of the twenty-four books Greenaway has created for Prospero's erudition. The narration consists primarily of the descriptive material published separately in Greenaway's book on the film. Whenever one of Prospero's books appears, we read its title printed at the bottom of the frame as the narrator describes its properties:

> This book ["The Book of Mirrors"] has some eighty shining mirrored pages; some opaque, some translucent, . . . some covered in a film of mercury that will roll off the pages unless treated cautiously.

In addition to using a narrator (Leonard Maguire), Greenaway has several methods for setting the books apart from the drama:

1. The books usually appear as visual inserts over the "cinematic" image of the narrative. The first reconfigures the screen. Because the computer images are, as Greenaway points out, roughly "the dimensions of the cinemascope-screen" (p. 29), "The Book of Water," surrounded by a black border, cuts across a previously square image (a standard aspect ratio of 1 to 1:33). This effect is repeated as Greenaway begins rhythmically cutting back and forth between full-screen-sized images and the books' letter-box format. As the sequence continues, the border changes colors (bluish-purple as we track through the bathhouse, gold around Prospero). The border is eventually replaced, the widescreen shot continuing "behind" the image of the book, creating frames within frames, sometimes three or four per shot. In the foreground, the books reframe the world, yet there is always a larger world within which they are read.[41]

   The books themselves have further frames within them, often animated. On one page drawings of clouds seem to move, spreading over the page (we hear thunder in the distance). A square appears in the center of the book, containing an image of a storm-tossed ship beset by thunder and lightning.

   In this brilliant opening scene, it is difficult to talk about "an" image; there are often several simultaneously. The pages of "The Book of Water" (taken from da Vinci) combine drawings, photographs, and descriptions. Each can move in relation to the other, the images "coming alive," the text being written as we watch.

2. The title of each book and its number are written in white calligraphy under the book. However, soon the titling exceeds the figurative "space of the books" and begins to crop up throughout the film. Time and again pages of text are superimposed over an image. Words scroll up from the bottom of the screen as Prospero speaks. When Antonio and Sebastian plot, not moving their lips as Gielgud's voice is heard, snippets of dialogue appear on the screen beneath them. Everything said or seen is first written, something made explicit by cutaways or superimpositions of Prospero's pen being dipped in blue ink, of words being written on a page.

No part of the film exists separate from words. (Even the upper and lower borders of the letter-boxed images become a site for writing; this is where Greenaway puts the books' titles.) For Greenaway, *Prospero's Books*

deliberately emphasizes and celebrates the text as text, as the master material on which all the magic, illusion and deception of the play is based. (p. 9)

The cumulative effect of these techniques is to call attention to the books as parallel texts, part of the film's context but at the same time "outside" the drama, shaping it while commenting on it. As always in Greenaway, the most fanciful constructs camouflage an unexpected undertow of emotion. As Prospero recounts his lost life as Duke of Milan, Greenaway interweaves a second story on a more private grief. As we track through Prospero's library, where scholars are hard at work, Prospero's exposition is intercut with descriptions of various books. The first is the "Alphabetical Inventory of the Dead" ("the first name is Adam and the last is Susanna, Prospero's wife"). The second studied by the scholars is the atlas "used when Orpheus journeyed into" Hell to bring his wife back from the underworld. The last is "The Vesalius Anatomy of Birth," a fictitious sequel to "the first authoritative anatomy book." But this "second volume, now lost, is even more disturbing and heretical" than the first.

It is full of descriptive drawings of the workings of the human body, which when the pages open, move and throb and bleed. It is a banned book that queries the unnecessary processes of aging, bemoans the wastages associated with progeneration, condemns the pains and anxieties of childbirth and generally questions the efficiency of God. (p. 20)

As we learn this information, we see Prospero's wife, Susanna, silently peel her stomach open to reveal an unborn child – the somber tone suggesting her death in childbirth.

Prospero's books, thus presented, interrupt, modify, contain, and elaborate upon Shakespeare.

III. Prospero's Books

The books in Greenaway's film are directly connected to his critique of the author figure. Greenaway casts a larger net than Resnais: where Langham in *Providence* uses his family as the source of his work, Greenaway's Prospero has four or five centuries of cultural texts to sort through. With the conceit of the books, Greenaway institutes Prospero as a postmodern figure, someone who creates – as Greenaway himself does – by picking and choosing from a world of works by other artists in other centuries. In this postmodern sense, the author himself may be nothing more than the fragments of texts from which he is made.

Greenaway does not find Prospero "particularly praiseworthy" (p. 12): "Prospero is in many ways the ultimate manipulator – a magus who contrives the whole story."[42] But he is not simply bad, either. Prospero is the product of "his relationship to his books" (p. 12). "Are we truly the product of what we read?" Greenaway asks.

> What was it, in those books, that made Prospero not only powerful but also a moralising scold and a petty revenger, a benevolent despot, a jealous father? (p. 12)

Like Greenaway or the postmodern reader/viewer, Prospero is both producer and product of a world made up of texts, not only a writer but a reader.

In *The Order of Things*, Michel Foucault discusses another character "made up of texts." Like Greenaway's Prospero, "Don Quixote reads the world in order to prove his books. And the only proofs he gives himself are the glittering reflections of resemblances."[43]

Like Quixote, Prospero in Greenaway's film finds himself in a text/ual world. More compelling in its artifice than it would be if real, "Prospero's island has become a place of illusion and deception" (p. 12).

> It will be no surprise that it is an island full of superimposed images, of shifting mirrors and mirror-images – true mir-ages – where pictures conjured by text can be as tantalizingly substantial as objects and facts and events, constantly framed and re-framed. (p. 12)

The books provide only the most obvious framework, calling attention to the way *everything* in the film is contained within a particular historical or discursive frame. As a postmodernist film like *Prospero's Books* makes explicit, the text is "a multi-dimensional space in which a variety of writings, *none of them original,* blend and clash."[44]

Peter Wollen, discussing *The Draughtsman's Contract,* argues that Greenaway "push[es] all the elements into an unreal and peculiarly inauthentic realm."[45] *Prospero's Books* re-creates "the high Renaissance world of masque, pageant, and emblem in exaggerated splendor,"[46] revealing the world as an artifice, a construct, a parade of texts – a masque of signifiers. Hundreds of figures line the path as Prospero walks from his bath to his library during the title sequence's tracking shot, each calling to mind a source or referent.

A masque is one way to corral a proliferation of signs. Stephen Greenblatt describes the function of masques in the period when *The Tempest* was written. As was true of England in the 1980s, at the time *The Tempest* was written

> England had experienced . . . population growth, . . . [and the] struggle for survival was intensified by persistent inflation, unemployment, and epidemic disease.[47]

The "crucial elements" in Elizabethan and Jacobean theatre were "techniques of arousing and manipulating anxiety," because "the ruling elite believed that a measure of insecurity and fear was a necessary, healthy element in the shaping of proper loyalties."[48] "Anxiety, in the form of threats of humiliation and beating," he adds, "had long been used as an education tool" (see Prospero's treatment of Caliban).[49]

> Not all theatrical spectacles in the late sixteenth century [however] are equally marked by the staging of anxiety: both civic pageantry and the masque are characterized by its relative absence.[50]

The absence of anxiety reinforces the beneficence of an absolute (and secure) monarch.

Prospero unleashes the masques when his power is confirmed. Unfortunately, for a modern audience, the masques' utter lack of anxiety translates into a lack of suspense. The already high level of spectacle throughout the film makes the endless parade of extras decidedly anticlimactic.

Despite the masques' interruption of the narrative (what Greenaway calls the "clash of 'the word' against 'the spectacle'"), pageantry is interestingly redesigned in contemporary terms.[51] The long parallel tracking shots, typical of Greenaway since *The Draughtsman's Contract,* make explicit the film's prebourgeois aesthetic. The use of such tracking shots in *Prospero's Books* underscores the fact that Prospero is himself a text in a world of texts.[52] Or, as Foucault asserts, that "he is made up of interwoven words; he is writing itself, wandering through the world among the resemblances of things."[53]

The corridors through which Prospero walks are lined with signs, a density of allusions characteristic of Greenaway and also characteristic of the Baroque. The parallels between the Baroque and postmodernism, as well as Greenaway's taste for the sixteenth and seventeenth centuries, have led some to tag Greenaway's later work "neo-Baroque."[54] The filmmaker himself cites the sixteenth century's "Great Mannerist Debate":

> its condition of doubt and misgiving and crisis of cultural confidence. Prospero is a Mannerist scholar – eclectic, subjective, obsessive, exhibitionist – a true believer in scholarship for scholarship's sake. We have worked accordingly.[55]

Beginning around 1590, Mannerism overlaps with the end of the Renaissance and the beginnings of the Baroque. It is defined by such (by now) familiar traits as a "self-conscious cultivation of elegance and technical facility," "a complex and intense intellectual aestheticism," and "a sophisticated indulgence in the bizarre."[56]

In a way that compares closely to the present, both Mannerism and the Baroque represent "a long moment of crisis, in which ordinary consolation no longer has much value."[57] Gilles Deleuze writes:

> At a time just before the world loses its principles . . . the Baroque solution is the following: we shall multiply principles – we can always slip a new one out from under our cuffs – and in this way we will change their use.[58]

In place of despair, we have magic. The Baroque finds comfort where Greenaway has found it – in excess and game playing, marked by "a proliferation" of improbable rules.

> Play is executed through [an] excess and not a lack of principles; the game is that of principles themselves, of inventing principles.[59]

This might hold true for the lightly playful *Drowning by Numbers,* but in *Prospero's Books,* Greenaway confronts the more troubling ethical issues of authorship and calls the master game-player to account.

As the film draws to an end, Greenaway creates one of *Prospero's Books'* simplest images. In a close-up against a black background sprinkled with a few twinkling lights, Gielgud speaks directly to the camera – "not a god or a magician or a Duke or a King," but "a dignified mortal" (p. 163).

> Please you, draw near.
> Now my charms are all o'erthrown,
> And what strength I have's mine own –
> Which is most faint: now, 'tis true . . .

As Gielgud speaks one of Shakespeare's most direct declarations of artifice, his hair shock-white against the "black velvet void" (p. 164), Greenaway pares away all spectacle. Slowly the image begins to recede, the frame growing smaller until it is the size of a television screen inside the cinematic screen, leaving us with this – an actor playing a part, a frame within a frame.

For Deleuze, "the essence of the Baroque entails neither falling into nor emerging from illusion but rather *realizing something in illusion itself*."[60] Refusing to sacrifice illusion, absorbed by artifice, Greenaway exposes it nevertheless.

It's all an honest magician can do, really. Show his hand.

7

Shock Tactics

The Cook, The Thief, His Wife and Her Lover (1989)

The Cook, The Thief, His Wife and Her Lover (1989) remains Greenaway's best-known film, and certainly the one most written about. As his most commercially successful film, *The Cook, The Thief, His Wife and Her Lover* was for many people the first Greenaway film they had seen and the film's extremes (particularly in plot and style) garnered much comment.

Greenaway's early films were perceived as being so unlike other films, so defined by style and structure, that it seemed as if the only category in which they could fit was that of "a Greenaway film." However, genre was lurking, one of the structures, submerged but still operative, holding Greenaway's penchant for myriad stories in check. *The Falls* can be seen as a documentary, *The Draughtsman's Contract* as Restoration comedy, *Drowning by Numbers* as a British black comedy, and *The Belly of an Architect* as the story of an American abroad. Yet in many ways it is *The Cook, The Thief* that comes closest of any film Greenaway has made to fitting within a traditional genre.

The Cook, The Thief has also been seen as an explicitly contemporary film, especially by those who knew Greenaway principally from *The Draughtsman's Contract*. The intervening films (*A Zed and Two Noughts*, *Drowning by Numbers*, and *The Belly of an Architect*) all take place in the present, but the insular symmetries of *Zed*, the timeless pastoral of *Drowning*, and *Belly*'s absorption in ancient Rome set them far from contemporary concerns. *Cook, Thief* not only takes place in modern Britain but takes life in 1980s England as its subject. *The Cook, The Thief* is, however, one of Greenaway's most vividly *British* films not, I would argue, because of its subject but because of its resemblance to other British films of its day. *The Cook, The Thief* is above all a prime exponent of the 1980s British gangster film.

Widely seen as a critique of Margaret Thatcher's economic policies and philosophy, *The Cook, The Thief, His Wife and Her Lover* is one of several notable films of the period that revive the gangster genre as a metaphor for the brute capitalism espoused by the Conservative government throughout the decade. Throughout the 1980s, British filmmakers reinvented the gangster genre in order to address issues central to the Thatcher period. This was done by looking at the past (*The Krays*, 1990; *Let Him Have It*, 1991) and the present (*Mona Lisa*, 1986; *The Long Good Friday*, 1980) through the structuring lens of genre.

Many of these films also have a sense of readdressing the 1960s, most often through the casting of such actors as Terence Stamp, Tom Courtenay, Tom Bell, John Hurt, and Michael Caine. The presence of icons of sixties British film begs a comparison between an era of youth, hope, and economic expansion and an era of retrenchment, economic catastrophe, and middle-aged defeat. The actors seem worn, tired, harder versions of the characters they played decades ago, as if they had become parents to their younger selves.

Yet unlike the films of the sixties that stressed a gray-on-gray, pseudodocumentary look, most of the eighties features are highly polished and carefully designed, attempting to pinpoint a moment through style. Only the films of Mike Leigh, Alan Clarke, and Ken Loach maintain the legacy of Free Cinema and the verité-influenced style of kitchen sink realism. By contrast, the emotional exploration of postwar Britain in most films of the eighties rests on making a fetish of period detail (consider films about the war and its aftermath such as *Hope and Glory*, 1987, or *Distant Voices/Still Lives*, 1988, or capital punishment films like *Let Him Have It* and *Dance with a Stranger*, 1985). In the gangster films, on the other hand, the details of sets and clothing serve a somewhat different function, one more typical of the gangster genre.

Frequently attacked as glamorizing violence, gangster films as a genre are obsessed with issues of style; the most famous movie-gangsters are those who make violence stylish. Strongly individualistic, gangster films personalize both violence and style, locating each in a powerful central figure. "Style" thus becomes two-edged, referring to a way of behaving as well as to facets of personal appearance emblematic of a level of status to which the gangster aspires. Violence becomes the means by which the gangster demonstrates an effective and often highly stylized way of dealing with the world; having done so, he is able to attain the stylishness (in dress, surroundings, and so on) that consolidates his status as star, the center of attention.

The theatricality of the violence in gangster films is often overlooked.

Frequently based on historical accounts of actual events, the gangster genre borrows a degree of realism from its sources. At the same time, the scenes of violence become elaborate set pieces, investing criminal acts with all the energy and excitement cinema can bestow on the transgressive. In the most interesting films, the audacious transformation of reality into dynamic spectacle is an act performed by the gangster himself.

As *The Cook, The Thief, His Wife and Her Lover* opens, the theatrical mode presses hard upon a realist setting, artifice foregrounded only to be displaced by the visceral quality of shock. As dogs in slow motion lick hunks of meat off the surface of a neon-lit street, stately music accompanies the camera as it cranes up a scaffolding to find two men in red footmen's uniforms standing sentry before a velvet curtain. As they ceremoniously open the curtain, two cars screech to a halt below (the sound of squealing rubber an icon of gangster films from the earliest days of sound film). We are returned to the street below (a location associated in Greenaway with danger and death [*A Zed and Two Noughts, Drowning by Numbers*, each designed, like *Cook*, by Ben Van Os and Jan Roelfs]), where several men dressed in anachronistic seventeenth-century cavalier-style clothes drag another man into the center of the screen. They strip him, smear his body with dog shit, and force him to eat it. The head gangster keeps up a running line of patter throughout the scene, his mocking tone positioning the mortifying humiliation as a child's lesson: "Come on, now. Open your mouth, open your mouth. Don't you appreciate your food? You must learn the rules." Snapping, "Take his pants down," Albert Spica, the dominant gangster, looms over the man, naked on the ground. "Oh dear, oh dear, didn't your daddy teach you to wipe your bottom?" Saying, "I've given you a good dinner, you can have a nice drink," Spica begins to piss on him. A woman's voice tells him to stop ("Come on, let's eat") and the men gradually leave off and move toward the back entrance of a restaurant. Two large open vans, one lit with blue and one with yellow, frame the scene.

The insistence on the sense of theatricality and self-conscious performance at the heart of the gangster film's gritty urban milieu is not an insight unique to Greenaway. Its near-constant reiteration in British gangster films, in fact, can be attributed to specific factors unique to the history of organized crime in Britain. In fact much of what Greenaway does in the opening scene of *Cook, Thief* can be traced back to the Krays.

In the early 1960s, Reginald and Ronnie Kray redefined the image of the British gangster. Their notoriety added key elements to the vocabulary of works on British gangsters. Several sources, for instance, comment on their theatricality: "In England the Krays are legendary, less for the enormity of their crimes than the relentlessly theatrical manner in which they carried on."[1] Influenced by American gangsters ("not the real ones, but gangsters in movies"), the brothers cared a great deal about appearance, about looking right. "The twins had a self-conscious style" complete with "sharp custom suits, manicures, house calls from the barber, [and] gold jewelry. . . . It was all an intricate performance, and they played it with total conviction."[2] The Krays showed that in late 1950s Britain not only was working class in style but that that style (especially as it applied to violence) could be used to seize power.

The Krays patterned their operation on American organized crime. While running a protection racket, the Krays invested in borderline-"legitimate" businesses such as nightclubs and gambling casinos, ventures that enabled them to court media coverage, promote themselves as celebrities, and brush shoulders with the rich and famous (Frank Sinatra, Joan Collins, Francis Bacon – George Raft was a personal friend).[3] Adding spice to the public's attraction to the Krays was their reputation as heads of "Britain's biggest and most violent crime empire."[4] One critic describes them as "celebrity Cockney thugs" in "the London pop demimonde" who "reigned with terror over the Carnaby Street 60s."[5] What the Krays contributed to British gang-based crime was a precipitous escalation in violence, including using machine guns when the police did not even carry handguns, and selecting weapons for their sheer outrageous appeal. *The Krays* (1991), a film made about the twins shortly after the release of *Cook, Thief*, re-creates some of their most notorious exploits. At one point Ronnie Kray pulls out a sword with great relish and carves a man's face open with it.

Gleefully mixing terror and glamour, the Krays, according to one writer, "lodged themselves in the national psyche as securely as the Queen Mother, Cliff Richard . . . and Cilla Black."[6] Another writer summed them up this way:

> They were identical twins locked in a bizarre symbiotic relationship – Ron was gay and Reg straight, Ron a grandstanding sociopath and Reg a violent businessman – that twisted them together into a single flamboyant entity.[7]

Or as Georgia Brown notes in a review of *The Krays*, "just think of them as Spica. . . . [in] *The Cook, The Thief, His Wife and Her Lover*."[8] The earliest film to feed off their image was released in 1970, the year after they went to prison. *Performance*, directed by Donald Cammell and Nicolas Roeg, has much in common with *Cook, Thief*. Considered shockingly violent, *Performance*'s title suggests the self-conscious theatricality the main character brings to his "work" as an enforcer for organized crime. In the words of his gangland boss, Chas (James Fox) is "an artist," a real "performer." As with most film gangsters, Chas's image of himself as someone special, a star within his profession, is connoted by his attention to personal appearance.

Clothes

In Hollywood classics such as *Little Caesar* (1930) and *Public Enemy* (1931), the first sign that a gangster has hit the big time is a trip to the tailor. The British gangster films borrow and elaborate on this trope. In *Mona Lisa* (1986), Bob Hoskins, recently released from prison, wears garish clothes that call attention to him (red vinyl jackets, too-tight jeans). The prostitute for whom he acts as bodyguard takes him to a men's shop and buys him clothes more suitable for someone waiting in the lobby of the finest hotels in London. Class, it is implied, is being invisible. In *Performance*, Chas is keenly aware of how clothes position one in relation to class. He keeps drawers of neatly folded clothes in his modern apartment, one holding nothing but row after row of cuff links, each set stored neatly in its open box. Pouring acid on an enemy's car, Chas is careful to remove his jacket and protect his shirtsleeves. As he heads for an appointment where he will rough up a businessman who has not accepted his gang's "protection," Chas's associates admonish him: "Put your tie on."

Both Chas and the Krays use dress to communicate their command of fashion as well as their disdain for the upper class.[9] The clothes worn in the sixties by the Krays (echoed in *Performance* and mimicked in *The Krays*) were fashionable in the sense of being new and expensive. ("Savile Row," the Kray boys shyly confess to their mum as they start to move up in the underworld.) The men's clothes in *Cook, Thief*, however, cannot be read in terms of actual eighties fashion, despite having been designed by "actual" eighties fashion designer Jean-Paul Gaultier. Startling appropriations of fashions centuries out of date, the clothes worn by Spica and his gang demand to be read in another way – not in terms of genre, but in terms of history, English and Dutch.

Writing on Gaultier's work in *Cook, Thief*, Nita Rollins argues that the "shock effect" of Gaultier's costumes "derives from [their] historicality."[10] Conceptualizing fashion as a form of self-expression, Rollins suggests that "Spica and his not-so-merrymakers" are "modeling themselves after Hals's painting of 1616, *Banquet of the Officers of the St. George Civic Company*."

Their discrepant habit of wearing military sashes – emblems of an antique honor – [acts as] a type of mirror to shore up their raggedy and derivative identities.[11]

Greenaway positions the Spica gang's relation to the Dutch Civil Guard somewhat differently. Where Rollins finds "civic-minded integrity" and "knight-errantry"[12] in marked contrast with Spica's men, Greenaway sees an "ironic picture of uniformed ceremonial bourgeois debauchery."

The Militia Clubs were male drinking-societies that had little to do with home-guard military defence against the Spanish. They were an excuse to dress up and get drunk with the boys. . . . Complaints of rowdiness, drunkenness, the boisterous firing of firearms, ill-disciplined used of gunpowder and insults to women were commonplace. . . . The giant reproduction of the painting in the restaurant is a template for bad behaviour – not good.[13]

Whether or not the Dutch guard in Hals's imposing portrait were in fact admirable or base, the meaning of the painting for a nouveau riche racketeer is simple: if it is old, big, and expensive, it signifies class.

Another historical model that might illuminate the gang's use of fashion would include not only seventeenth-century Holland but the willfully anachronistic clothes of the Teddy Boys of the 1950s. Perversely combining the greasy ducktail hairstyles of fifties rock-and-roll with Edwardian clothing styles from the turn of the century, Teds set themselves apart by wearing clothes that were utterly out of touch with other fifties fashions. Disdaining the fin-de-siècle aesthete's devotion to detail, their adoption of Edwardian styles remained determinedly partial and idiosyncratic. Purposely presenting themselves as being in opposition to fashion, Teds dressed not in order to move up in class, but to announce their indifference to "fitting in" or "moving up." For the gangster, dressing "out" of fashion becomes a statement of power, a refusal to be held to rules governing everyone else.

This "downward mobility chic" or anti-chic, epitomized by punk, more accurately describes the way Spica and his men wear clothes.[14] Like the Teds, they claim history for themselves, as a birthright. Yet the gangsters' relationship to and assumption of the historical styles we see in the Hals painting are brazenly indifferent both to contemporary fashion and to claims of "accuracy" or "authenticity" in relation to historical dress. Wearing a style that unifies them as a group by setting them apart from others, the gangsters defy the usual arbiters of taste and subvert their power to sanction. The result is a sartorial mishmash backed up by the ever-present threat of force.

The rebellion against fashion may be revolutionary, but the revolution is a conservative one. Deeply conservative, Spica and his gang are the shock troops of a reactionary right-wing proletariat. (Teds in popular mythography became Rockers, not Mods, and replaced their Edwardian suits with leather and Harleys.) Small indications of an underlying social conservatism abound throughout the modern British gangster film. Early in *Performance*, Chas's associates, driving to a "job," discuss the deplorable violence on television and its effects on children. Preparing to rape his wife, Georgina, on the hood of a car, Spica is shocked to find that she is not wearing underwear, that she has been out in public without "knickers." His constant inquiries as to whether she has washed her hands in the bathroom, and the homophobia rampant in the dialogue, are also part of a pervasive underlying social conservatism.[15]

Business

True conservatism in the British gangster film is synonymous with business. Intercutting the gangsters' daily terrorizing of small businesses with an argument in favor of a market-driven economy, every scene in the first part of *Performance* evokes Thatcher *avant la lettre*. Sounding like an eighties prime minister discussing the "fluid state of business ethics today," a bewigged barrister argues that what is really on trial is the "ethics of a community."

> Our national economy, even our national survival devolves upon the consolidation – by merger – of the smaller and weaker economic units with the larger and lustier pillars of our commercial [establishment].

At the mention of lust, Chas and his friends burst into a business and begin tearing up the place. As Chas berates the owner, "You know what you are? You're a disgrace, an incompetent disgrace, you're not fit to run a – " "Business is business," the lawyer continues, finishing Chas's sentence, "and progress is progress." According to Harry Flowers, Chas's boss, "small business in this day and age is against nature."

All the gangsters in *Performance* use business jargon as a euphemism for terror. As the barrister continues his description of this "admittedly bold but in no way unethical merger – I say merger, not takeover," Chas and his friends rip out electrical equipment, mock-complaining, "It's not maintained," "Obsolete." The depiction of organized crime as capitalism by other means dates back to Brecht and Weill's *The Threepenny Opera* and begins to appear routinely in postwar Hollywood films such as *I Walk Alone* (1947), where gangs have become "syndicates," complete with rules of incorporation and an overseeing board of directors. Granting protection to a bookie whose business has just been "redecorated" by his men, Harry congratulates him on having "been invited to join our associated group of companies." In a world where, as the barrister says, "words still have meaning," Flowers controls the vocabulary ("Took over? You was merged, my son") as he raises his glass in a toast "to Old England." The investment in this new discourse is considerable; Flowers's sidekicks react with shock when Chas murders the bookie (a former friend). "They'll call us gangsters. It'll be goodbye to business."

In all of the British gangster films, the concept of equating gangsterism with capitalism is given an American provenance. Lauding their continuing success, Harry Flowers in *Performance* exults, "We've got progress" in "this terrific democratic organization." And what is it attributable to? "Organization . . . Look at the Yanks." The criminal organization in *The Long Good Friday* has reached a pinnacle of success where they are able to consider a joint venture with the Americans, as are *The Krays*.

While Hoskins in *The Long Good Friday* looks to the Americans for validation in their proposed cooperative enterprise, Spica (like Greenaway) turns not to America but to Europe: particularly Holland (painting, clothes) and France (food). In *Cook*, the status bought with the proceeds of brigandage is the restaurant, Le Hollandais.[16] Spica's uxorious attempts at "partnership" (bringing Richard, the chef, vanloads of food, and cases of new silverware) do little to hide what is in fact a barely disguised takeover. Reminding Richard at first that "this is our anniversary – three months," Spica, when crossed, is quick to point out that without his "protection" "you wouldn't last long." Hoisting into place a huge new sign that links Spica's name with the chef's (Spica taking top billing), Spica's men short out the lights. In an aside, Richard notes, "Thanks to Mr. Spica, it is dark everywhere."

The restaurant business is itself a euphemism, haute cuisine inseparable from systematic killing. Spica arrives at the restaurant with two large vans of "fresh" (recently deceased) "food": dead meat, dead fowl, dead fish. Presented to the chef, Spica's largesse is rejected. As Richard curtly notes, a good chef selects his own supplies. As the naked man attacked by Spica and his men in the opening scene staggers toward the restaurant from the cold, dark street, Albert and Richard flank the cavernous doorway – a visual standoff between two men who deal in death. As with Smut in *Drowning by Numbers,* the foundation of Richard's art is death – just as the threat of death underlies Spica's power. But where Albert enthusiastically metes out suffering and death, Richard, unable to prevent it, soothes the victims and with great delicacy makes an art of the remains. Signaling for a chair, Richard ushers the beaten man in out of the cold, his staff providing cleansing comfort.

Ironically, violence poses the greatest obstacle to the gangsters' realization of their plans. As the Americans point out in *The Long Good Friday,* while some violence is necessary, too much is at odds with good business. In that film, a series of IRA murders masquerading as gangland hits make it appear as though the mob boss played by Bob Hoskins is not in control of his territory, scaring off the potentially lucrative trans-Atlantic deal. In *Performance* and *The Krays,* the issue of violence is more intractable. Harry's henchman notes that Chas is "an ignorant boy, an out of date boy" because he "enjoys his work" too much. Chas's description of his work – "Putting a little stick about, putting the frighteners on flash little twerps" – echoes the favorite phrase of the murderous Tory whip (and future prime minister) in the 1990s British television drama *House of Cards.* In the toilet at the restaurant, a marauding Spica arbitrarily accuses an older man of loitering and harassing young men. When the man threatens to complain to the management, Albert responds, "I am the management" and knees him in the groin. "That's what these people need," Spica concludes, "Short, sharp, shock treatment."[17]

The gangster's greatest power comes from the judicious employment of violence, against people, places, and things. Teaching someone a lesson, Chas and his men trap the man's chauffeur in the garage with the family Rolls-Royce. Mixing food and class and ownership with the verbal aplomb of Albert Spica, Chas draws his finger along the Rolls, and remarks to the bound and gagged chauffeur: "A tasty finish. A man of taste. Looks after his property, your owner? Does he? Does he?" Carefully donning gloves from a stylish leather bag, Chas pours acid all over the car, pausing for a moment when he reaches the chauffeur, tied to the car's grille. Opting not to waste the acid, Chas takes a different tack. Brandishing a straight razor, he shaves the chauffeur's head, mocking him at every step. "No soap on the gentleman's collar." A proper barber, Chas finishes up by pulling out a mirror and holding it at different angles for the chauffeur to see: "Trend settin', sir, wot?"

The much-noted violence of *Cook, Thief* has its roots here: the psychological humiliation, the physical abuse, the rhetorical questions. Whether it is Chas pouring acid on a car and shaving a man's head, or Ronnie Kray using a sword to slice a man's face into a permanent smile, or Spica pissing on a man smeared with dog shit, the British gangster film establishes this exaggerated, horrific violence as eminently British.

This is not to suggest a direct influence.[18] Greenaway frequently cites Jacobean drama as his "conscious model – most particularly *The Duchess of Malfi* and *'Tis Pity She's a Whore.*" What struck him "most poignantly" when he first saw *'Tis Pity She's a Whore* at the age of fifteen were

> the actions and activities of Vasques towards Hippolita and Putana . . . acts of the most dismissive, casual brutality and sadistic disdain for suffering that dramatically shocked, haunted and fascinated me.

As a schoolboy, Greenaway saw a direct emotional connection between these texts and his own experience at public school.

> I witnessed first-hand much ice-cold brutality and mental and physical humiliation sanctioned by "a blind-eye" authority.

He concludes from this that the "specific type" of "English" violence discussed here "has a long history – and was alive and thriving long before cinema took it to its bosom."[19]

In his film about the Krays, Peter Medak locates the roots of violence in the war – its horror, deprivation, and the perverse strengths that develop from the will to survive. In *The Long Good Friday,* the internecine conflicts of the mobsters pale in comparison with the widespread bloodshed resulting from the government's institution of martial law in Northern Ireland.[20] In *Performance,* closest perhaps to *The Cook's* anticonservative stance, it is the worship of business itself and the ease with which money is translated into popular culture, celebrity, and status that provide the most fertile ground for corruption.

There is even a moment when it is possible, in a comic vein, to see violence at its grossest level become routine, absorbed into Britain's daily life. Like the media-savvy Krays, Monty Python's Piranha Brothers court celebrity status. The chief investigator on the case, Superintendent Harry "Snapper" Organs, recounts that the police "kept tabs on their every movement by reading the color supplements." As with Spica or the Krays, the tales of Doug and Dinsdale Piranha's violence are legend. One small-time crook remembers the time he was summoned to see Dinsdale.

> Dinsdale was there, in the conversation pit, with Doug, and Charles Paisley, the baby crusher, a couple of film producers, and a man they called Kierkegaard who just sat there biting the heads off whippets. And Dinsdale said, "I hear you've been a naughty boy, Clement," and

he slits me nostrils open, saws me leg off, and pulls me liver out. And I said, "My name's not Clement," and then he loses his temper and nails my head to the floor.

But it is not physical violence that holds the greatest terror for those unfortunate enough to meet the Piranhas. The owner of "a high class nightclub for the gentry at Biggleswade . . . (and not a cheap clip joint for pickin' up tarts)" recounts how Dinsdale's brand of intimidation was nothing compared to Doug's. "Everyone was terrified of Doug. I've seen grown men pull their own heads off rather than see Doug." What did Doug do to inspire such dread? "He used – sarcasm. He knew all the tricks, dramatic irony, metaphor, bathos, puns, parody, litotes, and – satire."

Language

Like other key protagonists in British drama, Spica is a language monster. Unlike most movie gangsters, Spica (Michael Gambon) is not attractive.[21] One of the most comprehensive descriptions of Spica sees him as

a triumph of Greenaway's impulse to catalog: he is sadistic, bullying, nagging, crude, loud, callous, self-important, sanctimonious, anti-Semitic, racist, misogynist, homophobic, drunken, unlettered, and possessed of a poor French accent.[22]

It is a longtime convention of gangster films that the boss is a blowhard, the one who makes the wisecracks, who talks and silences the others. When one of the thugs makes a joke while Chas is shaving the chauffeur's head, Chas erupts, "I said shut your bloody hole." Spica speaks in monologues and shouts down anyone who tries to participate. His topics are an unappetizing mix of food, power, sex, and shit. Inviting Mitchell (Tim Roth), one of his henchmen, to eat a prairie oyster, Spica asks him to describe how it tastes (like "wet bread") and dwells on its consistency, "no, it's all squishy with gritty bits" and a skin on it. Instructing him to swallow it, Spica reveals it was a "sheep's bollock" – "The next time I ask you to work for me, Mitchell, I'll be expecting you to chew someone's bollocks off on demand."

William F. Van Wert describes "the way language overall is used in the film: stating, restating, inverting, following assertions with inverted rhetorical questions," the result "antagonistic, obsessive, [and] rhythmic."[23] *How* Spica talks is central to his character, not only in his use of language but the very quality of his voice. Critics noted over and over the unattractiveness of Michael Gambon's voice, its wheedling, nasal quality. How Gambon uses his voice is essential because Spica (as implied by his name) is a speaker. The physical characteristics of speech are what give you power over others, the voice's volume and timbre, its placement in the chest or throat, calling attention to the physical body from which it comes. Pacing and tone, conversely, give you power over language, the ability to inflect words (say, with sarcasm) in order to control or subvert their meaning. The written word, on the other hand, does not vary its meaning. Silent, fixed (in the character Michael's words, "reasonable"), it is indifferent to the reader's desire, impervious to intimidation or coercion, and less susceptible to co-optation, or subjection to Spica's will. This may account for Spica's hostility to the written word.

As Michael (Alan Howard) sits reading in the restaurant, Albert suddenly bursts into the shot and pulls the book out of his hand.

> What are you doin'? Reading again? This is a restaurant, not a library. The only thing you're allowed to read in here is the menu. You are insulting the chef. Reading gives you indigestion. Didn't you know that? Don't read at the table.

He sits abruptly.

> Y'know, I've just been reading stuff that'd make your hair curl. Out there. In the toilet. That's the sort of stuff people read. Not this. Don't you feel out of touch? Does this stuff make money? Y'know, I bet you're the only man who's read this book – but I bet you every man in this restaurant has had a read of that stuff out there. It makes ya think, doesn't it? You know, I reckon you read because you've got nobody to talk too.

Albert invites Michael to meet the wife – "She likes to read too." She likes to read in bed, and (the clincher for Spica) "she even likes to read on the john," he tells Michael as he leads him by the arm over to the table to meet his wife, Georgina (Helen Mirren).

Van Wert compares Greenaway's use of language to "sped-up Beckett or Pinter" and there is good reason why these particular playwrights come to mind.[24] Pinter in his work in the sixties in particular specialized in delineating the ways a speaker could humiliate someone with simple repetition. Picking up on something someone said, the more dominant figure rings as many changes as possible upon a carelessly used word or phrase, shading it first with surprise, then confusion, now with ridicule, now contempt. Repeated until it loses all meaning, a word becomes as opaque as a cricket bat and can be used to pound the hapless soul who originally dared speak. Al-

Figure 26. *The Cook, The Thief, His Wife and Her Lover* (1989) (Alan Howard, Richard Bohringer, Helen Mirren, Michael Gambon, and Tim Roth). (Museum of Modern Art/Film Stills Archive)

bert's use of repetition, though delivered in a fawning, solicitous tone, is fundamentally sarcastic. Introducing Michael to everyone at the table, Spica asks him his name. Pounding like a headache on the one word to which everyone is most sensitive, one's name, Spica responds,

> Well, Michael? Oh, is that a Jewish name, Michael? Do you eat kosher food then, Michael? Sit down, Michael, and tell us all about kosher food, Michael.

When Michael responds, "I'm sorry, but I'm not Jewish," Albert turns the conventional apology back on him, "Why be sorry? Why hide it? Sixty percent of the people in this restaurant are a touch Jewish."

Spica asks his usual rhetorical questions, but his attempt to elicit the listener's acquiescence in his own humiliation fails with Michael. Soft-spoken, literally silent until this point, Michael's association with books places him outside Spica's system where nourishment is inevitably transmuted into shit.

We first see Michael through Georgina's eyes. So wrapped up in the book he is reading, Michael doesn't notice when his food, balanced precariously in midair, falls off his fork. Michael's appetites, unlike Spica's, are not ravenous. A man of moderation (always wearing the same mousy brown suit), Michael is not only indifferent to what he eats, he does not need to read everything he sees. At his apartment, a golden library filled to the ceiling with books, he tells Georgina that although he is "cataloguing French history," "it's not necessary for the bookkeeper to read all the stock."

In his ultimate display of infantile rage against language, Spica forces Michael to eat his words. Gazing at Michael's library, Georgina asks, "What good are all these books to you – you can't eat them." In Spica's hands, words can literally kill, and he kills Michael with the written word. Having found Michael's apartment once Michael and Georgina have escaped the restaurant, Spica paces back and forth as one of his associates shoves pages down Michael's throat. Words spew out of Spica's mouth as pages torn from a book on the French Revolution are pushed into Michael's with a wooden spoon; he talks the whole time as Michael gags on his own blood. He's "too old for Georgie," Spica says, "same age as me." Spica does not want Mitchell to chew Michael's bollocks off after all – he is worried the headlines would say "Jewish bookkeeper savaged by sex maniac." "I want no evil gossip spread around about me." Albert prefers "a dignified revenge killing" where people could "admire the style." Losing his bearings outside of his territory, Albert falls to his knees: "Hold his nose . . . ram the bloody books down his throat – suffocate the bloody bastard." The men want to burn the place and destroy the evidence, but Albert, back at the restaurant demonstrating how to eat crayfish, does not want it destroyed. "I want Georgie to see it."

> What did he say? The French Revolution was easier to swallow than Napoleon? *His* favorite dish was oysters Florentine. Churchill liked seafood. All the great generals were keen on seafood. Hitler liked clams and Mussolini liked squid.

When Mitchell asks, "What did the bookseller eat?" Spica responds "How do I care? It all comes out as shit in the end."

Spica's constant verbal confusion of the realms of food and shit is presented as a gustatory perversion, to wit, coprophilia, getting a sexual kick out of blurring the boundaries between food and excrement.[25]

> Y'know, I'm an artist the way I combine my business and my pleasure. Money's my business, eatin's my pleasure – and Georgie's my

pleasure too – though in a more private kind of way than stuffin' the mouth and feedin' the sewers, though the pleasures are related – because the, the naughty bits and the dirty bits are so close together. It just goes to show how eating and sex are related.

Not to mention shit.

Spica identifies one dish as looking "like cat food for constipated French rabbits." Forcing dog feces into the mouth of the man in the opening scene, he sneers, "Don't you appreciate your *food?*" Telling Georgie not to smoke, he opines, "It ruins your taste buds, burns your tongue, and makes your pee stink. . . . I've smelt the loo after you've been piddling in there." And he concludes that she can't have children because she "don't eat properly": "You should drink more water and eat more kidneys." His concern with piss allows him to combine food, excretion, and racism:

> Some of them Indians are well-known for drinking their own pee. The same water would go round and round and round. Of course you're bound to lose some through evaporation.

Asking the grandmotherly Grace, "Now whose pee, whose pee would you drink first?" Albert turns an eye on his wife: "Georgie and I have our little sessions."

Spica's confusion of orifices centers on a fear of women's bodies, a fear defended by extreme violence. Food and shit, sex and women: the naughty bits and the dirty bits.

Women

> "Men stay kids all their fucking lives and they end up heroes or monsters. . . .
> Women have to grow up."
>
> *The Krays*

What is unique about *Cook, Thief* as a gangster pic is the centrality of the woman. Greenaway cites "violence towards women" as one of the "very dangerous taboo areas" that first attracted him to Jacobean drama, but explosive violence against women is also a well-known characteristic of gangster films.[26] In *The Long Good Friday, Mona Lisa,* and *The Krays,* women can be the pivots around which the narrative is structured, but the men control the action. Here Georgina makes things happen by choice. She is central because of her actions.

In *The Long Good Friday,* Helen Mirren plays the mistress of gang leader

Bob Hoskins. He needs someone with more social polish than he possesses to act as a kind of class-liaison in his dealings with politicians and potential investors. Where Hoskins involves Mirren in every aspect of the business, treating her as a partner and respecting her advice, Spica's relation to Georgina (also played by Mirren) is one of plain dominance. The class difference between Albert and Georgina is not as great as that between Mirren and Hoskins in the earlier film, but Georgina's sensitivity and taste are still notably better than Spica's, which are nonexistent. Entering the restaurant, Georgina is drawn to the little kitchen boy, Pup, singing in a corner. Albert, on the other hand, only ceases bellowing long enough to throw money at the boy, who immediately stops short. Instead of depending on her expertise when it comes to food – her knowledge of restaurant French, knowing when it is acceptable to eat with one's fingers, her appreciation of French cuisine (Richard compliments her excellent palate), Albert is angrily indifferent to what is "correct," either in table manners or pronunciation. As he reels off a list of dishes he would prefer to those Richard has prepared, Albert mispronounces everything, culminating with "poy-zann oh p-p-p-" "It's pwa-sohn," Georgina notes. He hits her repeatedly across the face with a menu – "Whad you say? What did you say? What did you say?" Georgie quietly reiterates, "Pwa-sohn." Although she seldom dares raise her voice, when Albert and his men attack the man in the opening scene, it is Georgina who insists, "Albert. Leave him alone."

Unlike *The Long Good Friday*, where the gangster and his woman are devoted to each other, in *Cook, Thief* Georgina is in the process of decoupling, establishing herself as an individual, separate from Albert. From the beginning, Georgina resists in little ways – for instance, smoking when Albert tells her not to. Entering the restaurant, he snatches a cigarette out of her hand and grinds it into the floor.

Georgina's resistance to Albert increases when she begins an affair with Michael, the man she has glimpsed from across the room in the restaurant. When Albert bursts into the lavatory where Michael and Georgina are having their first wordless assignation, Georgina covers herself by pleading, "I'm just having a quiet smoke." As Albert gropes her by the washbasins, she pointedly remarks, "Men who hang around ladies' lavatories are asking to have their illusions shattered."

When Albert, beginning to suspect, drags Michael over to the table to introduce him to Georgina, he tries to control people as he usually does, through language. Turning away a waitress who tries to return Michael's books, Albert tells Michael, "You won't need those. We're going to hold a conversation." Albert dictates the conversation, telling Georgie what to say. "You can start, Georgie. Tell Michael all about yourself. . . . Tell Michael you live in a big house and you spend four hundred pounds a week on clothes." Georgina recites, "I spend four hundred pounds a week on clothes." "You wear beautiful things . . . " "I wear beautiful things." "You eat in the best restaurants . . ." "I eat in the best restaurants." She repeats his promptings word for word, having learned to use repetition to reflect his tyranny back at him, making him look ridiculous. When he warns her to "try a little harder please," she continues with a list of the consumer services available to her courtesy of Spica's money. She goes to a good hairdresser, a good dentist ("*he's* Jewish," Albert interjects), and a good gynecologist – "You what?" – adding, "it's unlikely that I'll ever have a baby . . . the three miscarriages I've had so far have ruined my insides." Ignoring Albert's stunned attempts to silence her ("I don't think we need to discuss that subject, do you?"), Georgina plunges ahead. "Being infertile makes me a safe bet for a good screw." Spica howls, "Shut up, Georgie!"

As soon as Michael has been dismissed, Georgina is punished for her nerve. Twisting her arm behind her back, Albert barrels her into the kitchen, furious that she told such "intimate" details to Michael – "telling a complete stranger about us." "Not about us, about *me*," Georgina retorts, insisting on her individuality. No longer content with subtle resistance, she stands face-to-face opposite her husband, advancing on him step by step as she throws his prejudices back in his face. When he growls, "What's all this about a gynecologist. Who is he? It had better be a she – ", she lets fly,

> It's a man. He's Jewish and he's from Ethiopia. His mother is a Roman
> Catholic. He's been in prison in South Africa – he's as black as the ace
> of spades – and he probably drinks his own pee.

With a vicious punch in the stomach, Albert silences her and drives her back toward the alley, running over a dog with his car in his hurry to get away from the restaurant.

Georgina's affair with Michael is the most important way she resists Albert, claims the restaurant as her own space, and re-creates herself as an individual. The next evening we find Georgina and Michael naked, modeled in golden light in a green room behind the kitchen. Dead birds are suspended from the ceiling, feathers falling gently around the couple. Michael tells her, "He's broken the silence for us." (Albert, rarely silent, is as opposed to silence as he is to the written word.)

MICHAEL: I once saw a film in which the main character didn't speak for the first half an hour . . . I was completely absorbed as to what would happen because anything was possible.
GEORGINA: And then?
MICHAEL: He spoiled it. He spoke.

When Georgina wonders if this means he will lose interest in her, he responds, "It was only a film." As Georgina discovers herself through prohibited actions, Michael has discovered himself through a text. (The revelatory aspect of art is explicitly connected here not to books but to art cinema – Michael's story invokes the lingering love scenes and minimalist dialogue common to films as diverse as Resnais's *Hiroshima Mon Amour*, 1959, and Wim Wenders's *Paris, Texas*, 1984, the film Greenaway cites as the overt subject of this discussion.)[27]

Shedding their clothes, Michael and Georgina set themselves apart from Spica's world. While Michael's clothes are the most "normal" and consistent in the film, Georgina's attire is emblematic of the way the film courts the fabulous. The first time Georgina contradicts Albert is in the alley in the first scene and concerns his criticism of her for wearing a black dress. Soft-spoken and wary, she insists, "it's not black, it's blue." Entering the restaurant, her clean-lined coatdress is suddenly light gray, in the restaurant, red, and in the toilet, white. Her mini-boots, the fringe on her gloves, and her Givenchy-style hat of feathers are always black. A kind of protective coloring, Georgina's clothes stop reflecting their surroundings the farther she gets from Spica's influence.

Where the costumes for Spica and his men are intentionally anachronistic, because of the greater latitude given women's fashions, Georgina's wardrobe is distinctly à la mode. In her essay on the costumes in *Cook, Thief*, Nita Rollins points out how Georgina's apparel contradicts traditional theories of how women's dress is to be read. Because the off-the-shoulder, sleeveless designs highlight rather than conceal the bruises inflicted by Albert, Georgina's clothes do not serve as a testament to her husband's munificence. And as the film progresses, Georgina spends less and less time in them.[28]

Nudity becomes the preferred state for Georgina and Michael. Their resemblance to Adam and Eve bespeaks their reinvention or rebirth even as they are expelled from the garden – though here the trajectory is clearly a Dantesque one, taking them from the restaurant's red hell, through purgatory, to a starry heaven visible through the windows of Michael's room. Escaping from Albert's wrath, Georgina and Michael are pushed into one of

Figure 27. Georgina and Spica. (Museum of Modern Art/Film Stills Archive)

the vans of meat rejected by the chef and left to rot in the alley outside Le Hollandais. Surrounded by decaying carcasses, they reenact a medieval depiction of what Fallen Man shall come to, and undergo a skin-crawlingly palpable mortification of the flesh.[29] As with Spica's first victim, after their journey in the van, Georgina and Michael need to be hosed off to prevent the (literal) remains of Albert's business from contaminating their vulnerable, exposed flesh.

As they escape in the van, Albert roars the curse that will rebound on him: "I'll bloody find him, I'll bloody kill him, and I'll eat him!" The final thing Georgina needs to establish in order to separate herself once and for all from Albert is that she is not food.

Food

It so happens there is almost a British tradition in the 1980s of films involving gluttony-unto-death and vice versa. Cannibalism, excessive consumption, grotesque death – in the eighties people overstuff themselves until they explode. In *Monty Python's The Meaning of Life* (1983) this happens to a diner at a fancy restaurant; in the 1986 animated short *Babylon*, to an arms merchant at a Conservative fund-raising banquet. As the banquet speaker drones on in an insinuating whisper about patriotism, Empire, and "peace through deterrence," the merchant, swollen to a giant size, explodes, drowning everyone around him in blood and munitions. In 1987's *Eat the Rich*, a multigendered, multiracial, multisexual group of working-class misfits opens a restaurant for yuppies and serves them to themselves. In these earlier cannibal texts (including *Eating Raoul*, 1982, and *Sweeney Todd*)[30], people do not know what they are eating. In Greenaway's film, they do.

As with all gangsters, Spica goes too far. Trying to expand his entourage by inviting in other mob bosses and their women, Spica overextends himself. As he loses control the violence escalates. When two of his (unimpressed) guests wander into the kitchen, the woman sees Georgina with Michael and tells Albert. He stabs her in the face with a fork. Trying to find Michael and Georgina after they have escaped, Albert makes the boy Pup eat the buttons on his coat, then, literalizing the metaphor, cuts off the boy's belly button. Even Spica's men protest, one vomiting in the corner. His men begin to desert him and things spin out of control. When Spica's gang members begin manhandling the guests at Le Hollandais and chase everyone out of the restaurant, Richard and his staff finally stand up to Spica and expel him and his thugs.

In all of the British cannibalism texts, the restaurant staff are fundamentally sympathetic – the waiter in *Babylon*, the restaurateurs in *Eat the Rich*. Even Sweeney Todd can be seen as striking back against injustice. It is Richard, the cook, whom Georgina approaches for help when she wants revenge for Michael's death. Georgina's relationship with Richard has been comparable to hers with Michael; mostly silent, she and Richard meet over food. Entering the kitchen for an assignation with Michael, she pauses to taste the sauce. Seeing her hesitate, Richard adds more salt. She tastes again and nods, making eye contact with Richard, who leads her to Michael waiting behind a bakery rack. (Albert, barging into the kitchen moments later, tastes the sauce and spits it out – "This custard's salty.")

Her silent accomplice, Richard also serves as confirmation, verifying memories too precious to let slip away. Coming to see him after Michael's death, Georgina presses him to tell her what he saw happen between her and Michael: "How can I know that he loved me if there were no witnesses?

". . . How could I know it was real unless someone was watching." He responds with the repetition of a ritualized litany.

> I saw him kissing you on the mouth, on the neck, behind your ear. I saw him undressing you, I saw him kissing your breast, I saw him put his hand between your legs.

Asking what he saw her do, she begins to cry as he lists the acts of love she performed for Michael. He tells her, "My parents behaved like that." – "They did? You saw them?" – "And lovers in the cinema sometimes behave like that" – "No, that doesn't count." " – And in my fantasy lovers always behave like that."

A voyeur, Richard is essentially passive. Georgina wants to make eating *mean* something. Richard has always known the meaning inherent in food. When she asks him how he prices each dish, he tells her he charges for vanity: "Diet foods have an additional surcharge of thirty percent. Aphrodisiac – fifty percent." And he charges "a lot for anything black."

> People like to remind themselves of death. Eating black food is like consuming death. Like saying, "Ha ha, Death, I'm eating you."

In literalizing Richard's metaphor, Georgina, like many heroines of Jacobean tragedy, courts madness. Whether or not she will survive the brutality of Spica's world with her sanity as well as with her life is a question raised after Michael's death. Finding Michael murdered in his apartment (while she was visiting the hospital to see Pup), she lies down beside him, calmly telling him what she would like to have for breakfast. Waking up the next day (as Spica's criminal organization is unraveling back at Le Hollandais), she tells Michael's corpse the private suffering she has undergone at Spica's hands. (To have one of the most intimate moments in the film take place between a woman and a corpse is a brazenly Jacobean touch.) Approaching Richard the next day, Georgina fluctuates between grieving for Michael and asking Richard, with an unsettling clarity, to cook him. She holds grief at bay long enough to realize Spica's curse.

The film has been structured according to menus, each listing various dishes and the day of the week, and decoratively festooned with arrangements of fish, fowl, herbs, and meat. The last menu has a simple single sprig and announces that the restaurant is closed "for a Private Function."[31] (*A Private Function* is also the title of a 1985 film that links social climbing with postwar food rationing. Its punning title combines eating with bathroom humor in order to expose the hypocrisy underlying the fundamental conservatism of petit-bourgeois social aspirations.) Albert bursts through the doors of the restaurant, complaining about being locked out of his own restaurant while tearing up the invitation to what will be his last meal. Georgina is waiting for him.

It is usually women who are described in edible terms. Luscious, delectable, tasty, a dish, cheesecake, tomatoes, tarts: such terms bring to mind in this context the oft-repeated tabloid description of Helen Mirren as the "thinking man's crumpet." (In the American advertising copy for the film, Mirren is posed between an oversized knife and fork under the heading "Lust . . . Murder . . . Dessert.") Albert's paraphernalia for molesting Georgie includes "a toothbrush, a wooden spoon, a plastic train, and a wine bottle." (She tells Michael's corpse that after a time she would use the implements while Spica watched – "it hurt less"). When one of the women, attacking Spica, lets slip about Georgina's affair, Albert stabs a fork through her cheek. Georgina reverses this state of affairs.

Welcoming Albert to the restaurant, she declares, "Happy anniversary, Albert." Threatening her as usual ("Your bottom's going to be very sore for weeks"), Albert is taken aback to see the restaurant stripped bare of its garish decor, a single table left in the center of the room. Georgina tells him that in honor of this occasion, "an anniversary I shall always celebrate," she is giving him a present. Albert tries to maintain the vanished status quo: "It's me who gives you presents. You've always known that. Besides, you've never had the money to give me a present."

The doors to the kitchen open with a roaring sound and a pageant of Spica's victims parade in – the kitchen staff, Pup in a wheelchair, the woman with her face bandaged, and someone on a stretcher. As they lay the stretcher horizontally on the table in front of Albert, Georgina takes her place opposite. Pulling the sheet off the body, she reveals Michael's steaming brown corpse. "Jesus, God!" Albert gasps as he jumps back. "It's not God, Albert," Georgina says in her most reasonable tone. "It's Michael." When Albert pulls a gun, his last defense, it is wrested from him and his last supporters fall away. (Mitchell is carried out and the motherly Grace faints.) Georgina has the gun. "Try the cock, Albert. It's a delicacy, and you know where it's been." Shaking, Albert attempts to eat his words made corporeal before him. He vomits the first time. The camera circling around Georgina and Albert, Michael dead between them, Georgina urges Spica on in the language and manner he could never attain, "Bon appetit. It's French." Albert tries once more, putting the fork to his mouth to taste the ashes of his victory.

Spica's last bite brings the film's investigation of food-as-metaphor full

circle. As a last meal, Richard's pièce de résistance is presented not to pro-
long life (to nourish) but to condemn. Spica's obsession with food's transformation into shit is revealed as a fetish, distracting us from the body itself. What Greenaway refers to as "this rotten, worm-infested body" is itself
on a journey to putrefaction, a trip to decay only momentarily postponed
by a healthy diet.[32]

Greenaway's exposure of "the scandal" of the body – that we are heirs
to the inevitable failure of the flesh – is reaffirmed by his use of nudity. In
most gangster films, gangsters live fast and die young. It's part of their glamour. With his insistently middle-aged cast, Greenaway gives us another kind
of body. While, on the one hand, we may see Mirren as an exemplar of mature female sexuality (where sexuality is a matter of character and not
merely appearance), on the other hand, her body renders equally visible the
physical toll life has taken – the bags under her eyes, the bruises on her
cheeks. The nudity in turn is understood in relation to the costumes, the
most notorious of which is the "harness outfit" Mirren wears halfway
through the film. Widely reproduced in production stills and in the film's
advertising, this design of straps-on-straps gives the illusion of "hiding nothing" (Georgina's bruises being particularly noticeable in this scene). Halfway between lingerie and evening wear, a corset and bondage, this outfit
flirts with the threshold between covered and uncovered, flesh dressed and
bared. Gaultier's association with Madonna (who in the film *Truth or Dare*,
1991, popularized styles similar to those worn by Georgina) only emphasizes the discrepancy between Mirren's voluptuous but lived-in body and
Madonna's exhaustively sculpted physique. The last naked body we see
transcends the claims of fashion. Spica, in his pitiful finery, ruffled and
sashed, puffy, bald, confronts the body laid out before him. Accepting "Michael" into his mouth (completing the full allegorical sweep of food as sex,
food as death, food as human waste), Spica consumes his future.

As Albert takes his last bite, Georgina shoots him, spitting out the last
word – "Cannibal" – as the curtains drop and crazed cabaret music spins
us into darkness.

By resituating the Jacobean revenge drama within the gangster genre,
Greenaway has found a popular form in which violence, verbal and physi-
cal, is quite at home. In Greenaway's work, Michael Walsh suggests,
"Greenaway's grids, lexicons, and encyclopedias are not simply affectless
(as critics tend to say) but determinedly distanced from affect."[33] In *The
Cook, The Thief, His Wife and Her Lover*, Greenaway finds other ways to

block the emotional connection between the audience and his film. In one interview he has said, "I wonder sometimes, if you wear your heart so much on your sleeve, it must ultimately stay there."[34] Confronting the darkest brutality at the core of an exploitative system, in *Cook, Thief,* Greenaway uses shock to cauterize the heart.

Peter Greenaway Filmography

All films written and directed by Peter Greenaway except where noted.

1966: *Train*, 5 min.; *Tree*, 16 min.

1967: *Revolution*, 8 min.; *5 Postcards from Capital Cities*, 35 min.

1971: *Erosion*, 27 min.

1973: *H is for House*, 10 min. (reedited 1978). Narrators: Colin Cantlie, Peter Greenaway and family. Music: Vivaldi, *Four Seasons*.

Intervals, 7 min.

1974: *Windows*, 4 min. Narrator: Peter Greenaway. Music: Rameau's "The Hen." Calligraphy: Kenneth Breese.

Water, 5 min. Music: Max Eastley.

1975: *Water Wrackets*, 12 min. Narrator: Colin Cantlie. Music: Max Eastley. Calligraphy: Kenneth Breese.

1976: *Goole by Numbers*, 40 min.

1977: *Dear Phone*, 17 min. Narrator: Peter Greenaway. Calligraphy: Kenneth Breese.

1978: *1–100*, 4 min. Music: Michael Nyman.

A Walk Through H, 41 min. BFI. Narrator: Colin Cantlie. Cinematography: Bert Walker, John Rosenberg. Music: Michael Nyman. Calligraphy: Kenneth Breese.

Vertical Features Remake, 45 min. Arts Council of Great Britain. Narrator: Colin Cantlie. Cinematography: Bert Walker. Music: Michael Nyman. Theme music: Brian Eno.

1979: *Zandra Rhodes*, 15 min. COI.

1980: *The Falls*, 185 min. BFI. Produced by Peter Sainsbury. Cinematography: Mike Coles, John Rosenberg. Editor: Peter Greenaway. Music: Michael Nyman, with additional music by Brian Eno, John Hyde, Keith Pendlebury. Voices: Colin Cantlie, Hilarie Thompson, Sheila Canfield, Adam Leys, Serena Macbeth, Martin Burrows.

1981: *Act of God*, 25 min. Thames TV. Produced by Udi Eicler. Cinematography: Peter George. Editor: Andy Watmore.

1982: *The Draughtsman's Contract*, 108 min. BFI/Channel Four Television. Executive Producer: Peter Sainsbury. Producer: David Payne. Cinematography: Curtis Clark. Editor: John Wilson. Production Design: Bob Ringwood. Music: Michael Nyman. Cast: Mr. Neville (Anthony Higgins), Mrs. Virginia Herbert (Janet Suzman), Mrs. Sarah Talmann (Anne Louise Lambert), Mr. Thomas Noyes (Neil Cunningham), Mr. Louis Talmann (Hugh Fraser).

1983: *Four American Composers: "John Cage," "Robert Ashley," "Philip Glass," "Meredith Monk,"* 55 min. each. Channel Four Television/Transatlantic Films. Filmed at the Almeida Concerts, 1982. Produced by Revel Guest. Cinematography: Curtis Clark. Editor: John Wilson.

1984: *Making a Splash,* 25 min. Channel Four/Media Software. Produced by Pat Marshall. Music: Michael Nyman.

A TV Dante – Canto 5. Screenplay: Peter Greenaway and Tom Phillips. Produced by Sophie Balhetchet. Cinematography: Mike Coles, Simon Fone. Film Editor: John Wilson. Video Editor: Bill Saint.

1985: *A Zed and Two Noughts,* 115 min. BFI Production/Allarts Enterprises BV Nederland/Artificial Eyes Productions/Film Four International. Produced by Kees Kasander and Peter Sainsbury. Cinematography: Sacha Vierny. Editor: John Wilson. Production Design: Ben Van Os and Jan Roelfs. Music: Michael Nyman. Cast: Oliver Deuce (Eric Deacon), Oswald Deuce (Brian Deacon), Alba Bewick (Andrea Ferreol), Van Hoyten (Joss Ackland), Van Meegeren (Gerard Thoolen), Beta Bewick (Agnes Brulet), Catharina Bolnes (Guusje van Tilbrough), Venus de Milo (Frances Barber), Stephen Pipe (Ken Campbell), Joshua Plate (Jim Davidson).

Inside Rooms – 26 Bathrooms, 25 min. (Video). Channel Four/Artifax Productions. Produced by Sophie Balhetchet. Cinematography: Mike Coles. Editor: John Wilson. Music: Michael Nyman.

1986: *The Belly of an Architect,* 118 min. Callendar Company/Film Four International/British Screen Hemdale/Sacis. Produced by Colin Callender and Walter Donohue. Cinematography: Sacha Vierny. Editor: John Wilson. Production Design: Luciana Vedovelli. Music: Wim Mertens and Glen Branca. Cast: Stourley Kracklite (Brian Dennehy), Louisa Kracklite (Chloe Webb), Caspasian Speckler (Lambert Wilson), Flavia Speckler (Stefania Casini).

1987: *Fear of Drowning,* 30 min. Allarts (for Channel Four). Produced by Paul Trybits. Codirector: Vanni Corbellini. Presented by Peter Greenaway and the cast and crew of *Drowning by Numbers.*

1988: *Drowning by Numbers,* 119 min. Film Four International/Elsevier Vendex Film. Produced by Kees Kasander and Denis Wigman. Cinematography: Sacha Vierny. Editor: John Wilson. Production Design: Ben Van Os and Jan Roelfs. Music: Michael Nyman. Cast: Cissie Colpitts (Joan Plowright), Cissie Colpitts (Juliet Stevenson), Cissie Colpitts (Joely Richardson), Madgett (Bernard Hill), Smut (Jason Edwards), Jake (Brian Pringle), Hardy (Trevor Cooper), Bellamy (David Morrissey), Nancy (Jane Gurnett), The Skipping Girl (Natalie Morse).

A TV Dante – Cantos 1–8, 100 min. KGP Production in association with Channel Four/Elsevier Vendex/VPRO. Made in collaboration with Tom Phillips. Cast: Virgil (John Gielgud), Bob Peck, Joanne Whalley.

1989: *The Cook, The Thief, His Wife and Her Lover*, 120 min. Allarts/Erato Films/Films Inc. Produced by Kees Kasander. Cinematography: Sacha Vierny. Editor: John Wilson. Production Design: Ben Van Os and Jan Roelfs. Music: Michael Nyman. Cast: Albert Spica (Michael Gambon), Georgina (Helen Mirren), Michael (Alan Howard), Richard (Richard Bohringer), Mitchell (Tim Roth).

Death in the Seine, 40 min. Erato Films/Allarts TV Productions/Mikros Image/La Sept. Cast: Jim Van Der Woude, Jean-Michel Dagory.

Hubert Bals Handshake, 5 min. Allarts (for the Rotterdam Film Festival).

1991: *Prospero's Books*, 123 min. Allarts/Cinea/Camera One/Penta coproduction in association with Elsevier Vendex Film/Film Four International/VPRO/Canal Plus & NHK. Produced by Kees Kasander and Denis Wigman. Cinematography: Sacha Vierny. Editor: Marina Bodbijl. Production Design: Ben Van Os and Jan Roelfs. Music: Michael Nyman. Cast: Prospero (John Gielgud), Miranda (Isabelle Pasco), Caliban (Michael Clark), Ferdinand (Mark Rylance), Alonso (Michel Blanc), Gonzalo (Erland Josephson), Antonio (Tom Bell), Sebastian (Kenneth Cranham), Ariel (Orpheo, Paul Russell, James Thierree, and Emil Wolk). Book Narrator: Leonard Maguire.

M Is for Man, Music, Mozart, 30 min. BBC/AVRO TV/Artifax coproduction. Cast: Ben Craft.

1992: *Rosa*, 15 min. La Monnaie de Munt/Rosas Production. Choreography: Anne Teresa de Keersmaeker and Jean-Luc Ducourt. Music: Béla Bartók.

Darwin, 52 min. Telemax Les Editions Audiovisuelles/Allarts coproduction with Antenne Deux/Channel Four/RAI Due, Telepool/Time Warner.

1993: *The Baby of Macon*, 118 min. Allarts coproduction with UGC–La Sept, in association with Cine Electra II/Channel Four/Filmstiftung Nordrhein Westfalen/Canal Plus. Produced by Kees Kasander and Denis Wigman. Cinematography: Sacha Vierny. Editor: Chris Wyatt. Production Design: Ben Van Os and Jan Roelfs. Cast: Daughter (Julia Ormond), Bishop's Son (Ralph Fiennes), Bishop (Philip Stone), Cosimo Medici (Jonathan Lacey), Father Confessor (Don Henderson).

Notes

Introduction

1. Elizabeth Butz, "*The Draughtsman's Contract*," *The USC Spectator* 6:12 (Spring 1986).

2. Marcia Pally, "Order vs. Chaos: The Films of Peter Greenaway," *Cineaste* 18:3 (1991), 3. Greenaway often cites John Ford's *'Tis Pity She's a Whore* as "responsible for [his] interest in both the beginning of the seventeenth century [the period of *Prospero's Books*] and the end [*The Draughtsman's Contract*]."

3. William F. Van Wert, "*The Cook, The Thief, His Wife and Her Lover*," *Film Quarterly* 44:2 (Winter 1990–91), 43.

4. Pally discusses Greenaway's penchant for trying to impose order on chaos; Hacker and Price point out the centrality of artists and issues of representation. Jonathan Hacker and David Price, *Take Ten: Contemporary British Film Directors* (New York: Oxford University Press, 1991).

5. Quoted in Pally, 6.

6. Quoted in Pally, 6. Borges seems especially apt as a fellow explorer of this encyclopedic territory, mapping an equally fantastical terrain. Borges had a notable fondness for the *Encyclopedia Britannica,* and his disquisition on the "Chinese encyclopedia" cited by Foucault and discussed in Chapter 1 comes from an essay on "The Analytic Language of John Wilkins." An obscure figure one might wish to read as fictional, Wilkins was (in classic Greenaway fashion) a seventeenth-century English philosopher who tried to devise a universal language. Martin S. Stabb points out that Borges thought "we only delude ourselves if we think of any language [or system] as describing all of reality's infinite bits and pieces," although both Borges and Greenaway seem to enjoy the idea of the world being "infinitely divisible." *Borges Revisited* (Boston: Twayne, 1991), 35. To bring the allusion full circle, Borges also turns up in *Performance* (see *Cook, Thief*), where "one of the characters, a gangster, is seen reading Borges's *Personal Anthology*." Emir Rodriguez Monegal, *Jorge Luis Borges: A Literary Biography* (New York: Dutton, 1978), 465–66.

7. Quoted in Pally, 6.

8. Harlan Kennedy, *Film Comment*, January–February 1982, quoted in Hacker and Price, 198.

9. Van Wert, 43.

10. Elsewhere he has said, "I believe there is only one truly great film-maker" who can stand on a level with Shakespeare and Rembrandt, "and that is Eisenstein" (quoted in Hacker and Price, 214–15).

11. Interview with the author.

12. Quoted in Hacker and Price, 217.

13. In repeating Kael's line Greenaway was quick to add, "I acknowledge the wit" (quoted in Hacker and Price, 213).

14. Quoted in Hacker and Price, 217.

15. Hacker and Price, 195.

16. Hacker and Price, 195.

17. Quoted in Adam Barker, "A Tale of Two Magicians," *Sight and Sound* 1:1 (May 1991), 28.

18. This line is actually from Resnais's *Providence* (1977).

19. Interview with the author.

20. Quoted in Hacker and Price, 191. Greenaway nevertheless defends games: "Some people . . . believe that game-playing is not compatible with serious film-making. Film-making itself is a complex game of illusion and bluff played between the film-maker and his audience" (192).

21. "The Draughtsman is a middling artist, capable of making a likeness but hardly very profound and not very intelligent. . . . The two behavioral scientists in *A Zed and Two Noughts* – again not particularly bright in the head. . . . And Stourley Kracklite [in *Belly*] is easily hoodwinked by the Italians. . . . I suppose the coroner in *Drowning by Numbers* in some sense is also part of that, a man who just cannot get it together. . . . And [in *Cook*] Albert Spica, of course, is a totally mediocre man through and through. He takes mediocrity to a high art form and uses it for terrifying ends because he's such a philistine." Quoted in Marlene Rodgers, "*Prospero's Books* – Word and Spectacle: An Interview with Peter Greenaway," *Film Quarterly* 45:2 (Winter 1991–92), 18.

22. Quoted in Rodgers, 18.

23. Quoted in Hacker and Price, 195.

24. From here on, all Greenaway quotations are from an interview with the author, except when noted otherwise.

25. Quoted in Hacker and Price, 208.

26. Quoted in Hacker and Price, 208–9.

27. Quoted in Hacker and Price, 209.

28. Quoted in Hacker and Price, 209. He adds, "I have tried to destroy every article."

29. Quoted in Hacker and Price, 209. Because he made mostly mock-documentaries in the seventies, when Greenaway makes *Four American Composers* for Channel Four Television, the "real" documentaries are nearly indistinguishable from the fakes. Real people (especially John Cage) tend to become Greenaway characters.

30. Quoted in Hacker and Price, 209.

31. For Greenaway, the opportunity to see avant-garde films "was a second course

in European cinema and maybe more valuable than the first for these were experimental, rarely seen, personal, and cheaply-made movies" (quoted in Hacker and Price, 209).

32. Leon Steinmetz and Peter Greenaway, *The World of Peter Greenaway* (Boston: Journey Editions, 1995), 5.

33. Greenaway in Steinmetz and Greenaway, 17.

34. Greenaway describes the film as "an ornithologist's journey through the short passage from death until the arrival of the next life" (in Steinmetz and Greenaway, 17).

35. Greenaway in Steinmetz and Greenaway, 17.

36. Hacker and Price, 189.

37. Peter Greenaway, "The Early Films of Peter Greenaway," pamphlet, ed. Liz Reddish (BFI Production, c. 1992), 2; quoted in Hacker and Price, 212. In an interview with the author, Greenaway also mentioned Italo Calvino, Buckminster Fuller ("a man who could speak for eight hours without hesitation"), and Thornton Wilder, whose *The Bridge of San Luis Rey* inspired *The Falls*. About Wilder's novel, Greenaway says, "It's an extraordinary story and it really sets up Borges himself. But it's also told, unlike Borges, with a great sense of emotion. [When one of the characters dies, it] brings tears to the eyes, even when you read it now. It's a story about loss, a great sense of fatalism. So beautifully written, so elegantly written. . . . It's one of the books that I read quite frequently, every two years. Nothing else he wrote [is] anywhere like it."

38. "For Greenaway the lists or classification systems are excellent demonstrations of the vain, absurd attempts to create an objectivity and meaning in the world. He acknowledges that they are necessary . . . but believes that we should be aware of just how shallow they are, and that art itself is another example of how we build up and enforce such systems" (Hacker and Price, 190).

39. Quoted in Hacker and Price, 199.

Chapter 1: *The Falls* (1980)

1. Ninety-two is the basic structural unit for the film (in homage, like *A Walk Through H,* to John Cage). It also appears within various stories. The names of the ninety-two least-well-known birds make up the lyrics of "The Bird Song" (composed by Castenarm Fallast #24 and sung by Pollie Fallory #74); Bewick Fallcaster #48 composed ninety-two variations on tinnitus; #64 (Thomax Fallfresh) watches ninety-two trains a week; #87 (Vassian Falluger) composes an opera of the ninety-two bird names; and there are 92 VUE languages.

2. Jorge Luis Borges, "The Analytical Language of John Wilkins," *Other Inquisitions,* trans. Ruth L. C. Simms (Austin: University of Texas Press, 1964), 103, quoted in Michel Foucault, *The Order of Things* (New York: Random House, 1970), xv. In the Simms translation, instead of "frenzied," item "i" is "those that tremble as if they were mad." Borges attributes his knowledge of this encyclopedia to "Dr. Franz Kuhn," who identifies it as the "Celestial Emporium of Benevolent Knowledge" (103). However, Borges's true subject is

John Wilkins. According to Borges, Wilkins "abounded in happy curiosities: he was interested in theology, cryptography, music, the manufacture of transparent beehives, the course of an invisible planet, the possibility of a trip to the moon, the possibility of the principles of a world language" begun by "divid[ing] the universe into forty categories or classes, which were then subdivisible into differences, subdivisible in turn into species" (101–2).

3. Foucault, xv.

4. Foucault, xv, xvi. "The monstrous quality that runs through Borges's enumeration consists . . . in the fact that the common ground on which such meetings are possible has itself been destroyed" (xvi).

5. Correspondence with the author.

6. Interview with the author.

7. Correspondence with the author.

8. "*The Falls* is presented in ninety-two different languages of which this is the most recent English version."

9. According to Greenaway, the COI "is, or was, the 'information' arm of the Foreign Office." Analogous to the USIA (the United States Information Agency), its job was to "tell the rest of the world about the British way of life – how many sheep-dogs there were in North Wales, how many Japanese restaurants in Ipswich" (quoted in Hacker and Price, 210).

10. The confusion over the Fallaris' alleged deaths resulted "no doubt . . . from Tulse Luper's fictional account of the Fallari life history." Being twins, Ipsan and Pulat share a life – their story is #16.

11. Though the narrator points out "there is some evidence to suggest that Squaline Fallaize is a fiction."

12. Betelgeuse is a "first-magnitude red giant star in the constellation Orion" (*Random House College Dictionary*, rev. ed. [1975], 129). Betelgeuse is one of the stars counted at the beginning of *Drowning by Numbers*, suggesting there could be as many languages as there are stars in heaven.

13. Bwythan Fallbutus #42, author of *A View from Babel*.

14. *Hapax Legomena* is a film by Hollis Frampton, a cinematic encyclopedist admired by Greenaway.

15. For instance, Pollie Fallory #74 was an actress who did bird imitations with fluttering gestures and a closed mouth. Now she does the definitive version of the Bird Song, her body rigid, her voice high-pitched. She also, we are told, does woman imitations.

16. Fallanx, Fallcaster, Fallcaster, Fallusson, and Fallqueue, respectively.

17. Number 18, Aptesia Fallarme (whose name evokes artesian wells) is the most shocking juxtaposition of women and water. Because water poured out of her every orifice, "in summer, she was asked to stand on bare spots in the garden." Demonstrating her talent at private parties, she would fill tub after tub with water until H. E. Carter, the documentary filmmaker, would run in with a dressing gown. Trying to make money from her VUE affliction, she granted a manufacturer of plastic swimming pools the right to use her name.

18. Icarus is referred to in #3, #12, #33 (Brueghel's *Death of Icarus*), and #36.

19. Greenaway points out that "Crow Films was indeed no fiction, but the name of the film and television company that traveled around Wales with me filming all

the Welsh victims. The van with Crow Films emblazoned on the side was no cheat" (correspondence with the author).

20. Creative geography is central to montage and montage-based avant-garde films such as Dmitri Kirsanoff's 1926 *Menilmontant*. Van Rickardt, "the French patriot and pioneer airman who threw himself from the Eiffel Tower in 1889," is identified as a linguist and a baritone in the choir of the "Lycée Nouvelle Menilmontant."

21. The hang-gliding Castel Fallboys (#36), shown sitting in a window (which puts him at immediate risk), is (figuratively) a direct descendant.

22. Several biographies intersect: the Fallbutus family (grandmother, son, daughter, and two granddaughters #40–#44), and the Fallcasters, including Bewick Fallcaster's wife, mother-in-law, brother-in-law, father-in-law, and Orian Fallcaster of the several name-changes (#48–#53).

23. Mothers in labor are especially important. Melorder is going to jump into the shadow of a building because his "mother began labor in that shadow and had to wait until it came round again before she was finished." In addition to the Boulder Orchard and The Raven on the Goldhawk Road, a maternity hospital is a third possible epicenter of the VUE.

24. A tape recording of his voice is heard on the soundtrack under the voice of the female translator. We never see or hear Constance.

25. Often it is women who stay grounded: Constance Fallabur and Clasper Fallcaster (#50), the fiftyish mother-in-law of Bewick Fallcaster. Melorder's fate seems dire – his brother-in-law is Rappaport Gull.

26. Constance thinks the VUE is a fabrication – or was it the story about the Eiffel Tower? Her favorite Tulse Luper story is "The Cassowary." As a plane flies overhead, everyone who looks at it is transformed into a bird – a swan, crows, swallows, gulls. Many thousands turn into penguins. At this point in *The Falls* we know that it is somehow important (and comically incongruous) that the filmmakers find it relevant to tell us what Constance's favorite Tulse Luper story is. Only later will we find that it is more her favorite *bird* story (in fact, that all Tulse Luper stories are bird stories) and that a fascination with things avian is a cultural by-product of the VUE. The idea of people turning into birds is presented at this point (#2) as highly fanciful.

27. Far and away the most attractive characters in the film, Ipsan, Pulat, and Stachia are glamorously young, energetic, and good-looking. Photographed in glossy black-and-white stills, like fashion models, the two bare-chested brothers sport long hair and shades, and flank the broad-faced Stachia smiling openly at the camera. The vividness of all three is a jolt amid the elaborate fantasies piling up around them. The sharp-focused photography, however, does little to make the brothers less interchangeable – we never do find out which is which. In the introduction to the published version of the script of *A Zed and Two Noughts,* Greenaway revealed that the photo was loaned to him by friends; it is actually a picture of the Brothers Quay, Stephen and Timothy (London: Faber & Faber, 1986, 13–14).

28. The spelling of "Gaspara" may be a mistake, the name being pronounced "Raspara" throughout the segment. The name appears as "Raspara" in the published version: Peter Greenaway, *The Falls* (Paris: Editions Dis Voir, 1993), 90.

29. Hitchcock was a favorite subject of structuralist film theorists. We do not see any images from *The Birds* or of Hitchcock himself, though the famous publicity still of Hitchcock with a crow perched on the end of his cigar would go well with the pseudonymous photo featuring Tippi Hedren as bird victim: the master of the hoax and the product of his work, a victimized woman.

30. Besides the crimes mentioned above, suspicious deaths crowd *The Falls:* people die but the authorities "can't say how" (Agostino Fallmutt #71). Geoffrey Fallthuis #83, a fan of Anton Webern, "fell or was pushed" from a balcony, while Crasstranger Fallqueue's relatives have a tendency to fall out of windows while in police custody (#78). Some crimes are merely indecipherable: Cole Fallbird #35 is awaiting trial for misconduct with a minor – or a mynah (it's hard to tell).

31. Suffering from phantom pregnancies (she has a picture of Queen Mary I in her room), La Solitaire demonstrates the struggle to subject reality to the imagination.

32. Not a Fall, Gull has a story that winds through the stories of others: he is identified as Melorder Fallabur's brother-in-law (#3), the godson of Lacer Fallacet (#7), the second custodian of the Boulder Orchard (#14), and a personal friend of Corntopia Fallas (#19). In the published version of *The Falls*, Greenaway spells the name Rapper Begol. The name "Rappaport Gull" is an example of the mis-hearing of words and names, known as "false homonyms" or "metanalysis."

33. The slides we see were taken by the vet who was sent to stalk and destroy the turkey with a shotgun. Carlos is now awaiting trial for shooting the vet.

34. Illegitimate (like T. E. Lawrence), Audubon had several names during his life. In addition to his accomplishments as a painter and naturalist, he also worked as a taxidermist.

35. The others provide alternative titles to describe stories from *The Falls:* "The Madras Lemonade Glass" (Stachia Fallari), "The Tyddyn-Corn Clout" (Menenome and Olivine Fallbutus), "The Dogs on Bardsey Island" (Lacer Fallacet), "Protest at The Golden Egg" (Mashanter Fallack), "The Wash-House Corpse" (Raskado Fallcastle), etcetera.

36. Greenaway identifies Luper as "first a literary device." "He manufactured a collage-book called 'Tulse Luper and the Centre Walk' where biography was reduced to diagrams examined under topographical headings." *Fear of Drowning* (Paris: Editions Dis Voir, 1988), 53.

37. People search far and wide for an actual Tulse Luper, or a historical precursor. The name "Tulse Luper" may even evoke T. E. Lawrence, philosopher, writer, man of mystery and world-roaming man of action, who lived under a pseudonym (and died with another). As he was illegitimate, he could be said not to have had "a name." Known best by his nickname/nom de guerre, Lawrence was a man of many interests and languages, adept at secret negotiations and betrayals, and best known by his most elaborate and patently fictitious identity as a blue-eyed Arab. Like Lawrence, Luper's well-established reputation may not stop him from using another name or appearing in disguise.

38. Peter Brunette and David Wills, *Screen/Play: Derrida and Film Theory* (Princeton, NJ: Princeton University Press, 1989), 64.

39. Some likely successors include *Drowning by Numbers* (represented here by Propine Fallax #27, a.k.a. "the third Cissie Colpitts"), and *A Zed and Two Noughts* (the swan attack recounted in #28, Cash Fallbaez).

40. Jorge Luis Borges, "The Library of Babel," in *Labyrinths: Selected Stories and Other Writings,* ed. Donald A. Yates and James E. Irby, trans. J.E.I. (New York: New Directions, 1964), 54.

41. In addition to Vladimir Nabokov's *Pale Fire,* recent fictitious works of criticism and fictional versions of scholarly investigations (examining authors who do not exist or creating elaborate fictions about those who do) would include Julian Barnes's *Flaubert's Parrot,* A. S. Byatt's *Possession,* Caroline Schine's *Rameau's Niece,* and Tom Stoppard's *Arcadia.* Greenaway himself is particularly fond of Thornton Wilder's *The Bridge of San Luis Rey,* "the only novel I've read encyclopedically ten times" (in Steinmetz and Greenway, 18).

42. Correspondence with the author. As of this moment, the only other edition is a novel in ninety-two chapters, based on the film's narration (Greenaway, *The Falls*).

Chapter 2: *The Draughtsman's Contract* (1982)

1. Hacker and Price, 198. Sainsbury also insisted the film be cut from its original four-hour running time to its current 110 minutes (199).

2. Brian MacFarlane, "Peter Greenaway (interview)," *Cinema Papers* 78 (March 1990): 44.

3. "After the political revolutions, the foreign expeditions and the French and Dutch expansionism of the seventeenth century, the dawning age will be one of peace at home and imperial consolidation. The gentry will embark on a regime of clearances and enclosures, agricultural innovation and 'improvement.'" Jill Forbes, "*Marienbad* revisited: *The Draughtsman's Contract,*" *Sight and Sound* 51:4 (Autumn 1982), 301.

4. Quoted in Rodgers, 18.

5. Quoted in Hacker and Price, 192.

6. Discussing mythical gardens with Mrs. Talmann, Neville tells her Gethsemane would have had "no geometric paths and no Dutch bulbs."

7. Greenaway cites "Truffaut's infamous, but not entirely unjustified, remark – 'To be an English film-maker is a contradictory term'" (correspondence with the author).

8. Hogarth worked primarily between the 1720s and 1764; Reynolds and Gainsborough, between roughly 1750 and 1790.

9. Karen Jaehne, "The Draughtsman's Contract: An Interview with Peter Greenaway," *Cineaste* 13:2 (1984): 14. The exceptions are meals, "when [the camera] slides slightly from side to side," Greenaway notes. "But that is the only time and it is extremely inorganic. It is a mechanical movement" (p. 14). Actually there is an exception: when Mr. Noyes stirs up Talmann's insecurities regarding his wife and Mr. Neville, they pace back and forth in the dark, tracked by a lateral pan. But given the lack of visual depth, and Noyes and Talmann's constant centering in the image, it is difficult to recognize the camera movement as such. The lateral pans across the long tables at mealtimes are one of Greenaway's most characteristic stylistic traits. He developed them to their most notable degree in *The Cook, The Thief, His Wife and Her Lover* (1989).

10. Quoted in Jaehne, 14.

11. Greenaway, quoted in Jaehne, 14.

12. Jaehne, 14. Greenaway notes that the dialogue is based "on the contemporary playwrights of the period, Sheridan, Congreve." It is also "very much aware of 20th century idioms [and] preconceived ideas of what that period sounded like" (p. 14).

13. Ronald Paulson, *Emblem and Expression: Meaning in English Art of the Eighteenth Century* (Cambridge, MA: Harvard University Press, 1975), 121. Another shot that evokes the more public aspect of the eighteenth-century conversation piece occurs when everyone has assembled outdoors to await the arrival of Mr. Herbert and to peruse Mr. Neville's completed work. Paulson notes that such "ceremonies that teeter between public and private are in fact the essence of the English conversation piece. . . . The three elements of greatest importance are the surroundings or native habitat, the relationships between the people and between them and their milieu, and the function of these elements to define" (p. 121).

14. Paulson, 122. In one example cited by Paulson, the husband ordered his wife's and his daughter's images eradicated from the painting and kept himself and his accountant emphatically present, balancing the left side of the frame through sheer will. (*Paulus Determeyer Weslingh and his Accountant* [1775] by Julius Quinkhard, reproduced on page 125.)

15. Paulson, 122.

16. Paulson, 123.

17. Paulson, 123. Paulson invokes garden imagery to situate the conversation piece: "This is not the Garden of Eden but the garden man makes for himself in the fallen world" (p. 123).

18. Reproduced in Paulson, 127.

19. He goes on to cite "Eric Rohmer's *The Marquise von O* and, to a certain extent, even Fellini's *Casanova*" (Jaehne, 13).

20. Paulson, 20. The English-style garden "was a return to what was thought to be the garden of the ancient Romans, the gardens of Hadrian." See *The Belly of an Architect* (London: Faber & Faber, 1987), 233 n. 3. "Allusion," Paulson notes, is "the most literary of the devices employed by the English [in their gardens]" (p. 20).

21. Forbes, 301.

22. Quoted in Hacker and Price, 195.

23. Quoted in Hacker and Price, 195.

24. In Greenaway's opinion, "Most mainstream cinema tends to glamorize, deodorize, romanticize, and sentimentalize. I'm very keen to not do those things. . . . Human relations are considerably harder and harsher, and much more to do with contracts" (quoted in Pally, 8).

25. Jaehne, 14. Greenaway continues: "There are three reasons for this. First, the facetious reason: paintings don't move. Secondly, with a still camera you throw the emphasis on the dialogue and soundtrack. . . . Thirdly, it is a sheer reaction to the St. Vitus dance of filmmaking over the last years. It seems to me that most camera work is done for no good structural reason, or even good emotional or mood reason" (p. 14).

26. Asked "Who did kill the master of the house?" Greenaway responds, "I could be enigmatic and throw the question back, but for me, everybody was respon-

sible, because everybody had reason to gain from the death of Mr. Herbert. So, like *The Murder on the Orient Express*, everybody is guilty" (Jaehne, 15).

27. Paulson, 22, 20.
28. Simon Schama, *The Embarrassment of Riches: An Interpretation of Dutch Culture in the Golden Age* (New York: Knopf, 1987), 331.
29. Schama, 332.
30. The full line is: "This precious stone set in the silver sea, / which serves it in the office of a wall, / or as a moat defensive to a house." William Shakespeare, *Richard II*, act 2, scene 1.
31. Greenaway expands: "Let us – and quite rightly – suppose Mrs. Talmann is extraordinarily aware of linguistic play and sexual double entendre in her local world where potency is essential and her husband impotent. Then she will know that the right-handed-dextrous/left-handed-sinister metaphor is played with – to incorporate innuendo of manual sexual foreplay of the human testicles as regards *testis* being the Latin for witness – the exhibition of the testicles to prove and be a witness not just to masculinity (a penis would supply this information) but potency in a world of not infrequent judicial castration – those passed the 'test' having the 'right' to apply to be a Roman senator or later a Roman Catholic cardinal . . . and she would know which testicle (though not through weight but a non-crush anatomical strategy) hangs lower than the other. She would also know that Mr. Neville is a knowing draughtsman of the human nude. We can see in the film that he draws the male nude statue in the garden – and we have seen the statue-figure/genius loci/priapic Pan draw attention to his sex by ostentatiously urinating as a fountain and later arranging his genitals to comply with orthodox standards of aesthetic genital exhibition. Mrs. Talmann would recognise the artistic tradition, from certainly the time of Hellenistic sculpture, that would hang the right (and therefore dextrous and therefore arrogant) testicle lower. It would be a characteristic of the drawing-what-I-see-not-what-I-know Mr. Neville to include such a nicety – undoubtedly too with a mixture of pride in masculine identity and not a little self-regarding exhibitionism" (correspondence with the author).
32. Schama, 424. Pomegranates have a rich metaphoric legacy. "Eat the pomegranate for it purges the system of envy and hatred" (Mohammed). "A fruit which bears open its breast and offers its entrails deserves to be crowned," quoted in Mario Praz, *Studies in Seventeenth Century Imagery*, 2nd ed. (Rome: Edizioni di Storia e Letteratura, 1964).
33. Women need to know how to control language and how to negotiate fertility, not only for the indirect access to power a male heir can provide but, as Mrs. Herbert implies, to protect and provide for their daughters as well.
34. Paulson, 23.
35. Hacker and Price, 192.

Chapter 3: *A Zed and Two Noughts* (1985)

1. Interview with the author.
2. Interview with the author.
3. Scott Bukatman calls Cronenberg "the most coldly analytical film-maker now

working (this side of Peter Greenaway, at least)" *Film Quarterly* 49:1 (Fall 1995): 60.

4. *Merriam-Webster's Collegiate Dictionary*, 9th ed. (Springfield, MA: Merriam-Webster, 1986), 1209.

5. Quoted in Hacker and Price, 218.

6. Quoted in Hacker and Price, 218.

7. Sung by Henry Hall and credited to the BBC dance orchestra at the end of the film, the original recording of this and "An Elephant Never Forgets" have a strong 1930s feel to them. As with the photos of Tulse Luper, Greenaway came across these recordings by chance. "In 1964 I bought a job-lot of 78 rpm gramophone-records from a shop in North London." That "very diverse collection" contained these songs as well as the Mozart Concertante for Violin, Viola and Orchestra that provided "the basis for the musical structure" for Michael Nyman's scores for *The Falls* and *Drowning by Numbers*. (*Fear of Drowning*, 125).

8. Quoted in Hacker and Price, 218.

9. Marcel Proust, quoted in a "Critical Anthology" arranged by Philippe Resche-Rigon in *Vermeer*, ed. Albert Blankert, John Michael Montias, and Gilles Aillaud (New York: Rizzoli, 1986), 216.

10. Vermeer's grandfather and uncle were arrested for counterfeiting. The ringleaders who had hired them were beheaded. John Michael Montias, *Vermeer and His Milieu: A Web of Social History* (Princeton, NJ: Princeton University Press, 1989), 17–34. Webern was shot on a balcony by a sniper at the end of WWII.

11. Pierre Descarges, *Vermeer*, trans. James Emmons (Geneva: Editions d'Art Albert Skira, 1966), 15.

12. Descargues presents this as P.T.A. Swillens's argument against the painting (p. 132).

13. According to Montias, these include *The Girl with a Pearl Earring, Girl Reading a Letter at an Open Window*, and two that Greenaway particularly cites, *The Music Lesson* and *The Lady with a Red Hat* (pp. 265–66).

14. Descargues, 15. Descargues also notes that the methods used with other Old Masters fail with Vermeer. "The result is that, as Vermeer studies proceed, the number of Vermeers, instead of growing, only dwindles" (p. 15).

15. Christopher Wright, *Vermeer* (London: Oresko Books, 1976), 69, 47.

16. Arthur K. Wheelock, Jr., *Jan Vermeer* (New York: Abrams, 1981). By 1995, the preferred name used in the major Vermeer exhibit at the National Gallery in Washington, D.C., was "Johannes" Vermeer.

17. Montias.

18. In order to get down to 23 or 26, you would need to eliminate the early *and* the later works. Descargues defends such draconian measures (although his personal count is much higher), arguing that "Vermeer himself, by the very nature of his art, encourages us to reject anything that does not come up to the highest standard" (p. 20).

19. In a collection of excerpts on Vermeer, Philippe Resche-Rigon writes, "There is something about the silent immobility of Vermeer's images that seems to defy description. The response to that implied challenge, the attempt to find works [*sic*, words?] to echo the mute power of the image, has in fact been one of the

more intriguing directions taken by modern literature in general" (p. 215). An example is French critic Paul Claudel, writing in 1946, who describes Vermeer as "someone who is perfect, rare, utterly exquisite, and if more adjectives are needed then they would be those that exist only in another tongue, 'eerie,' 'uncanny'" (quoted in Blankert, Montias, and Aillaud, 218).

20. Descargues, 13.

21. Thomas E. Benediktsson and Janet K. Cutler, "*A Zed and Two Noughts*," *Film Quarterly* 47:2 (Winter 1993–94), 38.

22. Vermeer's compositions often have tables or other objects interposed between the front plane of the image and the women in the background, giving the impression that some of the women are cut off at the waist or the knees (*Girl Asleep, Girl Reading a Letter, The Lacemaker, Mistress and Maid*). Some women are shown full figure, seated (*The Glass of Wine*) or standing or, as in the three-figure *The Concert*, both.

23. *The Procuress* appears in *The Concert* and in *Young Woman Seated at a Virginal*. Edward Snow, *A Study of Vermeer*, revised and enlarged ed. (Berkeley: University of California Press, 1994), 188 n. 1.

24. Benediktsson and Cutler, 38. In the original painting, the fuzziness of the artist's hair and the vividness of the black and white stripes (linking him with Venus and the zebras) is nearer photorealism than anything else in Vermeer's work. Perhaps this is why Greenaway redesigns the work as an allegory of photography, with the artist as a photographer and not a painter. His Van Meegeren is bald.

25. Greenaway, *Prospero's Books* (New York: Four Walls, Eight Windows, 1991), 83.

26. Wheelock, 48, 47. Though, given the circumstances, Van Meegeren might have lied.

27. Wright, 57.

28. *Mistress and Maid* (a.k.a. *Lady with a Maidservant, Maid Handing a Letter to Her Mistress*, etc., c. 1667–68) is not to be confused with *The Love Letter*, in which a maid also hands a letter to a woman in yellow. (Nor is it *Woman Writing a Letter with Her Maid*.) This composition is tighter and more intimate.

29. For instance, Edward Snow so loves *Soldier and Young Girl Smiling*, he suggests that after Vermeer painted it, he spent the rest of his career compelled "to lose everything that is discovered in this painting, so that eventually it might be found again, transformed" (p. 90).

30. Even the punctilious Montias ventures a guess for love. After painstakingly establishing that Catharina Bolnes was a good match for Vermeer, he notes that all his research "still leaves Catharina's motivation unaccounted for. . . . Would it be unseemly to suggest that it was the force of love that attracted her to him?" (p. 100).

31. Weschler argues, "It's almost as if Vermeer can be seen, amid the horrors of his age, to have been asserting or *inventing* the very idea of peace" (p. 59). Weschler sees Vermeer's work as a fanfare for humanism, something that is not Greenaway's project at all ("Inventing Peace," *The New Yorker*, November 20, 1995, 56–64).

32. Weschler, 59.

33. Quoted in Hacker and Price, 218.
34. Benediktsson and Cutler, 38. For the concept of Vermeer as a master of the split second, we are led back to Weschler, discussing Snow's analysis of *Head of a Young Girl*: "Has the girl just turned toward us or is she just about to turn away?. . . . Such immanence . . . is of its essence. . . . The answer is that she's actually doing both. This is a woman who has just turned toward us and is already about to look away: and the melancholy of the moment, with its impending sense of loss, is transferred from her eyes to the tearlike pearl dangling from her ear. It's an entire movie in a single frozen image. . . . The speculation among some critics that Vermeer's model for this image may have been his daughter renders the conceit all the more poignant" (pp. 59–62). In a lecture on Vermeer, Greenaway quotes Godard: "Cinema is truth 24 frames a second."
35. Benediktsson and Cutler, 38.
36. Greenaway on cinematographer Sacha Vierny: "He is a brilliant cameraman. . . . The more he is encouraged to be experimental, the more excited he becomes. . . . He made a rainbow in [*Zed*] that competed with the sun" (quoted in Hacker and Price, 220).
37. Quoted in Hacker and Price, 216.
38. Quoted in Hacker and Price, 218.
39. As mythological creatures, Venus and Felipe are depicted behind bars in the zebra cage as they discuss their mythological zoo.
40. Benediktsson and Cutler, 36.
41. Greenaway's "initial inspiration" came from "the Oxford Scientific Unit whose specialised natural history footage I had often used in documentaries at the COI. [They] once showed me some material they had taken of common-fly grubs consuming a mouse carcase. They, and I, were truly fascinated by a phenomenon – not appreciated before and revealed only by the single-frame camera – one frame every five seconds – that the grubs worked in a close formation, 'grazing' on the mouse flesh methodically, making use of their combined enzyme-slime for decomposing the animal. I remember the biologist's remark that 'they rummage around the inside of the mouse like a tightly-packed herd of grazing elephants'. . . . I truly think this short piece of footage – perhaps 40 seconds – coupled with the biologist's remark, set me off to think of the possibilities of filming the decay of an elephant." As it happens, "no elephant appears in *A Zed and Two Noughts* – the plot demanded a different animal" (correspondence with the author).
42. Greenaway also made a film about decomposing dogs: "An early film called *Erosion*, filmed in Western Ireland in 1971, featured a number of dog-corpses washed up on beaches and thrown over cliffs. It gave rise to the story of the Photographer's Dog used in *The Falls* – Biography 7 – Lacer Fallacet" (correspondence with the author).
43. This is not a negative view of nature. In *Fear of Drowning*, Greenaway points out that "Insects – like snails – are instruments for turning decay into life" (p. 49).

Chapter 4: *Drowning by Numbers* (1988)

1. Quoted in Rodgers, 15.
2. Quoted in Rodgers, 15.

3. Quoted in Hacker and Price, 220.
4. Greenaway obligingly lists where all the numbers can be found in his book *Fear of Drowning* (pp. 25–31), although he warns that the list "is not definitive."
5. Quoted in Hacker and Price, 216.
6. Cissie Colpitts "was invented around 1976 for Tulse Luper," Greenaway notes. "She had to be his equal in wit and irony – someone to tell him that his conceits were making him conceited and his cleverness was making him smug" (*Fear of Drowning,* 53, 55).
7. The script of *Drowning by Numbers* "was originally intended to evoke the flat landscape of East Yorkshire – along the River Humber from Goole to Spurn Head where there are forty-seven water-towers in twelve miles" (*Fear of Drowning,* 75). Goole, in particular, "features in a lot of the movies. It's a town of water towers because the water pressure's so bad." Greenaway's wife is from Yorkshire; his maternal grandmother "is seventy percent of the model for the eldest Cissie Colpitts" (p. 41).
8. According to *The Falls,* "despite the serious attempts to amalgamate them into one person, there have in fact been three Cissie Colpitts in Goole since 1931." The first "was President of the Goole Water Tower film vault" and most likely knew "the Yorkshire cameramen who made up the Goole Experimental Film Society." (*Goole by Numbers* [1976] and *1–100* [1978] are also obvious forerunners to *Drowning by Numbers* among Greenaway's early short films.)
9. "Sylph," *Random House College Dictionary,* rev. ed. (1975), 1331.
10. Michael Walsh, "Allegories of Thatcherism: The Films of Peter Greenaway," in Lester Friedman, ed., *Fires Were Started: British Cinema and Thatcherism* (Minneapolis: University of Minnesota Press, 1993), 269. Walsh argues that *Drowning by Numbers* "makes ceremonials out of obsessional material, that it plays games with obsessional material, that it runs rings around obsessional material," and has "a comic and detailed awareness of its own concerns" (p. 268). In his comparison between Greenaway and psychoanalytic studies of obsessionals, Walsh describes how "the obsessional [Madgett in particular] devotes his life to death; he expresses the contradictions entailed in an effort to ally himself with death both by believing he cannot die and by waiting for death, systematically temporizing with his rituals and ceremonials, his counting and collecting" (p. 269).
11. Quoted in Hacker and Price, 210.
12. Describing a drawing of this scene (reproduced in Steinmetz and Greenaway, *The World of Peter Greenaway,* fig. 69), Greenaway notes: "Smut is bowled at by his left-handed (sinister) father, and the trajectory of the ball . . . is presently aimed at his son's heart." Following several biblical allusions, he points out that the boy in his drawing "does not even have a bat with which to defend himself" and asks, "Are fathers habitual bowlers of hard balls to damage their sons' self-esteem? My father called it a toughening-up process to prepare you for the hard knocks of the world where most of the umpires will not shout 'Foul!' unless rewarded" (Steinmetz and Greenaway, 69).
13. This is Rubens's *Samson and Delila.* The runners #70 and #71 introduce themselves as Van Dyke.
14. Quoted in Hacker and Price, 216.

15. Walsh, 270. According to Walsh, Madgett's failure with women should come as no surprise: the obsessional "self is barred from genital achievement by its fixation on mortality" (p. 270).

16. To continue the Cissie Colpitts saga, Greenaway proposes "a nine-part television series," a "prequel" to be called *Fear of Drowning*. "Each episode would increase in length, starting at twenty minutes and increasing by five-minute increments until the 115-minute *Drowning by Numbers*" (*Fear of Drowning*, 125). The scenarios for each episode are outlined in the book *Fear of Drowning*, 125–47.

Chapter 5: *The Belly of an Architect* (1986)

1. "The Piazza del Popolo is the work of Giuseppe Valadier, who laid it out between 1816 and 1820, from designs on which he had already started work in 1784" (shortly before the death of Boullée). "On the south side, opposite the church of S. Maria del Popolo, are the twin churches of S. Maria di Monte Santo and S. Maria Dei Miracoli . . . commissioned from Carlo Rainaldi by Pope Alexander VII in 1660." Christopher Hibbert, *Rome: The Biography of a City* (New York: Norton, 1985), 350. Piranesi's dramatically angled view of the twin churches in the piazza has an obelisk separating them. Greenaway's shot has no obelisk.

2. "It was too expensive. There were various other reasons – because I had a Dutch producer, because we had Dutch money, because the circumstances of using a Dutch location [made it] much easier" to make the film there instead (interview with the author).

3. Interview with the author.

4. "It's so Henry Jamesian, the naive, pioneering, blustering American who goes to the old world and gets completely controlled and manipulated" (Greenaway, quoted in Rodgers, 18).

5. Quoted in Hacker and Price, 220.

6. See James Naremore, *Acting in the Cinema* (Berkeley: University of California Press, 1988).

7. Quoted in Hacker and Price, 220.

8. Jean-Claude Lemagny, *Visionary Architects: Boullée, Ledoux, Lequeu* (Houston: University of St. Thomas, 1968), 16.

9. Lemagny, 16.

10. Dominique de Menil, "Foreword," in Lemagny, 11.

11. De Menil, 11.

12. Lemagny, 16.

13. De Menil, 11.

14. *The Compact Edition of the Oxford English Dictionary*, vol. 1, A–O, 365.

15. Lemagny, 26, 20.

16. Lemagny, 36.

17. Interview with the author.

18. Etienne-Louis Boullée, "Architecture, Essay on Art," trans. Sheila de Vallée, in Helen Rosenau, *Boullée and Visionary Architecture* (London: Academy Editions, 1974), 86.

19. Boullée, 87.
20. Boullée, quoted in Lemagny, 16–17.
21. "Boullée also exerted a specific influence, as recorded in Speer's book, on the Nazi period" (Rosenau, 26). For Rosenau, Boullée's imposing structures "can be regarded as 'megalomaniac,' expressing civil and collective relationships, rather than the individualism of the rising bourgeois classes" (Rosenau, 27).
22. Jean-Marie Pérouse de Montclos, *Etienne-Louis Boullée: Theoretician of Revolutionary Architecture,* trans. James Emmons (New York: Braziller, 1974), 44.
23. Correspondence with the author.
24. Correspondence with the author.
25. In a 1990 interview Greenaway identified David Lynch as his "favourite filmmaker west of the English Channel" – "I thought *Blue Velvet* was a masterpiece" (Hacker and Price, 212).
26. The model does not resemble Boullée's lighthouse as much as the "circular building" (Rosenau 79), the "truncated cone-shaped tower" (Lemagny 36–37), and the "Project for a Spiral Tower" (Pérouse de Montclos, pl. 99). It looks mostly like a smokestack.
27. According to Francesco Furrieri and Judith Chatfield, "antique sources identify [the statue, located in the Boboli Gardens in Florence] as a portrait of Pietro Barbino." Barbino "was a dwarf much beloved of the court of Cosimo I as he was clever, and known for his literary talents and his kindness." However, contemporary sources feel that the sculptor, Valerio Cioli da Settignano, "would not have depicted Barbino as such a ridiculous figure." The 1560 figure (which is also a fountain) is also called "Bacchus." *Boboli Gardens* (Florence: Editrice Edam, 1972), 37.
28. "For a time," Greenaway states, "I wanted to be a critic like Raymond Durgnat." He pursued this vocation "by writing totally unreadable articles like 'The Relationship between Chirico and Resnais.'" He adds, "I have tried to destroy every article" (Hacker and Price, 209).
29. Boullée, 107.
30. Boullée, 107. "It would be erroneous to class Boullée with the Romantics, since his individualism was based on a reasoned appreciation of function and ruled by the recognition of the laws of nature, founded on Newton's theories" (Rosenau 28).
31. Pérouse de Montclos summarizes Boullée's attitudes thus: "The most beautiful of natural bodies is the sphere, which combines the most perfect symmetry with the widest variety, for its surface is enhanced by the subtlest gradations of light" (p. 38).
32. Hacker and Price, 202 n. 38.
33. Rodgers, 17.
34. Rosenau, 20–21.
35. There is a tendency to discuss Boulée via comparisons with other artists. Carter Ratcliff notes that Joseph Cornell's affinity with Boullée can be seen in his use of architectural elements, for instance, in his preference for "domes instead of columns" (p. 43). And like Boullée's cenotaph, Cornell's "works, whether explicitly astronomical or not, tend with a dreamy restlessness to draw infinity inside their narrow confines" (p. 43). Cornell has many other interests in common

with Greenaway, including birds, maps, postcards, old photographs, lists, sixteenth- and seventeenth-century Dutch masters, and astronomy. "Joseph Cornell, Mechanic of the Ineffable," in Kynaston McShine, ed., *Joseph Cornell* (New York: Museum of Modern Art, 1980), 60.

36. Pérouse de Montclos, 28. To underscore the connection between Boullée and Piranesi, Lemagny points out that Boullée's work "shows the influence of Legeay, a disciple of Piranesi, or perhaps a rival" (p. 16). De Montclos tells us that Jean-Laurent Legeay was Boullée's second teacher (p. 27). "In urging his pupils to complete [their projects] with a perspective drawing, Legeay ... created the link which had been lacking between the architect and the architectural painter" (pp. 28–29).
37. Richard Rand and John Varriano, *Two Views of Italy: Master Prints by Canaletto and Piranesi* (Hanover, NH: Dartmouth College; Hood Museum of Art, 1995), 53.
38. Pérouse de Montclos, 37. Ratcliff describes Piranesi's aesthetic as "the picturesque of spiritual homelessness" (p. 60).
39. Quoted in Hacker and Price, 207.
40. Rand and Varriano, 53.
41. Rosenau, 20. She dates the *Carceri* as 1760, the *Antichita Romane* as 1756.
42. Ratcliff, 60. This description is equally apt for many scenes in *Prospero's Books*.
43. Rand and Varriano, 59.
44. Hacker and Price identify the number 7 as important in the film (p. 204 n. 39).
45. Claudine Isé, "Black and Light: Madness and the Cogito in *The Story of Adele H.,*" *The USC Spectator* 12:1 (Fall 1991), 19.
46. Derrida's *The Post Card* shares many concerns with Greenaway's work. On the back cover, Derrida writes, "This satire of epistolary literature had to be ... stuffed with addresses, postal codes, crypted missives, anonymous letters, all of it confided to so many modes, genres, and tones. In it I also abuse dates, signatures, titles or references, language itself" (Chicago: University of Chicago Press, 1987).
47. Isé, 20.
48. Peter Brunette and David Wills, summarizing Derrida in *Screen/Play: Derrida and Film Theory*, 61.
49. "Madness appears as a rupture or a breakdown in the discourse, and for Derrida these ruptures are an inevitable product of [the Subject's] attempt to appear coherent and unitary rather than fragmented and disseminative" (Isé, 19).
50. Isé, summarizing Derrida, 20.
51. Ratcliff, 60.
52. Susan Buck-Morss, quoting Adorno's *Uber Walter Benjamin. The Dialectics of Seeing: Walter Benjamin and the Arcades Project* (Cambridge, MA: MIT Press, 1990), 58.
53. Buck-Morss, 160.
54. Greenaway writes, "This nose-stealer was real. I appropriated him from a newspaper article." In the catalogue for the 1996 exhibit "Spellbound" at the Hayward Gallery in London, the newspaper story is reproduced under the title "Sad Nose" (correspondence with the author).
55. Rodgers, 18.
56. Buck-Morss, 111.

57. Rodgers, 17.
58. Rodgers, 18.
59. Rosenau, 27. As an architectural term, *enceinte* can mean an enclosure; popularly, it refers to pregnancy. *Carceri* can also mean enclosures or enclosed spaces; popularly, it is translated as a reference to a prison. See William L. MacDonald, *Piranesi's* Carceri: *Sources of Invention* (Northampton, MA: Smith College, 1979), 23–24.
60. Hibbert, 368–69.

Chapter 6: *Prospero's Books* (1991)

1. Greenaway, *Prospero's Books*, 9.
2. Greenaway, *Prospero's Books*, 9.
3. Greenaway, *Prospero's Books*, 43.
4. J. L. Austin, *How to Do Things with Words* (Cambridge, MA: Harvard University Press, 1962).
5. Walter J. Ong, *Orality and Literacy: The Technologizing of the Word* (New York: Methuen, 1982), 31.
6. Ong, 32. Ong also notes that sound cannot stop, can only exist in time, and cannot be dissected as sound and still exist in an aural dimension (p. 32).
7. Ong, 37. He cites 1610 specifically; *The Tempest* was written in 1611, when *Prospero's Books* is set. For Ong, the traces of an "oral culture" continued "roughly until the age of Romanticism or even beyond" (p. 41).
8. Ong, 45.
9. Ong, 117.
10. Ong, 31.
11. Barker, 28.
12. Ong, 32.
13. Ong, 43–44.
14. Ong, 55. While James Clifford and others have taken exception to many of Ong's positions, his arguments seem particularly apt in relation to Prospero's use of speech and the written word.
15. Ong, 59.
16. See Ong, 31, 33–36.
17. Ong, 33.
18. Michel Foucault, on psychiatrists listening to madmen who are defined by their speech, in *The Archaeology of Knowledge and the Discourse on Language*, trans. A. M. Sheridan Smith (New York: Pantheon Books, 1972), 217.
19. Harold Bloom, *The Anxiety of Influence* (New York: Oxford University Press, 1973).
20. Greenaway, *Prospero's Books*, 9. Greenaway repeats this in somewhat different form in an interview with Adam Barker: "There is a deliberate amalgamation or confusion between Shakespeare, Gielgud and Prospero – they are, in effect, the same person" (Barker, 29).
21. Greenaway has often mentioned Resnais as one of the few filmmakers he respects, although when it comes to *Providence* his attitude is one of regretful disappointment, at best (conversation with the author).

22. James Naremore, *The Magic World of Orson Welles* (New York: Oxford, 1978), 279. Naremore argues that Welles's film "contains some of the most beautiful readings of Shakespeare ever recorded for film – especially in the case of Gielgud's soliloquies." He singles out "Henry IV's celebrated speech on sleep, for example" (pp. 278–79). Gielgud's speech has an unusual amount of vibrato, more commonly found in singing.

23. Dirk Bogarde, *An Orderly Man* (London: Chatto & Windus/The Hogarth Press, 1983), 235.

24. A third valedictory film built around Gielgud is Kenneth Branagh's somewhat maudlin short film *Swan Song* (1994).

25. Barker, 29.

26. Ong, 40–41.

27. Barker, 29.

28. Rodgers, 15. At one point in his script Greenaway asks us to attend as the ink dries (p. 63).

29. Bogarde, 235.

30. Roland Barthes, "The Death of the Author," *Image-Music-Text,* trans. Stephen Heath (New York: Hill & Wang, 1977).

31. Bogarde writes that when he saw the film at its French premiere, "it made me laugh, much to the anger of some of the French press who hissed at me furiously like geese, thinking, I suppose, that I was being irreverent" (p. 240).

32. Bogarde, 232–33.

33. Greenaway, *Prospero's Books,* 9.

34. Greenaway, *Prospero's Books,* 8. All subsequent references are to this edition.

35. The film's credited calligrapher is Brody Neuenschwander.

36. Some or all of these tropes are also present in the illustrations on pages 10–11, 18–19, 22–23, 34–35.

37. Greenaway argues that "the image-manipulation" made possible by this technology goes beyond mere "collage. For the paintbox can change the shape, form, contrast, colour, tone, texture, ratio and scale of any given material" (p. 28).

38. He describes the result as "a nicely tuned conceit to illuminate the role of deception . . . practiced by a playwright . . . and maybe by a film-maker in the manufacture of cinema, and maybe indeed practised by a film-maker in his description of the manufacture of an image" (p. 33).

39. The Juggler as "a naked bright-orange bacchante with wide hips who juggled balls and fruit, scientific instruments and defenseless small animals." She "juggled figures" for Sycorax, having been the witch's "book-keeper, her cabbalistic counter, her numbers advocate" (p. 29). She eventually switched to juggling "mathematical solids," "indication . . . if by now indication is needed – of The Juggler's original role as Sycorax's numerologist and geometrician" (pp. 29, 33).

40. Kircher's pyramids are reminiscent of the visionary architecture of Boullée. Greenaway captions the illustration as suggesting "the observations of an academic relying on travellers' tales" (p. 98).

41. "This framing and re-framing becomes like the text itself – a motif – reminding the viewer that it is all an illusion constantly fitted into a rectangle . . . into a picture frame, a film frame" (p. 12).

42. Barker, 29.

43. Foucault, *The Order of Things*, 47. "Every episode, every decision, every exploit will be yet another sign that Don Quixote is a true likeness of all the signs that he has traced from his book." For Foucault, a figure caught in a world of texts is compelled to live them out: "It is incumbent upon him to fulfil [*sic*] the promise of the books" (p. 47). Many critics have found Foucault especially relevant in discussions of Greenaway, perhaps nowhere more so than in this film. Two examples should suffice: first would be Foucault's "relentless exposure of 'the author' and 'the subject' as romantic and regulatory fictions"; second is Foucault's "insistence on 'truth' as the effect of a system of exclusions, as the product of a discourse that defines what can and cannot be said" – in other words, discourse, "that rich and vexing term which enables Foucault to convey how power works *as* knowledge, how language . . . actually constructs and positions us in terms of a panoply of social norms and perversions" (Wendy Brown, "Jim Miller's Passions. A Review," *differences* 5:2 [1994], 147).
44. Barthes, 146. My emphasis.
45. Peter Wollen, "The Last New Wave," in Friedman, ed., *Fires Were Started: British Cinema and Thatcherism*, 45.
46. Wollen, 45.
47. Stephen Greenblatt, *Shakespearean Negotiations: The Circulation of Social Energy in Renaissance England* (Berkeley: University of California Press, 1988), 137.
48. Greenblatt, 135–36.
49. Greenblatt, 135.
50. Greenblatt, 133.
51. Correspondence with the author.
52. See Brian Henderson, "Towards a Non-Bourgeois Camera Style," in *Film Theory and Criticism*, 2d ed., ed. Gerald Mast and Marshall Cohen (New York: Oxford University Press, 1979), 832–47.
53. Foucault, *The Order of Things*, 46.
54. Even the film's choreography mimics Deleuze's description of "the Baroque dance in which the dancers are automata" (p. 68).
55. Correspondence with the author.
56. *Encyclopedia Britannica*, 784.
57. Gilles Deleuze, *The Fold: Leibniz and the Baroque*, trans. Tom Conley (Minneapolis: University of Minnesota Press, 1993), 68. Deleuze also identifies Prospero as "the Mannerist hero par excellence" (p. 67).
58. Deleuze, 68, 67.
59. Deleuze, 67–68.
60. Deleuze, 125. My emphasis.

Chapter 7: *The Cook, The Thief, His Wife and Her Lover* (1989)

1. Interview with Gary and Martin Kemp, *Interview*, November 1990.
2. *Interview*.
3. Georgia Brown, "Mum's the Word," *Village Voice*, November 13, 1990.
4. Andrew Alderson, "The real story of the Krays and Tory peer," *Sunday Times*, August 8, 1993, p. 1.

5. Brown.

6. John McVicar, "Violence Is Golden," 20/20 (London), December 1989.

7. *Interview.*

8. Brown.

9. In both *Performance* and *The Krays* the characters are eager to improve their financial position without trying to change class. These gangsters dress to fit in *and* to stand out, being trendsetters in the new post-1950s consumer culture. Chas in particular uses his clothes to prove that he is as good as his "betters" while maintaining his accent to prove he is not in awe of them and does not want to be them.

10. Nita Rollins, "Greenaway–Gaultier: Old Masters, Fashion Slaves," *Cinema Journal* 35:1 (1995), 68.

11. Rollins, 72.

12. Rollins, 75.

13. Correspondence with the author.

14. Rollins points out that most theoretical sources on fashion (Veblen, etc.) have no way of accounting for the appeal of "downward mobility" in fashion (pp. 67–68).

15. Michael Walsh mentions Spica's surprising "sanctimoniousness" in constantly checking on whether or not Georgina has washed her hands after using the toilet (p. 275). The particular prevalence of homosexuality in British gangster films is probably attributable to the Krays. Openly gay at a time when it was still illegal, Ronnie Kray is reported to have once said, "I am not a poof. I am a homosexual" (McVicar). In 1993 (after the film *The Krays* was released), it was revealed that the special protection the Krays enjoyed from the police was in part due to a relationship Ronnie had had with a member of the House of Lords, ironically a prominent Conservative. "The gangster twins were able to forge Britain's biggest and most violent crime empire relatively unhindered, until they were finally convicted of murder in 1969" (Alderson, 1). Following the Krays, homosexuality became central to British gangster films in ways not seen in American films. This cannot be attributed solely to changing times in films of the 1980s; it is already present in *Performance* in 1970. When Chas offers to go after the bookie Joey, Flowers yells at him to "keep personal relations out of business. Your relationship with Joey was double personal, right?" Although they are never explained, references to homosexual relationships permeate the organization. When his shop is "redecorated" (smashed up), Joey says he'd "give a grand to have that Harry-pervert-Flowers here right now." (Chas arrives and asks, "Will I do?") When Joey ambushes Chas in Chas's apartment, he has written POOF on the wall in red paint, and tortures Chas to make him "say it." As the gang gathers to figure out what to do with Chas once he has killed Joey, Harry is in bed. A youth in a towel is in his bathroom, a photo of two nude young men on a nearby dresser. Despite the routine use of homophobic slurs (poof, pervert, fairy, etc.), the hypermasculinity of the gang coexists rather comfortably within a homosocial as well as a homosexual setting, as it does in *The Krays*. Mary Desjardins discusses homophobia in *The Krays* in "Free from the Apron Strings," in Friedman, ed., *Fires Were Started.*

16. Le Hollandais re-creates a familiar triumvirate. French and Dutch and British,

as with L'Escargot in *A Zed and Two Noughts,* Le Hollandais joins in a word food, country, and home (Alba's country estate, Albert and Richard's contested restaurant). Van Wert points out, "What is English in this film is both Jacobean revenge tragedies and Margaret Thatcher's England; what is Dutch in the film is both the preponderance of gifted portrait painters and table painters as well as the name of the restaurant as well as an allusion to Kees Kasander and the Dutch connection Greenaway has established. What is French in this film is both the refinement of cuisine, aspired to but never reached, as well as the barbarism of the French Revolution and its ensuing reign of terror, exemplified by Michael's books" (p. 48).

17. *A Shock to the System* (1990) is another Thatcher-era film where murder is business-as-usual in the corporate world.

18. Greenaway had not seen *Performance* or several of the other films discussed here when he made *The Cook, The Thief* (correspondence with the author).

19. He adds, "Watch [Lindsay] Anderson's *If . . .* and [Peter] Brook's *Lord of the Flies* for confirmation" (correspondence with the author).

20. *Performance* equates gangster tactics with government tactics (something explicit in *The Long Good Friday*). Chas tells the Pakistani owner of a pornographic cinema, "I don't think I'm gonna let you stay in the film business," as he kicks him in the groin and takes his money. The owner comments, "British justice," as we cut to a grainy black-and-white image on the screen, showing two men about to whip a woman's exposed backside.

21. Greenaway wrote the characters with actors in mind and kept their names when the casting changed. Albert is named for Albert Finney (Greenaway's first choice for the role), who would play an American-style gangster in the Coen brothers' film *Miller's Crossing* (1990). Surprisingly, Michael, the bookworm, was designed for Michael Gambon.

22. Walsh, 272–73.

23. Van Wert, 43.

24. Van Wert, 44. Other 1960s playwrights come to mind as well: the scabrous John Osborne (*Look Back in Anger*); the absurdism of Joe Orton, as well as the menace of early Pinter (the casual thugs wandering through *The Caretaker* and *The Birthday Party;* and the combination of fear, control, and abuse of women in *The Homecoming* and *Accident*). Spica can be seen as the middle-aged spread of the Angry Young Man, Jimmy Porter gone posh, Arthur Seaton of *Saturday Night and Sunday Morning* with power, a Ted triumphant.

25. Kaja Silverman points out how "perversion" in general subverts "many of the binary oppositions upon which the social order rests." *Male Subjectivity at the Margins* (New York: Routledge, 1992), 187.

26. Violence against women has provided shock value in gangster films from the time James Cagney shoved a grapefruit in a woman's face in the American *Public Enemy* (1930) to John Hurt's slugging a hysterical female hostage in Stephen Frears's *The Hit* (1984) – which also served as a comeback vehicle for 1960s star Terence Stamp.

27. Correspondence with author.

28. Rollins, 70–71. Rollins quotes Thorstein Veblen on why women wear couture: the woman "does not perform this wasteful expenditure and undergo this dis-

ability for her own personal gain in pecuniary repute, but in behalf of someone else to whom she stands in a relation of economic dependence." Thorstein Veblen, *The Theory of the Leisure Class* (London: Allen & Unwin, 1957), 180–82.

29. Van Wert identifies this shot as being based on "Masaccio's *The Expulsion of Adam and Eve*" (p. 47).

30. In the theatre, Christopher Bond's version of *Sweeney Todd,* about a barber who, abused by authority, cuts his customers' throats and feeds the remains to a salivating public, appeared in 1973 and was made into a musical by Stephen Sondheim in 1977. Sondheim noted that Bond's version had "elements from Jacobean tragedy." Director Harold Prince defines Todd in terms that would fit Spica: impotence and rage. Quoted in Craig Zadan, *Sondheim and Co.,* 2nd ed. (New York, Harper & Row, 1989), 243, 245. *Sweeney Todd*'s Industrial Revolution setting is echoed in *Cook, Thief*'s kitchen set, its cavernous factory-level scale suggesting the machinery behind the studiedly "posh" Old World elegance of the restaurant, and in Michael Nyman's score with its rhythmically striking anvil. Walsh mentions the kitchen set in particular when pointing out that through its horizontal tracking shots "the film reminds us that we are looking at a studio space temporarily and yet thoroughly made over into a restaurant; this is linked with a 1980s economy of consumption and entertainment in which fashionably transitory restaurants actually did colonize studio-like spaces, often staying in them for a period only slightly longer than the production of a film" (p. 274).

31. Greenaway notes: "The isolated sprig is a sprig of rosemary for remembrance – of Michael," adding that rosemary is "an ideal seasoning for pork with which the cooked human body, I am told, is the closest to be compared" (correspondence with the author).

32. Rollins, 71. Rollins vividly compares Greenaway's depiction of the mortal, aging body to fashion (pp. 71–72).

33. Walsh, 270. Greenaway's style distances us not only from violence but also from the nudity that becomes more pervasive in his films (*A TV Dante, M Is for Music, Man, Mozart, Prospero's Books*).

34. Quoted in Hacker and Price, 213. Greenaway adds, "There is a Coleridge quote – 'What excites us to artificial feelings makes us callous to real ones.' I hold in regard the notion of 'passionate detachment'" (correspondence with the author).

Selected Bibliography

The bibliography on Greenaway in Hacker and Price (pp. 226–27) is especially useful for early coverage of Greenaway's work in British newspapers and journals.

Austin, J. L. *How to Do Things with Words.* Cambridge, MA: Harvard University Press, 1962.

Barker, Adam. "A Tale of Two Magicians." *Sight and Sound* 1, no. 1 (May 1991): 27–30.

Barthes, Roland. "The Death of the Author." In *Image-Music-Text.* Trans. Stephen Heath. New York: Hill & Wang, 1977, pp. 142–48.

Benediktsson, Thomas E., and Janet K. Cutler. "*A Zed and Two Noughts.*" *Film Quarterly* 47, no. 2 (Winter 1993–94): 36–42.

Blankert, Albert, John Michael Montias, and Gilles Aillaud, eds. *Vermeer.* New York: Rizzoli, 1986.

Bogarde, Dirk. *An Orderly Man.* London: Chatto & Windus/The Hogarth Press, 1983.

Brown, Georgia. "Mum's the Word." *Village Voice*, November 13, 1990.

Brunette, Peter, and David Wills. *Screen/Play: Derrida and Film Theory.* Princeton, NJ: Princeton University Press, 1989.

Buck-Morss, Susan. *The Dialectics of Seeing: Walter Benjamin and the Arcades Project.* Cambridge, MA: MIT Press, 1990.

Butz, Elizabeth. "*The Draughtsman's Contract.*" *The USC Spectator* 6, no. 12 (Spring 1986): 1–2.

Ciecko, Anne T. "Peter Greenaway's Alpha-Beastiary Ut Pictura Poesis: *A Zed and Two Noughts.*" *Post Script* 12, no. 1 (Fall 1992): 37–48.

Deleuze, Gilles. *The Fold: Leibniz and the Baroque.* Trans. Tom Conley. Minneapolis: University of Minnesota Press, 1993.

Derrida, Jacques. *The Post Card.* Chicago: University of Chicago Press, 1987.

Descargues, Pierre. *Vermeer.* Trans. James Emmons. Geneva: Editions d'Art Albert Skira, 1966.

Desjardins, Mary. "Free from the Apron Strings: Representations of Mothers in the Maternal British State." In Friedman, ed., pp. 130–44.

Forbes, Jill. "*Marienbad* revisited: *The Draughtsman's Contract.*" *Sight and Sound* 51, no. 4 (Autumn 1982): 301.

Foucault, Michel. *The Archaeology of Knowledge and the Discourse on Language.* Trans. A. M. Sheridan Smith. New York: Pantheon Books, 1972.

The Order of Things. New York: Random House, 1970.

Friedman, Lester, ed. *Fires Were Started: British Cinema and Thatcherism.* Minneapolis: University of Minnesota Press, 1993.

Greenaway, Peter. *The Belly of an Architect.* London: Faber & Faber, 1987.

The Cook, The Thief, His Wife and Her Lover. Paris: Editions Dis Voir, 1989.

The Draughtsman's Contract. L'Avant-Scene, no. 333, 1984.

Drowning by Numbers. London: Faber & Faber, 1988.

"The Early Films of Peter Greenaway." Pamphlet, ed. Liz Reddish. BFI Production, c. 1992.

The Falls. Paris: Editions Dis Voir, 1993.

Fear of Drowning. Paris: Editions Dis Voir, 1988.

Prospero's Books. New York: Four Walls, Eight Windows, 1991.

Prospero's Subjects. Japan: Yobisha, 1992.

Rosa. Paris: Editions Dis Voir, 1993.

Watching Water. Milan: Electa, 1993.

A Zed and Two Noughts. London: Faber & Faber, 1986.

Greenblatt, Stephen. *Shakespearean Negotiations: The Circulation of Social Energy in Renaissance England.* Berkeley: University of California Press, 1988.

Hacker, Jonathan, and David Price. "Peter Greenaway." In *Take Ten: Contemporary British Film Directors.* New York: Oxford University Press, 1991, pp. 188–227.

Hibbert, Christopher. *Rome: The Biography of a City.* New York: Norton, 1985.

Isé, Claudine. "Black and Light: Madness and the Cogito in *The Story of Adele H.*" *The USC Spectator* 12, no. 1 (Fall 1991): 18–27.

Jaehne, Karen. "*The Draughtsman's Contract*: An Interview with Peter Greenaway." *Cineaste* 13, no. 2 (1984): 13–15.

Kennedy, Harlan. *Film Comment,* January–February 1982.

La Piana, Siobhan. "Homosociality and the Postmodern Twin." *Constructions* (1990): 15–33.

Lemagny, Jean-Claude. *Visionary Architects: Boullée, Ledoux, Lequeu.* Houston: University of St. Thomas, 1968.

McShine, Kynaston, ed. *Joseph Cornell,* New York: Museum of Modern Art, 1980.

Montias, John Michael. *Vermeer and His Milieu: A Web of Social History.* Princeton, NJ: Princeton University Press, 1989.

Naremore, James. *Acting in the Cinema.* Berkeley: University of California Press, 1988.

Ong, Walter J. *Orality and Literacy: The Technologizing of the Word.* New York: Methuen, 1982.

Pagan, Nicholas O. "*The Cook, The Thief, His Wife and Her Lover*: Making Sense of Postmodernism." *South Atlantic Review* 60, no. 1 (January 1995): 43–55.

Pally, Marcia. "Order vs. Chaos: The Films of Peter Greenaway." *Cineaste* 18, no. 3 (1991): 3–8.

Parke, Catherine N. "The Director's Contract: Peter Greenaway and the Riddle of History." *Eighteenth Century Life* 11, no. 2 (May 1987): 114–17.

Paulson, Ronald. *Emblem and Expression: Meaning in English Art of the Eighteenth Century.* Cambridge, MA: Harvard University Press, 1975.

Pérouse de Montclos, Jean-Marie. *Etienne-Louis Boullée: Theoretician of Revolutionary Architecture.* Trans. James Emmons. New York: Braziller, 1974.

Pilard, Phillipe. "The Greenaway Case: Un Anglais pour cinephiles." *Franco-British Studies* 15 (Spring 1993): 10–17.

Rodgers, Marlene. "*Prospero's Books* – Word and Spectacle: An Interview with Peter Greenaway." *Film Quarterly* 45, no. 2 (Winter 1991–92): 11–19.

Rollins, Nita. "Greenaway–Gaultier: Old Masters, Fashion Slaves." *Cinema Journal* 35, no. 1 (1995): 65–80.

Rosenau, Helen. *Boullée and Visionary Architecture.* London: Academy Editions, 1974.

Schama, Simon. *The Embarrassment of Riches: An Interpretation of Dutch Culture in the Golden Age.* New York: Knopf, 1987.

Silverman, Kaja. *Male Subjectivity at the Margins.* New York: Routledge, 1992.

Snow, Edward. *A Study of Vermeer.* 2nd ed. Berkeley: University of California Press, 1994.

Steinmetz, Leon, and Peter Greenaway. *The World of Peter Greenaway.* Boston: Journey Editions, 1995.

Van Wert, William F. "*The Cook, The Thief, His Wife and Her Lover.*" *Film Quarterly* 44, no. 2 (Winter 1990–91): 42–50.

Vickers, Nancy. "Dante in the Video Decade." In *Dante Now: Current Trends in Dante Studies,* ed. Theodore J. Cachey, Jr. Notre Dame, IN: University of Notre Dame Press, 1995, pp. 263–76.

Walsh, Michael. "Allegories of Thatcherism: The Films of Peter Greenaway." In Friedman, ed., pp. 255–77.

Weschler, Lawrence. "Inventing Peace." *The New Yorker,* November 20, 1995, pp. 56–64.

Index